Ray E. Cramer

A Teaching Music through Performance in Band
20th Anniversary Edition

Also available from GIA Publications

Teaching Music through Performance in Band
Volume 1 (Second Edition) • G-4484
Resource Recordings:
Grades 2-3 • CD-418   Grade 4 • CD-490
Grade 5 • CD-817   Grade 6 • CD-818

Volume 2 • G-4889
Resource Recordings:
Grades 2-3 • CD-446   Grades 4-5 • CD-551

Volume 3 • G-5333
Resource Recordings:
Grades 2-3 • CD-473   Grade 4 • CD-510

Volume 4 • G-6022
Resource Recordings:
Grades 2-3 • CD-552   Grades 4-5 • CD-603

Volume 5 • G-6573
Resource Recordings:
Grades 2-3 • CD-623   Grades 4-5 • CD-638

Volume 6 • G-7027
Resource Recordings:
Grades 2-3 • CD-683   Grades 4-5 • CD-684

Volume 7 • G-7436
Resource Recordings:
Grades 2-3 • CD-780   Grades 4-5 • CD-816

Volume 8 • G-7926
Resource Recordings:
Grades 2-3 • CD-849   Grade 4 • CD-876

Volume 9 • G-8433
Resource Recordings:
Grades 2-3 • CD-899   Grades 4-5 • CD-945

Volume 10 • G-8876
Resource Recordings:
Grades 2-3 • CD-960   Grades 4-5 • CD-980

Teaching Music through Performance in Band
Solos with Wind Band Accompaniment • G-8188

**Teaching Music through Performance
in Middle School Band**
Volume 1 • G-8871
Resource Recording • CD-963

Teaching Music through Performance in Jazz
Volume 1 • G-7268
Resource Recording • CD-772

Volume 2 • G-9031
Resource Recording • CD-1001

**Teaching Music through Performance in Jazz
for Beginning Ensembles**
Volume 1 • G-9022
Resource Recording • CD-1000

**Teaching Music through Performance
in Beginning Band**
Volume 1 • G-5337
Resource Recording • CD-485

Volume 2 • G-7264
Resource Recording • CD-750

**Teaching Music through Performing
Marches** • G-5684
Resource Recording • CD-563

Teaching Music through Performance in Orchestra
Volume 1 • G-5565
Resource Recording: Grades 1-3 • CD-536

Volume 2 • G-6091
Resource Recording: Grades 1-3 • CD-615

Volume 3 • G-7191
Resource Recording: Grades 1-4 • CD-751

Teaching Music through Performance in Choir
Volume 1 • G-6534
Resource Recording: Levels 1-4 • CD-650

Volume 2 • G-7100
Resource Recording: Levels 1-5 • CD-719

Volume 3 • G-7522
Resource Recording: Levels 1-5 • CD-869

**Teaching Music through Performance
in Middle School Choir**
Volume 1 • G-7397
Resource Recordings:
Set 1 • CD-854   Set 2 • CD-927

Ray E. Cramer

A Teaching Music through Performance in Band
20th Anniversary Edition

GIA Publications, Inc.

Chicago

For a complete, searchable index of works covered in the Teaching Music Series, as well as audio clips of more than 1000 pieces, visit the website TeachingMusic.org.

A Teaching Music through Performance in Band
20th Anniversary Edition
Ray E. Cramer

www.teachingmusic.org

Layout: Martha Chlipala

GIA Publications, Inc.
7404 S Mason Ave
Chicago IL 60638
www.giamusic.com

G-9344
ISBN: 978-1-62277-219-3

Table of Contents

It's a Long Way from Delong

Ray E. Cramer

Introduction

Upon graduation from high school in 1958, I loved music and playing my horn, but I wasn't sure where I wanted to go or what I wanted to do in life. In school I had enjoyed some wonderful learning experiences, especially from two great music teachers you will hear about later. I had applied and been accepted to two university music schools, but I still remained undecided. At the encouragement of my high school band director, I decided to attend Western Illinois University and work towards a music education degree. I asked myself, "What does being a teacher mean?" The answer came over the next years that followed as I discovered that teaching is a complex, varied, challenging, demanding profession. It requires teachers to be knowledgeable, enthusiastic, dedicated, flexible, understanding, and focused on worthy goals. Teachers must be able to recognize the good and potential in students. Teachers must be realistic in their expectations but also be ready to take students further and help them achieve more than they think they can achieve. I have never been sorry I made the decision to become a teacher. It would be my desire if one reader of this article would find inspiration from my humble beginnings and find satisfaction with a career choice in music teaching. If you are willing to work hard and put yourself in a circle of influence of dedicated, motivated, and inspirational teachers, good things will happen for you.

To help you understand my early years, know that my parents and my older brother and sisters were tremendous role models for me during my youth. You see, I was the "late arrival" in our family—often called the "tag-along." They were all supportive and helpful in making sure I made good responsible choices, formed a solid work ethic, and developed a cooperative attitude. As is often the case with a younger sibling, my brother and sisters always felt I did not receive the same kind of disciplinary treatment they did when they were growing up. I just told them I never did anything wrong to receive punishment. *(smile)* I'm not sure they really believed that at all.

The classroom instruction I received all through my school years was excellent. The teachers were knowledgeable, committed to their subject field, and exhibited care in ensuring the growth of each class member. As long as you were willing to work hard and show progress in their classes, success was assured. After all, isn't that what we want our students to strive for in our own teaching situations?

Growing Up on a Farm

According to my Mother (I certainly don't remember anything of the event), I almost came into this world in the dark. It was the middle of the night on June 28, 1940, during a vicious thunderstorm so common in the Midwest during the summer months. As I was growing up, my Father related to me how difficult the 15-mile drive to the hospital in Galesburg, Illinois, was in the storm, having to drive around several downed trees and power lines in the middle of the road. (It's funny how much more violent the storm became each time the story was told.) When we arrived at the hospital, there was no electricity and the hospital was cranking up the generators. Just before I made my entrance into the world, the power was restored. So I did see the light from the beginning, so to speak.

I grew up on a farm in west central Illinois near the very, very small town of DeLong. (It is still there, but an even smaller version than when I was a boy.) It was not a large farm by today's standards of modern farming, where it is not unheard of to farm hundreds of acres, or even thousands. Our farm included all those things important to young boys: woods with a stream flowing through, a pond for fishing, swimming, hockey, and a great barn with hay mows to build forts and tunnels. There were also the usual animals, cows, hogs, chickens, and my various pets, including a dog, cats, a crow, a raccoon, a squirrel—and my favorite, a skunk (deodorized, of course). Not all of these pets were around at the same time, but my parents kept thinking I was going to open a zoo!

There was not a musical instrument in our home except for a decrepit, hand-cranked Victrola on which my older sisters played 78 rpm records of some very strange popular music from the late '40s and early '50s.

All of my siblings became farmers. My sisters married farmers, and my brother was a farmer. My grandfather and great grandfather were farmers, so it seemed highly logical that I would also farm. That would have been fine with me, but a musical "false start" intervened, at least temporarily.

I attended a rural, two-room school through my elementary grades; grades 1–3 were in one room and grades 4–6 were in the other. I walked to and from school, a distance of about a mile from our farm. Of course, I told my children that it was through blinding blizzards and heavy rain storms. The walk became more challenging with each telling. Over the passing years, I have looked back and realize that I had very good teachers all through elementary school. My teachers expected me to work hard and complete my work satisfactorily. Yes, there was discipline and expectations, but with positive direction and devotion from the teachers.

My Musical False Start

At some point during my sixth grade year, the district elementary music teacher visited our rural school. The teacher had brought a few instruments along to demonstrate to our class and encouraged members of the class to begin lessons on their chosen instrument. Most of my friends chose the typical instruments (flute, clarinet, saxophone, trumpet, drums), but when the teacher asked if anyone was interested in the trombone, no one raised their hand. I thought the glissando was cool (the only thing the teacher could demonstrate), so I thought: Why not? I could be first chair right from the start.

My father sold two pigs to buy me a used Pan American trombone. It had a few minor dents and it wasn't too shiny, but hey, it was MY HORN. It didn't take me too long to discover that it wasn't much fun learning notes, rhythms, and positions on the horn, so the glamour of the glissando faded quickly. Besides that, it was taking time away from playing with my friends and doing the chores my father expected me to do. So, I quit! (I have always been quite embarrassed about that.) My father was not too happy about having sold two pigs to buy the horn and have it sit unused in my bedroom. My mother did her best to encourage me to not give up playing, but to no avail. I was a happy camper having extra time to play and enjoy the pond, the streams, and the timber land.

Then, during the summer months prior to my entering junior high school, a strange thing happened. One afternoon, there was a knock on our front door. When I went to see who it was, there stood a rather tall, young man who I had never seen before in my life. In those days, no one worried about opening a door to a stranger, so I did. This gentleman had a really nice smile and introduced himself as the new band director in our district. His name was Don Zimmerman, and he did not beat around the bush. With a friendly handshake, he asked me why I had not signed up for junior high band. Gulp.

Caught red-handed and feeling very guilty, I replied without really thinking that I was bad, I wasn't having any fun, and I wasn't as good as some of my classmates who seemed to have done well. (Is there a message here about actually practicing?) With his disarming smile, he asked me if I still had my horn. By this time, my Dad and Mom had come to the front porch where we were talking, and my Dad promptly replied that yes, it was up in my bedroom. Mr. Zimmerman asked if he could give me a lesson right then. As I went to get my horn, he proceded to get his trombone out of the car. We sat on the front porch, and he helped me attain the best sound while having more fun than I had in all of my music lessons in the preceeding months before I quit. When we finished, he simply looked at me and told me that he thought I would have a very good experience playing in the junior high school band. He told my Mom that if she would bring me to town once a week, he would give me lessons without financial obligation. My Dad was happy knowing that just maybe that two-pig investment might pay off after all.

Junior and Senior High School (Knoxville, Illinois)

My Father used to tell people that we lived at 11th and Plum...11 miles plum out in the country. That was a bit of a tale, as I think it was only 8 miles from Knoxville, but who is counting when all we saw from Knoxville to our farm was field after field of corn and soybeans, with an occasional hayfield thrown in the mix.

My junior high school experiences were filled with music and football. Yes, I loved playing football all through junior and senior high school. Music, of course, was also a huge part of my school activities. The private lessons I took with Mr. Zimmerman were fundamentally based and musically driven with high expectations for achievement, but always with a smile and positive input, and never threatening or condescending. I was motivated by the challenges he placed before me. There was a continual quest for improvement that came from within, an inner desire for achievement that resulted in tremendous satisfaction. During football season, this sometimes became a problem when my lips got bruised or cut in games. We had no face guards of any kind until my junior year in high school, so direct smacks to the chops were commonplace. The single plastic guard added to the helment did little to help the lips, but I did have fewer bloody noses. Being a brass player, this did affect my practice time, but I really enjoyed practicing. In fact, I enjoyed practicing so much that every now and then my Father would send me to the barn to practice. That gave him a little more peace and quiet, but the animals in the barn didn't appreciate my playing quite so much.

Junior high band was just as Mr. Zimmerman said it would be...great fun. He had a way of making each person in the band feel special. Every student in band was important, regardless of the chair they occupied. The literature

chosen for the band was always top-notch. The band played with great care and conviction. There was no way we wanted to let Mr. Zimmerman down for the hard work he put into our success.

In addition to full ensemble, he promoted the importance of small ensembles and solo performances by the members of the band. His vision for the entire music department was not restricted to band. He also led all of the high school choral groups with the same focus on solid fundamentals, tone quality, and musical sensitivity. He was a busy man, but he also felt we needed a string program. Keep in mind this was not a large school system; there were less than 240 students in the high school. Nonetheless, he started a string program. The string program took off with great enthusiasm and numbers were quickly added. Four years later, the orchestra was invited to perform at the MENC National Conference in Saint Louis, Missouri. This was a full orchestra and served as a model for what could be achieved even in a small school system with the great leadership, organization, and support by the school and community. To this day, I find it hard to realize just how much this dedicated teacher was able to accomplish in our school.

During the latter part of my 8th grade year, several of the more advanced players in the junior high band were invited to participate in the high school band's final concert. The first chair trombone player, Eddie Breece, became my trombone idol. I thought he was the coolest person and the best trombonist I had ever heard. More importantly, he did not take offense at this young trombone player from junior high band sitting in his section. Rather, he was most encouraging and helpful. Little did I know that the following year when I went into high school, I would be sitting in the chair that Eddie Breece had occupied all through school, first chair. I was not sure what Mr. Zimmerman was thinking as I was promoted ahead of several upperclassmen in the section. I guess when they found out I could play my part without a problem, they took it all in stride.

I practiced a lot. Every day I would lug my horn home on the school bus so I could spend the evening preparing the lessons I would have with Mr. Zimmerman. When it came time to select solos to perform at contest, I was given "Thoughts of Love" by Author Pryor. I thought this must be a mistake, as Eddie Breece had performed that solo the previous year as a senior. I thought my teacher had made a poor decision knowing I was just a freshman. He handed me the solo just as school was dismissed on a Friday afternoon. He told me to work on it over the weekend and we would have a lesson on the solo on Monday after school. I have always loved a challenge, so I spent many hours working on the solo during the entire weekend. My advantage was that I had listened to Eddie Breece play that solo several times the previous year, so I had a pretty good idea what it should sound like. On Monday after school when it was time for my lesson, my teacher was pretty shocked when I played the entire solo by memory. That was good and bad, for from that day on my teacher's expectations had for my playing rose to a whole new level.

Following my sophmore year, I was so disappointed to learn that Mr. Zimmerman had taken a new job in a much larger city to become the orchestra director. I will not forget the words of encouragement he shared with me at my final lesson. He told me there was nothing I could not accomplish in music as long as I stayed focused and continued devoting the time and energy needed to be successful. He also said that the leadeship exhibited by us upperclassmen would be very important in the continued success of the band. We took that to heart and were very pleased when Charles Knapp took over the band and orchestra program during my final year of high school. He was a strong leader and a wonderful musician, and he provided inspiration and guidance for an already well-established program. He was a new teacher, but his teaching, leadership skills, and solid musicality propelled the program to new levels of excellence. He devoted his entire career to Knoxville High School. Mr. Knapp was the person who encouraged me to go into music as a profession. As I menioned earlier, I loved participating in football as well as music, so I was a bit conflicted about the career path I wanted to follow.

College Study, the Navy, or Farming? That Was the Question!

Mr. Knapp encouraged me to audition at the University of Illinois and Western Illinois University, where he had attended college. I was accepted at both schools and received a tuition scholarship at Western Illinois. At the time, I felt I wanted to attend the University of Illinois because I was most familiar with that school. I attended their two-week summer music camp and participated in the Illinois All-State Band twice, which was held on the University of Illinois campus each time. The big problem was financial. My Father was not rich, our farm was small, and it was a struggle just making ends meet from one year to the next. Sometimes the ends did not meet at all.

My oldest sister was married to a young man who was in the Navy. When he would come home on leave and talk about his life in the Navy, it seemed pretty ideal: good pay, exciting travel, and cool uniforms. My sister seemed very happy and was able to live in several nice locations during his time in the Navy. At the time, I thought I was in love, so the idea of possibly getting married and enlisting in the Navy seemed like a reasonable and logical choice. And most importantly, the Navy would pay my way!

My love life lasted about as long as an ice cube on a sidewalk in mid-summer. My Western Illinois scholarship was still valid. I figured that with summer jobs, I could afford to pay my own way, so off I went to WIU. I told Mr. Knapp that I would give it a couple of weeks and if I felt comfortable, I would try it for a year. It turned out to be a great decision, for after just a few days, I was hooked like a big fish and never looked back, only forward.

Western Illinois had excellent professors, new music department facilities,

and the band director was a motivated, inspirational teacher and a great musician. I learned so much from Dr. Suycott and felt I could not have received a better undergraduate education. Durng my time at Western, I played in every ensemble the school offered. Through Dr. Suycott's encouragement, I also developed a great interest in composition. Having no keyboard skills at all when I began my college training meant that I had to spend a lot of time in the practice room to pass my piano requirements for graduation. Anyone else have a similar story?

When it came time to think of graduate study, I only had one school in mind—the University of Iowa. My reasons for this choice fell into three categories:

1. A wonderful composition department
2. The chance to perform and learn from Professor Frederick C. Ebbs, Director of Bands
3. Receiving financial help with a Fellowship in Composition

It seemed like a chance to continue my education in an area I was convinced I would be successful—a budding young composer for band.

Being a composition major, playing in five ensembles (that included the Hawkeye Marching Band), and trying my best to survive music history, trombone lessons, form and analysis, and literature study with Professor Voxman put me on a road to possible disaster. However, I soon discovered that my own expectation for success in composition was fading; I quickly realized that I had neither the talent, time, nor keyboard skills to succeed. So I made the correct decision to give up being a composition major. I did not want to give up any of my playing opportunities, knowing full well those experiences would help me be a better band director.

The practical rehearsal techniques I was observing by playing under the leadership of Professor Ebbs proved to be the most important aspect of my work at Iowa in preparing me to become a band director. The way he rehearsed, his musical insight, concept of tonal production, and creation of beautiful sounds and colors from the band became my building blocks for the future. I learned the importance of learning the names of students and developing relationships with them that made them feel comfortable with their dedication to master ensemble skills and promote pride in attaining excellence. Little did I know that only a few years later, Mr. Ebbs would invite me to become his Assistant Director of Bands at Indiana University.

Meeting Molly, My Future Wife (What a Blessing)

All the things you just read about the importance of my time at the University of Iowa, while extremely important in shaping my future career, pales in comparision to meeing my future wife, Molly Marie Murphy. As we celebrate our 53rd wedding anniversary the month this publication is released, the role Molly has played in my life throughout these 53 years has been a gift from God and a fantastic blessing. It was a chance meeting (I believe it was orchestratetd by the Lord) when my good friend and colleague in the trombone section of the orchestra stopped by his girlfriend's apartment to pick up her horn prior to rehearsal. When she walked out of the house, she not only had a horn in hand but was accompanied by this five-foot bundle of energy with a smile as big as Ireland who climbed into the back seat where I was sitting and introduced herself as Molly. It was a short drive to campus, but it was enough time for me to think this young lady was special.

I thought about calling Molly for the next week and asking her out for coffee. I finally gathered up enough courage to call her and asked if she would like to go for coffee. She agreed, and we had a wonderful time getting to know each other on that first date. When I dropped her off at her apartment, I asked if she would like to go to a movie with me the next night. Once again she agreed, and we went to see the new Alfred Hitchcock movie, "The Birds." The following night, we went for a hamburger and a stroll around a park by the Iowa River. By the end of the evening, we felt we knew each other well enough that we decided (or perhaps it was by a mutual understanding) that we would get married. Three dates, three nights in a row, coffee, a movie, a hamburger with fries, and I was now broke. So for the next several dates, Molly bought the coffee, a small Dairy Queen, and transmission oil for my old car so we could get to the Dairy Queen.

We were going to wait a year before getting married, but I had secured a job in West Liberty, Iowa, which was only 15 miles from Iowa City, where Molly was finishing up undergraduate school. Telephone calls and trips to Iowa City over the first few months that fall made us decide to get married just after Christmas. It had to be after Christmas, as I did not want to miss the Midwest Clinic. I could not have chosen a better mate. Molly was most understanding and supportive of my work, and I was most supportive of her work as a teacher. We waited for a few years before having children, but when we did, I found out what a fantastic mother she was for our children. It is our FIRM belief that a happy marriage creates a happy life!

West Liberty High School (1963–1965)

As I was finishing my degree at Iowa, the job search began. Fred Ebbs recommended me for an assistant position in Long Island, New York, in a large school system that he knew well. It seemed like a wonderful opportunity and quite a different situation than the one-year position I held in Bardolph, Illinois, where I was the instrumental teacher for the entire school system. I

was waiting to hear from the administration in New York about being hired when a position opened up in West Liberty, Iowa, which was only 15 miles from Iowa City, where Molly would be completing her undergraduate degree the following December. I interviewed for the West Liberty job and was offered the position right away. Decision time again. I really did not want to be in New York with Molly in Iowa City, so before hearing from New York, I accepted the West Liberty position. This ended up being a very smart decision as I later found out that the New York position was not going to be offered because they did not get the funding to add the position I was considering.

West Liberty was a small, rural community with a wonderful mix of farm and town students. It was a wonderful school system with excellent teachers throughout the building. The high school band program was small, but with good instrumentation. We worked diligently on building solid fundamentals, and by the spring the band was playing pretty well, earning its very first Division One rating at the concert band contest. The next year, the band increased in size with the addition of a hard-working group of students from the junior high. We added a "stage band" (that is what jazz ensembles were called in the early '60s) the second year, which the students loved and which was a new experience for me, as I had a limited background in this genre.

All in all, the West Liberty job was a wonderful opportunity for me to gain valuable skills in rehearsal techniques and develop my own manner of building pride and vision for the program. Also during my second year at West Liberty, Molly had finished school and was able to secure a job in the West Liberty elementary school. We would have been quite happy to stay at West Liberty for a longer period, but again Fred Ebbs told me about a larger school system in soutwest Iowa that was looking for a new band director. He thought I should take a look at this program to see what I thought. Even before an interview, Molly and I drove across the state to visit Harlan just to get an impression of the town and the area. We were impressed by the town and the beauty of southwest Iowa. During that visit, I had a chance to talk with local residents to get their impression of the school system. They all felt like it was a great school system run by competent administrators and teachers. I interviewed and was offered the job, so off we went to Harlan, Iowa.

Harlan High School (1965–1968)

Harlan, located in southwest Iowa, was a town with a population of about 5,000 (twice the size of West Liberty). The economy and the support for the schools were just fantastic. The superintendent of schools, Mr. Frazier, believed that academics and all school activity programs needed to be of the highest quality. This attitude made for positive efforts by faculty and students, resulting in a very rich teaching enviornment. The year I took the job, the school

15

system had jumped in size from class B to class A. While the school's increase in numbers was due to the closing of several small schools in the county, the enrollment in the band program did not increase at all because there were no insturmental programs in any of those smaller schools.

What I did discover with the students in the band program was an eagerness for improvement and respectability. Several of the other schools in our conference had excellent bands. The students in the Harlan band were diligent workers, and they were determined to become a strong band. When you work with motivated students, taking them to a higher performance standard, the responsibility is on your shoulders to instruct and inspire. The band improved quickly. I was blessed with wonderful leadership from the upperclassmen, and the younger students had received excellent training in their elementary and junior high school instruction. Another factor that helped the program grow was the fantastic support of the parents. The students in the band were pretty evenly divided between those who lived in town and those who lived in the country. The parents were very cooperative in making sure their children were present at extra rehearsals either before or after school.

It was my goal to establish a well-balanced program where the students would have the opportunity to participate in a variety of band-related activities. The central focus was the concert band, where I stressed solid fundamentals in tone production, tuning, articulation styles, balance, blend, and musicality. I knew that once the students understood the importance of those basic fundamentals, they would transfer to every ensemble activity in the program. I placed a high priority on the importance of solo and small ensemble participation. Every student in the band was required to play in a small ensemble. While solo playing was highly encouraged, it was not required. Even so, a very large percentage of the band chose to work on solos as well. I am a firm believer that small ensembles play an important role in building depth and confidence in the total band program.

During my three years in Harlan, the band grew in size and respectability. The program participated in concert, marching, and jazz festivals, always with good results. Solo and ensemble contest saw every student in the program participating either in an ensemble or solo performance. It was in this job that I commissioned my first work for concert band. It was a wonderful experience for the students and the community. The composer was in attendance for the premiere, and the large audience turnout for the concert was extremely rewarding for the band.

My wife and I loved the community and the many friendships we developed during our three-year stay. It was during this time that we started our family. Both Heather and Jeremy were born in Harlan. When Heather was born, the marching band was scheduled to take a trip to a marching festival in the Black Hills in South Dakota. The baby came a month early, so the band went to South Dakota with my assistant, and I stayed home with Molly while

Heather was being born. Like many small towns in rural Iowa, when the local radio station found out that the local band director missed the trip with the marching band, it became an on-the-air local color story. Little did I know that it also became a "news" item on other radio stations around the state. When I called Molly's mother to tell her she was a new grandmother, she said, "I have been waiting on your call as I heard on the radio Molly was in the hospital having the baby." Thirteen months after Heather was born, Jeremy came into the world. Shortly after he was born, we moved to Parma, Ohio, where I served as director of bands at Parma Senior High School.

Parma Senior High School (1968–1969)

When I met Dick Davis, music supervisor of the Parma system, at Midwest Clinic, he told me of the new Normandy High School that would be opening the following fall in the Parma School District. I knew of the fantastic background of this school system and of the great band tradition and excellence of the two established high schools already in the system. In fact, I had just heard a performance of the Parma Senior High School Band at Midwest Clinic and was very impressed by the incredible talent and musicality of the band. Later in the spring, I received a call from the music supervisor inviting me to Cleveland to interview for a band position in the system. Based on our discussion in Chicago, I assumed I was going there to interview for the band job in the new high school. I was met at the airport by the music supervisor and Barbara Rankin, director of the Parma Senior High School Band that I had heard at the previous Midwest Clinic. On the way to Parma from the airport, I was informed that I was actually being interviewed for the Parma Senior High School job, not the new high school position. I was told that Barbara Rankin was leaving Parma, getting married, and moving to California. Needless to say, I was shocked. I broke out in a cold sweat and thought I should just have them take me back to the airport so I could fly back to Iowa and continue to enjoy working with my Harlan High School Band. I'll never forget Barbara saying to me, "This is just like Harlan, Ray. It has a small-town feel, friendly people, and great students to work with just like you have in Harlan." Parma, located right next to Cleveland, was nothing like Harlan, and the students I had heard play a few months previously in Chicago were nothing like my Harlan students! I was thinking, "What am I doing here?!"

Barbara was correct on one point: The students were terrific, very talented, and a pleasure to work with through the one year I spent in Parma. What a fantastic program Barbara Rankin had built in the 12 years she was at Parma. They had been the Ohio Band of the Year the previous 10 years, have performed at the Mideast Clinic and the Midwest Clinic. The enrollment of the school was 3,600 students in 3 grades, and all of the students in the 90-member symphonic band studied privately with professional musicians in the Cleveland area, including the Cleveland Symphony. A large percentage of the students in the concert band also studied with area professionals. I soon realized that I was facing a new challenge: Could I convince these outstanding student musicians who were so loyal to their previous director that together we could establish musical goals that would continue to bring accomplishment and satisfaction?

As I look back on that experience, it was a great opportunity for me to grow professionally. I had never worked with such talented young musicians. My decisions on repertoire would be critical to the success of the ensemble, and my rehearsal pacing would have to be elevated to new levels of focus and productivity. It turned out to be a great year. The band members were cooperative, worked hard, and continued to grow musically as I challenged them through my selection of literature and high expectations. I found they thrived on these ingredients.

I would have been very happy to remain in that position for many years, but in the spring of 1969 when Fred Ebbs visited us in Cleveland (his mother lived in the area and he came to visit her), he shared with me that his assistant at Indiana University was leaving to take a job in Oklahoma and asked if I would be interested in applying for that position. Teaching at the universithy level had always been a goal of mine, but I had no idea the opportunity would come quite so quickly. After discussing the possibility with Molly, I decided to apply. An invitation to interview and a trip to Bloomington became a reality. What was even more surprising was a letter from Wilfred Bain, Dean of the School of Music, offering me the Assistant Director of Bands job at Indiana Univeristy. So along with my wife and two young children (ages 1 and 2), we headed off to yet another new challenge.

Indiana University (1969–2005)

Little did I know upon our arrival in Bloomington, Indiana, that it would begin a 36-year engagement. That position afforded me many opportunities for incredible experiences with faculty and students, and rich musical memories that will be foremost in my mind until the day I leave this earth. To try and put this 36-year experience in a few short paragraphs would be impossible. Perhaps in a few years after I fully "retire" (Tim Lautzenheiser says I am "retreaded," not retired) a book about my IU years and my "other" job at the Musashino Academia of Musicae in Tokyo, Japan, could possibly become its own publication. But now is not the time for that project.

Indiana University is a special school and home to one of the great schools of music in the country, the Jacobs School of Music. Going from Parma Senior High School to IU was a dream come true, but I have to admit I was one nervous "youngster" at the beginning of that first year.

My initial responsibilities included assisting with the marching band (write drill, chart, music rehearsal), conducting the second concert band, and

teaching courses in music education. It was a very steep learning curve, and yes, I "learned" quickly that the university experiences and demands were a bit different than what I had experienced in my high school teaching. Preparing and rehearsing an all new pre-game and half-time show for every home game (by hand, without any of the current computer programs now available) and throwing in rainy weather that kept you from outdoor practice along with the "pressure" that came with putting together a drill routine in one or two rehearsals taught me to apply the KISS system: Keep It Simple Stupid!

I loved the students, their energy, enthusiasm, musical talent, and desire to excel. It provided a new vision for what I already loved doing, but with new goals firmly established in my own mind. My thought was that I would stay at IU for a few years and then seek my own Director of Bands position at another university. My responsibilities kept changing, and I soon was named Director of the Marching Hundred, with the added responsibility of being in charge of all athletic bands in addition to the assignments previously mentioned.

I interviewed for a couple other university positions, but none provided the excitement and musically rewarding experiences I already had at IU. The next few years flew by very quickly, and in 1982, I was named Director of Bands. I had new responsibilities, higher expectations, a more demanding schedule, but with a new sense of commitment to an instution that I loved. Indiana provided so many experiences for me that will forever be etched clearly in my mind and heart. Yes, at some point in the future, the Lord willing, I hope to have the chance to write in much more detail about my IU years. There is so much more to tell—or as Paul Harvey used to say, "And now here's the rest of the story."

Musashino Academia of Musicae (1990–Present)

In 1984, the Indiana University Symphonic Band was invited to perform at the joint ABA/JBA convention that was being held in Tokyo, Japan. Our first rehearsal upon arrival was held in Beethoven Hall on the campus of the Musashino Academy of Music. During that rehearsal, I met some of the school administrators and shared the podium with three Japanese guest conductors who would conduct on our concert in Tokyo. The hall was very fine with great acoustics. What surprised all of us was seeing all of the university buildings jammed into a very small space that perhaps only covered a square city block. After spending the past 15 years on what I considered to be one of the most beautiful campuses in the country, I was not expecting the closeness of all of the buildings. The streets were so narrow that our tour busses could not drive to the school. We had to park 2 blocks away on a major street and walk to the school. However, we were treated very well by school officials and the university students. We left the rehearsal with a good feeling about how the rest of our 16-day tour would go. We were not disappointed in any way. Throughout the tour, we were treated like celebrities and everyone loved the experience.

The general feeling by all the band members was that someday they would love to visit again.

I knew Musashino Academy of Music had a fine band. I had heard recordings of their ensemble and was impressed by the clarity, technical profiency, pitch control, and the literature they were performing. During the late spring of 1990, I received a call from Robert Bergt, a friend who was head of the music department at Valparaiso University. I didn't realize at that time that he was the full-time orchestra director at the Musashino Academy of Music. Musashino had asked him for recommendations for American Collegiate band directors who might be interested in coming to Musashino for a semester to conduct their top wind ensemble. Mr. Bergt had given my name to the president of Musashino, and the president asked Robert to call me to see if I would be interested. This caught me completely by surprise, but I was intrigued and interested in this possibility. After a discussion with Dean Webb, head of the IU School of Music, permission was given to accept the invitation and arrangements were made to have my resposibilities covered during my semester's absence. Thinking this would possibly be a one-time opporunity, I went into it thinking that I would just enjoy the experience and the culture of Japan. This fall will be my 26th year of involvement with this excellent music school. It is in reality a music conservatory, as the students obtain degrees in music education or music performance. My 26-year association will perhaps have to be part of the "Indiana story," as the many and varied experiences are far too numerous to put into this chapter.

Perhaps my biggest challenge in Japan was dealing with the language issue. I very quickly found out during the first rehearsal that the students understood very little English. When I asked them to please begin at measure 42 and gave the downbeat, only one student played. That's when I realized they did not understand what I had said! Right then, I knew I was going to have to learn how to say "please start at measure 42" in Japanese. Thus began a new learning curve for me as I struggled, made mistakes, and eventually found a way to express myself through enough Japanese phrases to make the rehearsals proceed with the required pacing and understanding. This made my life and the students' lives much more comfortable.

My wife and I leave again for Tokyo in a few weeks, which will be our 19th time we have traveled to Japan for the 3-month engagement at Musashino. Over the years, we have developed very close personal friendships and a wonderful relationship with the university. We have enjoyed these engagements, and each visit has taught us more about the history and cultural traditions of the country. Tours with the ensemble have taken us to every part of Japan. The band has also enjoyed their two appearances at the Midwest Clinic (in 1995 and 2006).

The students are always polite, cooperative, and dedicated in performing to the best of their abilities. The Musashino Wind Ensemble has been a leader

in the country for many decades. It was not until I did some research that I learned that the wind ensemble was established one year after the Eastman Wind Ensemble was founded by Fred Fennell. It is now common practice that high school and university bands have follwed suit in estabishing smaller ensembles.

As long as my health remains strong, I will continue my association with Musashino. Next year will be very exciting for the school, as they will be moving into an all-new campus facility. Special concerts and activites are being planned for the opening of the new school, including commissions and guest artists. My association with the school has been a special blessing that has extended my professional career.

Conclusion: Only God Knows

In conclusion—How often have we heard that, meaning "the end" or "the last"? That would be an understatement, for I am not sure just what that means for me at this point in my life. When is "old enough to know better" supposed to kick in? Thankfully, it has not hit me just yet! I still love working with bands and having hands-on experiences with musicians who love to play and make music together. As long as I can communicate with people in a lucid and productive manner, then I will continue being involved in teaching/conducting, "the good Lord willing and the creek don't rise." It has been and continues to be a most rewarding profession. I can honestly say I looked forward to going to work every day. I thank God for the opportunities he has provided me and I look to the future for whatever He has in store in the years to come. Thanks so much for your interest and love for teaching. Please stay in this profession. We need YOU, and the young musicians you inspire need YOU. I close with these two quotes:

"Teaching is perhaps the essence of my function as a conductor. I share whatever I know and whatever I feel about the music."

—Leonard Bernstein

"You cannot get through a single day without having an impact on the world around you. What you do makes a difference, and you have to decide what kind of difference you want to make."

—Jane Goodall

CHAPTER 1

Our GPS for Success: It's All About the Literature

Ray E. Cramer

As I recall my early years of teaching, perhaps the most difficult decisions I faced were those requiring the choice of literature for my bands at the junior and senior high school level. Mostly I relied on experienced directors or my college band director for suggestions. At the time, it seemed to me the most important questions about making those choices involved the following:

1. Will students like the music?
2. Are my players competent enough to perform it?
3. Do we have enough "rehearsal time" to learn the music?
4. Will the parents and school personnel appreciate the music?

While these questions continue to be important in any band director's decision process, I know they only cover a small part of the complex problem of choosing fine literature. Selecting quality music must be the top priority in our responsibilities as teachers and conductors. Once those decisions have been made, the top priority must then be to teach the music, not the piece. A main focus of the *Teaching Music* series is to provide a list of quality band music to assist in establishing a *plan* and *procedure* for you and your students to achieve musical satisfaction and the excitement that comes from attaining a goal. When realized, this will have a positive impact on your students, parents, and school colleagues. After all, our basic aim is to make the preparation and performance of music exciting for *everyone*. To accomplish this task we need to energize our teaching so that our students may see in us knowledge, creativity, positive communication, enthusiasm, and above all, musicality.

Before we look at this list of selected works, it will serve us well to examine the criteria that we typically use in making decisions regarding music of artistic merit. Please understand that this is a representative list and certainly does not reflect the only choices that can be made for each grade level. It is a starting point and a place from which to embark on our goal of *teaching music through performance in band*.

Without question, there are many philosophical viewpoints regarding the selection of quality music. Some are rather direct and simplistic, while others require careful examination based on a set of guidelines. Kurt Weill (1900–1950), a contemporary German composer, once said, "I have never acknowledged the difference between 'serious' music and 'light' music, there is only good music and bad music." A highly respected band director once made this simple statement regarding literature selection: "Play only music you can respect." And a distinguished composer of band music simply asks, "Does the music *say* anything or *go* anywhere?" While each of these statements has its own merits, let's concentrate on a few basics for clarification in covering the wide range of material on our list.

Just for a moment consider the age-old question, "What comprises music of artistic merit?" The obvious conclusion is that the music must characterize itself by having special effectiveness or is set apart by qualitative depth, and must stand on its own. Criteria used in this study for evaluating literature can be broken down into a few basic considerations. Does the music have:

1. a well-conceived formal structure?
2. creative melodies and counterlines?
3. harmonic imagination?
4. rhythmic vitality?
5. contrast in all musical elements?
6. scoring which best represents the full potential of the wind ensemble?
7. an emotional impact?

If we are going to teach *about* music and *through* music while *performing* music, then we must incorporate all of these elements into our rehearsal planning as we prepare our students for performance.

Let's look at a few selections from each level on our list and highlight just why they are included.

Snakes! • Thomas Duffy • Grade 2

Snakes! is a wonderful example of how exciting and accessible a contemporary work can be without great range and technical demands. This piece shows great creativity and explores a whole new gamut of different sounds, textures, and colors. Young players can have a wonderful learning experience and become totally involved in the music making process.

Air for Band • Frank Erickson • Grade 3

This piece has been performed by the youngest of bands and by fine university bands around the world. *Air for Band* is beautifully scored, exhibiting the richness of tone we have all come to appreciate in a fine band.

The melody is constructed in such a manner to draw attention to its outstanding contour and expressive quality. It is a musical gem.

First Suite in E-Flat and Second Suite in F • Gustav Holst • Grade 4

Both of Holst's suites for band have been hailed by many as the cornerstones of contemporary band literature in this century. Examine them carefully by the seven simple elements given above and you will quickly discover the genius and creative talent of this great composer. These magnificent works have withstood the test of time and will continue to do so based on the strength of their musical sensitivity.

Divertimento for Band • Vincent Persichetti • Grade 5

Persichetti's *Divertimento for Band* represents a whole new genre of literature for band. Composed in 1950, *Divertimento* was his first composition for band and brought forth several new concepts in writing for winds.

First, there was a greater emphasis on individual tonal colors represented by each section of the ensemble; second, the scoring was much more transparent; and third, the percussion section took on a more important function, particularly in regard to melodic representation.

Divertimento work set the pace for a whole new era of compositional style and tonal color for bands. Other major composers took note of this potential and began contributing major works of their own to our medium during the decade of the 1950s.

Variants on a Medieval Tune • Norman Delio Joio • Grade 5

This is a masterful setting of the famous Renaissance melody "In dulci jubilo." Dello Joio's variations are magnificently conceived and demonstrate sensitive writing for solo and full-ensemble scoring. The contrast in style, dynamics, and tempos contribute to the piece's musical energy as it moves toward a dramatic finale. *Variants on a Medieval Tune* provides an ideal vehicle for teaching how music from the Renaissance period can be utilized in a most effective contemporary setting.

Lincolnshire Posy • Percy Grainger • Grade 6

As determined by two different doctoral studies from the past twenty years, *Lincolnshire Posy* is considered one of the most respected and well-known works for band composed in the twentieth century. Little explanation as to why it is included on this list seems necessary; however, Grainger's skill and creative talent are certainly best portrayed in this fabulous score. The careful representation of the original folk songs and how they were sung, the rhythmic vitality and challenges, the colorful scoring, and the emotional sensitivity all contribute to the artistic merit of this masterwork. Certainly there is much to be taught about the piece as well as of the life of a great composer.

There is so much *great* music to share with our students, so why should we settle for less? We need to capitalize on every aspect of music to bring the "whole package" into our performance experiences to enhance student involvement and musical fulfillment. Correct notes are obviously important, as are attacks, releases, good balance, blend, careful intonation, clarify in texture, and articulation style; but these are all stepping stones to generating musical electricity and excitement. To accomplish this, we must, as teachers and conductors, give our students *more* than basic musical stepping stones; they need our musical heart and soul, which can only be communicated by sharing everything we have compiled about the period, style, composer, and structure of the composition. In other words, we must involve the students totally, teach them *about* the music, and *through* the music we choose. Ours is an awesome responsibility; but our energy and enthusiasm for the task must infect those under our charge.

A Tribute to Teachers

In the fall of 1963 Leonard Bernstein presented "A Tribute to Teachers" on his first *Young People's Concert* of the season. His comments were powerful then and remain just as significant today. He said:

You may think it is strange that I have chosen to open this new season of *Young People's Concerts* with the subject of *teachers*. After all, aren't these programs always about *music*? And what have teachers got to do with music? The answer is: everything! We can all imagine a painter or writer who is self-taught, but it is almost impossible to imagine a professional musician who doesn't owe *something* to one teacher or another. The trouble is that we don't always realize how important teachers are, in music or in anything else. Teaching is probably the noblest profession in the world—the most unselfish, difficult, and honorable profession. But it is also the most unappreciated, underrated, underpaid, and underpraised profession in the world. And so today we are going to praise teachers. And the best way I can think of for me to do this is by paying tribute to some of my own teachers…and…all the great teachers on earth who work so hard to give young people a world that is better, richer, and move civilized.

None of us knows who among our students will become the next Leonard Bernstein, Percy Grainger, William Revelli, Herbert L. Clarke, William Bell or Frederick Fennell. However, it is *our* responsibility to be the strongest musical influence in their lives as we possibly can be. Through that effort comes inspiration and joy in making music a vivid and vital part of our students' lives. I have always found meaning and a challenge in the following quote of Aaron Copland:

> So long as the human spirit thrives on this planet, music in some living form will accompany and sustain it and give it expressive meaning.

Enjoy the trip through your musical journey, remembering to follow your GPS to success: literature!

CHAPTER 2

Performing Music of Multicultural Diversity

Ray E. Cramer

Introduction

Not so many years ago, instrumental music educators probably felt if they performed marches, overtures, tone poems, suites, and an occasional solo with band accompaniment they were doing their part in contributing to a student's diversified education. In one sense they were, by providing music of variety and character. Please do not misunderstand me, this is still important today at any level of band participation and programming. How well I remember some of my early band experiences during the decade of the '50s, when the band would perform some of the "new" works by John Morrisey, Paul Yoder, Clifton Williams, Frank Erickson, and, of course, those really strange pieces by Persichetti, Gould, and Grainger. I had not yet even heard the Hindemith Symphony. Some band composers of that era would introduce multimovement works which carried titles aimed at representing music from different periods or countries and use rhythmic devices one would associate with other cultures.

My reason for relating these early band experiences is not to point a disapproving finger at the people entrusted to teaching and leading my early development in instrumental music. They were excellent teachers and conductors who inspired, motivated, and produced outstanding results in the small rural community of Knoxville, Illinois. In fact, I should mention the names of Don Zimmerman, my first trombone teacher and director, and Charles Knapp, my last high school teacher and director. Both of these gentlemen were excellent role models for all of us and brought great success to our small school during a time when most music programs were struggling to find identity and direction. Our fine band was exposed to the best literature available at the time. We were encouraged to strive for excellence in performance and challenged as people and musicians. During my high school education there were numerous opportunities to hear professional musicians especially when they were invited to perform with our band. It was also an honor to be conducted by respected university directors and to hear concerts by such noted bands as the University of Illinois, University of Iowa, and Northwestern University. There were many other fine university bands during this period but it was just too difficult to travel to their campuses.

I point all of this out only to bring a strong message to conductors everywhere at every level. These same goals and opportunities exist in abundance today through videos, CDs, CD-ROM, and various computer programs which are easily obtained and affordable. However, we must never arrive at the point where we think, only these products will help our students achieve our desired goals. Personal interaction with professionals, attendance at live performances, inspired teaching, and energetic leadership will inevitably make the most positive impressions on young musicians. Teachers and conductors with vision and creativity will continue to produce effective programs and students who wish to continue in the footsteps of their mentors. However, there is a larger picture today which can have a dynamic impact on our programs. One of the means to ensure future growth and support of music education as we move into the twenty-first century is by exploring the challenges of performing music of multicultural diversity.

Communication

Information sharing is quick and easy today. I grew up on a farm with a crank telephone on the dining room wall and our phone number was two shorts and a long. It is rather amazing to me how quickly you can communicate via e-mail with a computer sitting on your desk. Even more astounding is the information available on almost any subject at the touch of a finger. The very concept of these two books, Teaching Music through Performance in Band, is to put information about compositions, composers, style, form, historical perspective, technical considerations, musical elements, and even suggested listening into the hands of conductors preparing these pieces for performance. How easy it becomes for conductors to incorporate this information into the daily rehearsal. Our whole responsibility as conductors is to share information with our students through gesture and verbal skills. You might think your students will not hold still for these lecture sessions. It is not intended for a conductor to share all of this information at one time, but rather to creatively bring these facts into the rehearsal procedure. It is astonishing just how much information is retained by eager students. They need to understand communication as a basic human need. It's just that we do it in different ways and need to teach this to our students so they embrace diversity instead of finding differences.

All of this serves as an introduction to a popular movement in education today which involves bringing diversity to programming and exposing our students to the various aspects of world music. This concept is not possible without your sincere interest and vision in sharing music of multicultural diversity. In a real sense, conductors have been engaged in this practice all along, but more recently the emphasis has been on carefully reproducing colors and stylistic trends inherent to the country or culture being represented. As you may well suspect, this is not always easy, especially in terms of finding out just what is involved in securing instruments to accurately produce the desired sounds. However, if only in a few circumstances you can bring to your students and audiences these special sounds and styles, their concert experience will have been enhanced.

Symbolism

In music, just as in art and literature, interpretation is left up to the individual who is listening, looking, or reading. Creatures of the world are in a constant state of struggle for survival with each other for sustenance, leadership, and territorial domain. However, they do not struggle for things which stand for sustenance, leadership, or domain. In the arts, on the other hand, we constantly examine symbols which represent different things as individuals respond through aural and visual perceptions. From early civilization, symbols have caused great confusion in deciding just what they represent. By the very nature of the meaning, symbols are used or regarded as representing something else. One can understand why there has been, and will continue to be, great confusion over exactly what a pictograph meant when discovered on a cave wall. Admittedly, when I listen to some concerts where music I know well is being performed, I am confused by what I know is marked in the score and what I am hearing from the ensemble. In music, symbols are taken for granted, but the crux of the musical process is obviously in the interpretation of these symbols by the conductor. A conductor's musical achievement rests solely on his or her realization of those symbols in manipulating sound. This is our primary function as a conductor: to control sound. Without this fundamental process, the re-creation of the composer's intent and the stylistic trends representing the country or culture, cannot be successfully achieved.

Student Involvement

You may ask, "Just what benefit is there in attempting to bring various aspects of world music to my students?" All of us, from time to time, become involved in various kinds of performance pressures and a general "get-the-notes-learned" mentality. Is it all that important? Of course we want our bands to play correct notes, but the real answer to that question depends on your own personal attitude. An individual who is curious about discovering new things and places will usually be inclined to share this excitement with others.

Young people are tremendously inquisitive by nature. With proper guidance and motivation, new subjects, topics, and musical elements of different cultures can become quite an exciting project. One thought which immediately comes to mind is the preparation of a program where music and art can join in a presentation of one or more cultures in a single event. Art could be displayed throughout the lobby with appropriate information written about paintings or sculptures. Perhaps a student could be assigned to each display information about food, dance, clothing and housing of the culture it represents. A brief pre-concert lecture could be given by students or faculty explaining various aspects of the musical program to follow. Perhaps a video or slide presentation could accompany the music. Included in this would be specific examples of musical elements or sounds on which the audience could focus their attention. I can see a tremendous event where many areas of the school would be represented. This collaboration would result in a win/win situation for everyone involved.

How do we learn about other cultures without the opportunity of living there? Of course, it would be ideal if everyone could experience living in a different culture. Most of us must rely on the usual forms for education about a country or culture, namely through its literature, art, music, or by viewing video resources. Through these various media presentations, we have a fantastic opportunity to produce a very special event through our own gifts, talents, and research.

The Elements of Music

The widely accepted elements of music today are still rhythm, melody, harmony, and timbre. These elements are vividly described and discussed in the wonderful book by Aaron Copland, What to Listen for in Music. As one begins to explore the parameters of performing music from other cultures, these four basic elements of music must remain in the forefront of a conductor's preparation. The realization of the performance, as always, develops in the interpretation of the symbols.

In 1984 our Indiana University Symphonic Band traveled to Japan to perform at the ABA/JBA joint convention. As one would expect, we deemed it appropriate to include on our program numbers written by Japanese composers. Additionally, we invited two Japanese directors to guest conduct these works in concert. Needless to say, this proved to be highly educational for me and for the band. While the notes and technical demands of the compositions had been carefully prepared, it quickly became apparent there were other musical considerations which I would have known only by growing up in their culture.

Knowledge

One of the compositions was Asuka by Tensunosuke Kushida. This wonderful piece depicts a traditional ceremony which takes place in an ancient temple in Japan. The score called for a "bell tree" and "wood block" as special colors used in various sections of the music. In fact, they were scored in such a manner that they became focal points of the piece. As our guest conductor was rehearsing the number, after the place where these "color" instruments were being used, he immediately stopped the band and gave a very strange look towards the percussion section. It was obvious he was not pleased with the kinds of sounds our percussionists were produceing. The conductor must have anticipated this happening for he had carried an athletic bag to the rehearsal. He proceeded to unzip the bag and motioned for me to come forward. He then gave me a present which consisted of Japanese "wood blocks" that looked like giant claves. They were made of extremely hard wood and were approximately three inches wide, two inches thick, and twelve inches long. He next gave the percussion section a lesson on how to achieve the exact sound he was seeking, which was quite deep and piercing. Finally, I was given a pair of traditional Japanese "bell trees." These bell trees looked like miniature Christmas trees with a handle and tiny bells hung around the outside of the tree. Shaking them produced the most unusual jingle I've ever heard. These traditional Japanese instruments totally changed the nature of Asuka. Years later, when my wife and I lived in Japan for a time, we had several opportunities to hear these instruments as they were played in temple ceremonies. Perceiving the use and sound of these instruments, I realized how misinformed I was in my concept of performance practice. With proper research I could have attained the knowledge to achieve the interpretation the composer intended.

A similar instance happened a few years ago when a fine young composer on our Indiana University faculty, David Dzubay, wrote a piece for the Indiana University Wind Ensemble titled Incantations. This piece is also about a Japanese shrine ceremony in which different types of drums are used in the ritual. For our American premiere, because I did not have access to traditional Japanese drums, we used regular bass drums and tom-toms of various sizes to produce the multi-pitches required. Now, after having lived in Japan and observing the culture, I know these drums were not what would be used in a Japanese shrine ceremony. Unfortunately, our school did not have the drums necessary for use in the premiere. A year later when I returned to Japan to conduct the Musashino Academy of Music Wind Ensemble, we performed this work using traditional Japanese horizontal drums. These drums produced the kind of sound one would hear in visiting a shrine ceremony. When adding the Japanese drums I also asked the percussion section to employ the proper performance technique required in playing these instruments. To further enhance the concert the percussionists were clad in the attire one would see in such a ceremony. With the utilization of the proper equipment, correct playing techniques, and traditional attire, this fine work took on a whole new expression.

During the 1995 MidWest Clinic, the Musashino Academy of Music Wind Ensemble performed Methuselah II which features the percussion section. This is quite an exciting number which can be performed on a wide variety of percussion instruments found in any part of the world. However, this performance was unique because it used traditional Japanese drums performed with established Japanese drumming techniques. The performers again wore traditional attire of the country and the performance brought about a spectacular response. The performance was overwhelming because it was beautifully performed and the students embodied the spirit, culture, and traditions of a rich heritage.

These kinds of experiences are possible for any group at any level, given the proper guidance and direction. You should choose material carefully and bring information to the students about the music and the style and culture from which it is derived. Is it possible to conclude that expression is a basic need, as is hunger, warmth, pain, love? Yes, it just comes in different forms. The ability of a student to appreciate the differences in expression will lead them to a life of tolerance, respect, and open-mindedness. The inclusion of music from other cultures and bringing attention to the beauty of the different forms and techniques brings our students closer to the complete acceptance of humanity.

Included in this publication are many pieces of multicultural diversity. I would like to point out several of these compositions in each grade level and encourage you to explore the cultural diversity. Since all are included in the "Teacher Resource Guides" I will not add any further information except to point out the national origin of the piece. Some are written by composers who are actually from the represented countries while other works are written to represent other styles and cultures.

GRADE TWO

Composition	Composer	Country
Sandy Bay March	Brian West	Australia
The New ANZACS	Brian Hogg	Australia
A Little French Suite	Pierre LaPlante	France
Old Scottish Melody	Charles Wiley	Scotland
Three on the Isle	Hugh M. Stuart	England
Korean Folk Song Medley	James Ployhar	Korea

GRADE THREE

Composition	Composer	Country
Fantasy on "Sakura, Sakura"	Ray Cramer	Japan
Retreat and Pumping Song	David Stanhope	Australia
Brazilian Folk Dance Suite	Arr. William E. Rhoads	South America
Renaissance Suite	Tielman Susato/Curnow	Germany
Rhosymedre	R. Vaughan Williams	Wales
An Irish Rhapsody	Clare Grundman	Ireland

GRADE FOUR

Composition	Composer	Country
Trail of Tears	James Barnes	Native American
Japanese Tune	Soichi Konagaya	Japan
Autumn Walk	Julian Work	African American
Variations on "Scarborough Fair"	Calvin Custer	England
Dreamcatcher	Walter Mays	Native American
Africa: Ceremony, Song, and Ritual	Robert W. Smith	African American

GRADE FIVE

Composition	Composer	Country
Four Scottish Dances	Malcolm Arnold/Paynter	Scotland
The Solitary Dancer	Warren Benson	America
Paris Sketches	Martin Ellerby	France
Ricarcare a 6	J. S. Bach/Fennell	Germany
Russian Christmas Music	Alfred Reed	Russia

GRADE SIX

Composition	Composer	Country
Gazebo Dances	John Corigliano	America
Huntingtower Ballad	Ottorino Respighi	Scotland
Winds of Nagual	Michael Colgrass	Central America
Dance Movements	Philip Sparke	England
Dance of the New World	Dana Wilson	America
Circus Polka	Igor Stravinsky	America

Conclusion

There are many popular songs with titles expressing the joy one finds in the experience of music. For example, "Music, Music, Music," "Say It with Music," "Music Makes the World Go 'Round," "The Sound of Music," or "The Music Will Not End." Music is the message, the medium, and the motivator. The world becomes smaller and more intimate every day. Distant places and cultures are no longer something we see and read about only in the National

Geographic. The concert band, as we know it in the Western Hemisphere, has gained in popularity around the globe. The increased presence of bands has spawned a new generation of international composers who have given us compositions that add significantly to the rich depth of our literature. All too often wind literature has received undue criticism from those who point to orchestral literature as having such great depth of repertoire. There is no question a tremendous wealth of material exists for this medium. The orchestra has enjoyed a long and distinguished heritage.

Since 1950, however, the amount and quality of material written for the band is unsurpassed. The most respected composers from around the world have written and will continue to write for the band medium knowing full well their music will be performed and at a high level of execution. The music will be well received and will become immediately accessible to bands everywhere. Review a list of Pulitzer Prize winners in music over the past twenty-five years and note the number of composers who have written compositions for band. The wind band has made astounding advancements during the second half of the twentieth century. Band directors must carefully prepare in order to guide their ensembles into the twenty-first century. The key to success, as always, depends on the material we put before our bands. We must all believe everything we accomplish in our programs is through the music we choose. It is the music which brings goals into focus, is inspirational, and brings discipline and personal growth to our students.

In this publication you will find a list of one hundred compositions, divided into five grade levels, with twenty selections in each grade. This chapter contains a chart with six works from each level which represent different countries and/or cultures. There are many others on the list which also represent music of multicultural diversity. As you choose material which represents other cultures you must become well informed about sounds, timbres, stylistic trends, and the equipment needed to achieve authentic performances.

Music is a journey. The band is our vehicle and the literature we choose to place before our students is the fuel which enables us to travel from one adventure to another. Perhaps the most important rule for directors to follow is to choose only literature which you respect. We cannot expect our students to become excited about what they are performing if they sense we do not respect the music. Will Rogers once said, "Even if you're on the right track, you'll still get run over if you just sit there." The music will keep us and our programs moving in the right direction. As we approach the twenty-first century the possibilities for incorporating various aspects of world music into our programs will only add high-test fuel for greater power and efficiency in the operation of our instrumental programs. Above all else, have fun with your students as you share the excitement and enthusiasm for making music through performance in band.

CHAPTER 3

Podium
Personality

Ray E. Cramer

Introduction

Since the first time a baton was used to "lead" musicians in rehearsals and performances, there has been a fascination with conductors and how their personalities impact music making. We all have a personality that directly affects how we relate to people every day of our lives. Regardless of the profession in which we are engaged, the success of our work directly reflects the nature and passion of our personalities.

When I was a relatively new teacher (many years ago), I attended a conference that was being held for hundreds of teachers who were being honored for each having received an outstanding young educator award. The guest speaker was the president of 3M. It was an inspiring speech, and certainly he said many things that I have remembered over subsequent years. The main topic of his presentation was to encourage people to utilize the power of personality to ensure success in any field of endeavor. He shared information that he had read from a doctoral study pertaining to the importance of personality in assessing one's success.

According to the information shared in his speech, there are three basic ingredients that contribute to one's success in any work. There is the need for *intelligence, knowledge of subject matter* and, of course, *personality*. If you were to attach to each of these a percentage of importance as they relate to success, the response would probably be like mine; it seemed logical and clearly apparent to me that each was an equally important component of success.

As the president continued his speech, all of us in attendance were astonished as he finished relating the information found in this document. The paper revealed that intelligence has a very low percentage assigned to it. People in any chosen field will have the basic intelligence to be successful, or they will choose another field. For example, if I do not have an I.Q. to be able to achieve the skills necessary to become a research scientist, I will direct myself toward another profession where I know my basic intelligence will allow me to be successful.

People proceed through a training program designed to give information necessary to allow them to attain success because of the knowledge gained through study and application. So no matter what the chosen field, either there is the intelligence to complete the requirements for that program or another field is chosen. However, regardless of the level of intelligence and amount of knowledge one has, unless a dynamic personality is added to the mix, success will not be achieved at its highest level.

I am sure you will be astonished, as I was, when it was related to us that in this doctoral study only 7 percent of success in any field of work could be attributed to *intelligence* and *knowledge* concerning the chosen field. It was made abundantly clear in this dissertation that 93 percent of one's success is directly related to the *power of personality*.

Concert Components

The Audience

When an audience is gathering for a concert performance of any kind, there is a level of anticipation and expectation that accompanies the waiting crowd. Without question, there will be a great difference between the level of expectation of the audience assembling in Carnegie Hall and those assembling in the gymnasium of a local school. Yet there are certain elements present that will always remain the same. The members of the ensemble all desire to perform (or at least we hope they do) to the best of their ability. The ensemble and the conductor believe in the music, have worked diligently in preparation, and are excited about the opportunity to exhibit their musicianship through performance. The concert will ultimately demonstrate the ability of the performers to benefit from the process of preparation as individual players and the ensemble as a unit. The concert attendees will listen to the concert and determine the success of the program as being the direct result of the leadership the group has had from the person standing on the podium. There is no getting around the fact that, after the performance, the pre-concert expectation affects whether the audience praises or criticizes the conductor. After all, it was the job of the conductor to have the players prepared for the concert.

The Conductor

Despite the many ingredients that are part of the recipe for performance success, a conductor must never forget the importance of making good impressions even before the downbeat takes place. From the moment the ensemble is finished tuning, the audience waits for the entrance of the conductor to begin the program. As the conductor enters, the audience begins to make mental notes as they evaluate the presence of the conductor. Does the conductor walk slowly or quickly? Is there a smile or an expressionless stare? Does the conductor make eye contact with the audience or ignore their presence? What is the posture of the conductor walking to the podium? Does the conductor acknowledge the ensemble and the audience or merely step on the podium to begin the first number?

This first contact with the audience speaks volumes about the personality of the conductor and his/her approach to the performance. A good conductor will:

- Walk with spirit (a bounce in his or her step) and be confident, assured, and poised to portray an image of positive control.
- Make that all-important eye contact with the audience and give them a reassuring smile that shows appreciation for their being present to take part in the musical presentation about to begin.
- Acknowledge the ensemble on stage by having them stand.
- Have the performers turn to face the audience when they stand and share a smile of their own.
- Shake hands with the concertmaster or concertmistress which, by this simple act, expresses appreciation to the entire ensemble for preparing the program.

All of these pre-performance protocols are very important in helping to establish a positive rapport with the audience. There are enough "barriers" already in place that tend to create a wall between the performers and the audience. Barriers create a feeling of separation and tend to reduce the musical impact of the performance. For example, the conductor and the members of the ensemble are in formal attire; the audience is not. The ensemble is performing in a brightly-lit environment while the audience sits mostly in the dark. The ensemble is above the audience on a raised stage and you, the conductor, are even higher, standing on the podium. There are so many things to consider – and the downbeat has yet to be given.

The previous paragraphs have focused mainly on the perception of the audience as they wait for the start of a program. They have anticipated this concert in a wide spectrum of emotion ranging from those of nervous parents there to support their children (and thank you to those important folks) to people who paid high-ticket prices to hear their favorite symphony or watch their favorite conductor.

The Performers

A few lines must be added regarding the thoughts and expectations of the performers who sit on stage waiting for the concert to finally become a reality. The veteran professional musician and a young student musician performing for the first time have very different expectations for what is about to take place. Obviously, their feelings will vary greatly in a wide spectrum of anticipation (perhaps, also, in the number of last-minute trips to the restroom). For the sake of discussion and since *Teaching Music through Performance in Band* is geared to those of us in the education of young musicians at the secondary and university level, I direct the following comments to non-professional musicians.

Young musicians are generally so nervous before a performance that, more often than not, nerves get in the way of their best effort. I had a college band director who used to say, "If the music is well rehearsed and basic fundamentals carefully observed, then the performance will be maintained at a high level of proficiency." If the student members feel the music has been well prepared and they are confident of their own performance level, then confidence overcomes nerves. With younger groups, it pays to follow a few sound principles just prior to a performance:

1. Allow for adequate warm-up time with the full ensemble.
2. Utilize the same materials and tuning procedures you employ in a regular rehearsal.
3. Keep the ensemble focused but without tension.
4. Don't give ensemble members a lot of free time just prior to taking the stage, as this usually creates situations that can lead to faulty mental and physical preparation.
5. Don't let the ensemble sit in the performance area for an undue length of time prior to starting the performance. This just creates added stress and tension among the musicians.
6. Make the students feel at ease and relaxed through your confidence and attitude in the warm-up room.
7. After acknowledging the audience and having the ensemble stand and be seated, do not wait too long before you give the downbeat.
8. Just before you give the downbeat, make sure you give the band a warm, confident smile that says you have complete confidence in their ability to perform well.
9. Maintain eye contact with the ensemble prior to the downbeat and well into the first phrase before you look at the score.
10. Finally, make sure you have mentally sung the opening phrase to yourself so you have the tempo well in mind before you give the preparatory beat.

Path to the Podium

All of us have a story to share of our "path to the podium." For most, it is one of careful planning and progression through an approved course of study in music education that led to our work as conductors. Somewhere along the line our paths crossed with a teacher and/or conductor who inspired, motivated, and instilled in us a desire to consider a career in music.

For others, however, the path to the podium came after working in some related music field or as a member of a professional orchestra. There are numerous examples in our orchestral heritage of conductors who emerged from the ranks of the orchestra membership to become quite famous conductors: Toscanni, Monteux, Ormandy, Barbiralli, and Wallenstein, to name just a few. Some who decide on a conducting career may have arrived at this decision through a deepening desire to explore the profession or, in some cases, by sheer accident. On the other hand, most of us in the band conducting field grew up playing in a band and proceeded through a degree program which eventually led us to a conducting position in an educational institution. Music has been an integral part of our existence for all of time and will continue in that capacity for as long as there is life on our planet. I cannot imagine life without music. So as we begin the new century – and millennium – we must continue to strive for excellence in teaching. We must constantly evaluate our role as music educators and conductors. Music enriches lives, so we must continue to build positive musical connections with people at every age level.

Productivity through Personality

Expectations

Does the band that you stand in front of on a regular basis understand your expectations for them as an ensemble? The students certainly sit in front of you with *their* expectations, so you must first determine if you are both on the same page. I have been in front of some bands where it was pretty apparent my expectations did not match those of the students. The matter at hand, then, is how to establish a common ground so that in the end everyone will feel a sense of satisfaction in what has been accomplished. It doesn't hurt to let students know your goals for them as an ensemble. This can be done in a variety of ways, but certainly you can just simply state your objectives. These objectives may be long range or short range, but the most important criterion is the manner in which you go about attaining these goals. Make sure you are honest and reasonable relative to the age, ability, and potential of the players in your band.

During the past thirty years I have had the opportunity, and the great pleasure, to guest conduct many different bands throughout the United States and in several foreign countries. One of the things I often find interesting and enjoyable is when three or four small schools join together for some type of festival which combines the talents of several bands. These are wonderful events which give the students and communities involved a unique musical experience. Often, when discussing literature selection for these "festival bands," the directors involved select music quite above the ability of their individual bands. I fully understand their rationale. Each of the participating schools probably has a small ensemble, many times without a complete instrumentation. When they combine forces, there is a full instrumentation and an increased number of players. It is, therefore, logical to be drawn into the belief that music of a much higher grade level can be performed. While each of the schools primarily perform grade three material, for example, there is now the false assumption that this bigger ensemble, with all instrumental parts covered, can choose music from a much higher grade level. And of course, the guest conductor is to accomplish this feat with a short one-day rehearsal schedule! We all know, however, that no matter what people think, there is no *magic* in the little white stick!

Each of us in our own programs, regardless of the level, must be realistic in what our students can successfully achieve. Of course, there are many factors involved: the individual ability of the performers, the amount of rehearsal time available prior to each performance, and the difficulty of the music selected for the program. The key words for me are "successfully achieve." There must be a sense of musical satisfaction at each juncture of the road for programs to move from one level to the next.

Preparation

In any given situation, it goes without saying that the better the preparation for the rehearsal the more productive it will be. The psychology involved in the approach to a rehearsal can be a tremendous advantage for the conductor. After all, the conductor is the one who has studied the score; made decisions on balance, dynamic subtleties, phrasing, tempo, and timbre; and anticipated potential problems in technique and rhythmic complexity. Using a "bull's-eye" approach, everything from the warm-up to the final selection in the rehearsal is carefully thought out and planned. Therefore, at the end of the rehearsal everyone involved will feel as though the intended goals of the day have been met.

I cannot stress enough that all too often we forget we are dealing with young students who have their own likes and dislikes, loves and hates, and good and bad habits. Sometimes all of the best preparation and effort seems to be for naught. We must not allow ourselves to become so agitated and frustrated during the rehearsal that we lose our control and vision for that particular day. The worst thing you can do is begin to react and say things in such a negative manner that not only will that day be lost but it may also take a long time to get attitudes and positive feelings flowing once again.

The conductor certainly has a broad spectrum of approaches from which to choose in creating the atmosphere desired for a rehearsal. One can be either tyrannical in his/her approach or the other extreme of completely passive. Conductors have found success at both ends of this spectrum. However, every conductor must have an approach in this sensitive area that best represents each individual personality.

I once attended a conducting workshop given by Frederick Fennell when he was still conducting the Eastman Wind Ensemble. I was exhilarated, motivated, and inspired to become a Fennell clone (long before the infamous sheep). So I rushed home to my aspiring Class B high school band and attempted to employ everything I had learned. I assumed it would enable my ensemble to respond in the same manner I observed in this select college band under the baton of Mr. Fennell. For the next several rehearsals, what actually transpired with my band was the group became less proficient and focused while our next concert was fast approaching. During a private lesson with a sophomore contrabass clarinet player (Richard Hansen, now the Director of Bands at St. Cloud State University), I mentioned how frustrated I was becoming at the poor progress of the band and that, in fact, I felt the group was quickly losing ground. In the most innocent way, Mr. Hansen told me, "You know, Mr. Cramer, you just haven't been yourself lately." With all due respect to my good friend and colleague Mr. Fennell, it hit me like a slap in the face that I can *only* be effective as I work through my *own* personality. This is a valuable lesson for every conductor to learn; be yourself and utilize, to the full potential, *your personality* and not that of someone else.

With a focused and positive approach to the music, the ensemble and the individual members will obtain a much more satisfying result. There seems to be a general consensus of opinion that conductors, through the force of individual personalities, make things happen. The music making under their leadership becomes convincing and meaningful. Here is what Leonard Bernstein had to say on this subject:

"Almost any musician can be a conductor, even a pretty good one, but only a rare musician can be a great one. The qualities that distinguish great conductors lie far above and beyond technique alone. These are the tangibles of conducting, the mysteries, and the feelings that conductors strive to learn and acquire. If they have a natural perception, it will increase and deepen as they mature. But, even the pretty good conductor must have this attribute in their personality and that is the power to communicate through arms, face, fingers and whatever vibrations may flow from them."

Work Ethic

Are you a diligent person? Is there a persistence and urgency about your rehearsal technique with which the students can readily identify? A conductor who possesses these traits will instill in his or her students a similar work ethic, one that will produce positive results in a timely manner. In each rehearsal there needs to be a feeling of accomplishment. Nothing builds success like success. So even if you begin with the most conservative goals, if these goals are met the ensemble will feel good about the time and energy invested. Perhaps one of the greatest assets we need to cultivate in working with young musicians is patience. We need to take to heart the phrase that is often found written on restaurant menus: "Please be patient; quality food takes time to prepare." While we all have experienced young students who seem to make giant strides overnight, it usually follows that most young musicians advance at a slower rate, and we need to respect their differences. Losing our patience slows down progress. One of my Indiana University colleagues, Eugene Rousseau, is the ultimate example of persistent patience. His even disposition and patience never seem to waiver when working with his students. Yet his expectations remain high. He continues to be encouraging with all his students as they develop to their full potential.

Help your students become diligent workers as you demonstrate your willingness to be diligent in your work with them. They will identify this outstanding characteristic of your personality and respond to your motivation and example.

Discipline

Nothing productive can ever be accomplished if there is chaos and uncontrolled behavior. Teaching/learning cannot take place without order and control. All of us can cite examples of programs and conductors at every level who emphasize control techniques using harshness and the old "iron fist" approach to discipline. Some have successful programs. There are, however, many others no longer teaching because this technique did not work for them. I know the subject of discipline and control continues to elicit extensive writing. I have no intention of getting too deeply into this area for fear of traveling an already well-worn path, but a few comments are appropriate.

The handling of discipline is uniquely individual. So much of what we do or say is directly connected to the way we were "controlled" as young children by our parents and teachers. My personal experience was growing up in a home where there were expectations of how I was to act and treat other people. My parents never hesitated to discipline when they felt my actions deserved punishment. However, one of my sisters enjoys teasing me by saying that if I got spanked it was with a broom straw and that she got the handle. Now, I know that was not true, but the point is there was a line to be towed and we were expected to follow the rules. Likewise, in school I had my share of strict teachers as well as those who maintained a fairly lax classroom. It seemed to me that I learned more, and felt greater satisfaction about my work, when the class was well organized, focused, and the teacher set expectations for the class to follow and achieve.

I firmly believe students need, desire, and welcome direction in their lives. Teachers who helped to shape and formulate my future direction and goals in music had a wide range of discipline techniques. There is of course *discipline*, and then there is *discipline*. Some people may become mean-spirited, vindictive, and insensitive in their approach and seem to have little success. Yet others can be strict disciplinarians and still achieve successful and lasting results. The key is the manner in which discipline is administered. It must be carried out in such a way that students know the teacher really cares for them and believes in what is being taught. When students sense they are not respected as individuals who can contribute to the program, all is lost. Work your own special "magic" by carefully evaluating how you can be the most effective using *your personality* in the way you want to approach your students. Genuinely care for your students and instill in them a sense of personal pride in what they are doing. You will be rewarded far beyond your expectations.

Consistency

As teachers, this area keeps us constantly scrutinizing our handling of students. We need to be consistent in all that we do and say, but this is so difficult to carry out. Yet we must strive for this in the most honest and forthright manner that we can.

I once commented to a respected colleague that he always appeared to be so consistent in how he treated people on and off the podium. (Even though it has been over thirty years since he made the following statement, it is still firmly etched in my mind.) He said, "I am the same person whether I am on the podium or not. Why should I deceive my students into thinking I am two different people? If my personality doesn't work in one place, why would it work in the other?" Through consistency in our actions and expectations, we can maintain uniformity and accountability in dealing not only with students in rehearsal but in all of our professional and personal relationships.

Verbal Communication through Personality

Things to Avoid

I am sure we could all write a book filled with the "things" we wished we had *not* said in the rehearsal room. There are things I have said in the heat of a tense rehearsal that I wish I could take back. The frustration level can become very intense at times, and we let thoughtless words slip out. Usually the moment we express ourselves this way we know it is going to cause pain to someone. Verbal barbs can cause deep wounds though they seem small at the time, but they rarely work in any shape or form. We must guard against this kind of overreaction.

The only recourse you have when you realize there has been a serious error in your choice of words is to go to the person and offer an apology. The best course of action is to say "I'm sorry" when you have caused pain to an individual student or even the entire ensemble. Students will understand and accept this. When you don't let your pride get in the way of a sincere apology, the students' respect for you will deepen. Using humiliation, fear, cruelty, name calling, sarcasm, or any form of unkind behavior is neither necessary nor effective. These negative approaches will only produce ineffective results.

Psychological Perceptions

There are many in the teaching profession who studied psychology extensively. I wish I had paid closer attention and worked harder in the required psychology courses I had in undergraduate school, for they contained a great deal of "perfectly sensible" ways to deal with students. However, like many students at that age, I just did not see the importance of these non-music-related courses. If I had paid more attention to the subject matter, it just might have saved me from some avoidable, early bruises to my ego – not to mention embarrassing moments.

Do you allow your negative attitudes to show? If you are like most people, then you are probably guilty of harboring a negative attitude from time to time. If you are experiencing problems with attitude, then you must leave them at the door of the rehearsal room. So often attitudes are shaped by situations that have nothing to do directly with the rehearsal and the students. Avoid a condescending attitude or manipulative and demeaning conversation when speaking with students. Everyone wants and needs to feel respected as individuals, regardless of age. Couch your criticisms carefully and offer positive encouragement in liberal doses. A good rule to follow is to use many positive comments for every negative comment that you make.

I am sure every conductor when stepping to the podium desires to be "liked" by the entire ensemble. There are, of course, those who at least on the surface give the impression they couldn't care less if anyone liked them. Nevertheless, inwardly we all want to be liked by our students and people we deal with on a regular basis. Conductors who want to be "buddies" or one of the "gang" and allow themselves to be called nicknames will find control and attention hard to come by in the rehearsal room. Very few directors have the ability to pull off this kind of rapport. More often than not it fails. Not every student is going to like you (hopefully more will than not), but the important thing is they must respect what the program represents and what you represent. Remember, respect is a two-way street, so develop a sincere respect for students and they will want to respect you as well. Even those students who do not necessarily like you can respect you deeply for your knowledge, your vision, your diligence, your enthusiasm, your exuberance and, most assuredly, your love for music and music making.

Effective Participation through Personality

Motivation

Every great teacher/leader/conductor must possess the ability to motivate and inspire young people. Students who are motivated and excited will consistently perform at a higher level of execution than students of perhaps even greater ability but without the advantage of inspired leadership. We must always keep in mind that our students look to the podium for confident and knowledgeable direction. A major factor of motivation is our own personal attitude. Students must know, without a doubt, that we are sincere in what we are trying to achieve. Even though we show determination and diligence, it will be our sincerity, enthusiasm, and positive attitude that produce concentrated effort from our students.

Self-Esteem

The more I read about youth today, the more I realize that one of the most important aspects of their daily lives is the need for self-esteem. Self-esteem can be shattered very easily, so we must be careful in dealing with this issue. Many students feel intuitively that their teachers like them, but it is equally or perhaps more important that they feel respected by their teachers. I often tell my own students preparing for a teaching career, "You must like your students to work with them." We need to become perceptive teachers capable of "reading" our students. In doing so we can better cope with situations in the classroom before possible confrontational situations occur. How do students look when they walk in the door? What is their posture? Do they make eye contact with you or their peers? Listen to what they are saying to their friends. If the morale of your membership is high, then positive things will transpire in your program.

Students will work effectively if they are having fun. It is important to understand that having fun while accomplishing musical goals is critical; it's not just chasing the notes. The higher the level of accomplishment, the greater the satisfaction. Tireless effort will come forth if students are enjoying the challenge placed before them. As conductors, a keen sense of humor is necessary for enjoyable rehearsals. I'm not suggesting that you should tell an endless stream of jokes from the podium, but certainly any rehearsal is ripe with opportunities to develop your "podium side" manner.

Non-Verbal Communication through Personality

Posture

As I was growing up, my mother reminded me on a fairly consistent basis to "stand up straight." She was doing her best to establish good posture habits, but I am sure she also knew that a person who tends to "slump" could project a negative image. If we want to portray a positive personality, a correct posture will visibly add to that image. Don't shuffle but walk with a brisk, powerful stride that projects confidence and strength. Perhaps one of the most enjoyable and informative conducting sessions I ever attended was taught by a mime. I learned so much about using my body and face to express many different emotions, all without saying a word. The importance of posture and how posture can project strong images to the audience was eye opening. Stand tall and use your physical presence to the fullest as you exhibit power and strength in your conducting.

Face and Eyes

It is pretty difficult to mask emotions when all people have to do is look at the face and into the eyes. The face and eyes usually express one's true feeling. It was probably a parent who first said, "I can read you like a book," referring to the facial expression of a conscience-stricken child.

As conductors, we must learn to take full advantage of our faces and eyes. We can "say" so much without saying anything at all. Avoid using inappropriate faces that might humiliate a student in front of his or her peers. This never results in anything except frustration and discouragement. Following is a rehearsal situation that happens quite often. Which reaction would you choose to use?

> A student has been working diligently in rehearsal, not goofing off, but makes an incorrect entrance in a piece being rehearsed. The student is one of the better musicians in the band and a leader. The conductor now has a couple of choices: (1) stop the rehearsal for an opportunity to once again exhibit your power and position by making this error an example of poor practice habits and lack of concentration or (2) recognize the student's facial expression (which says, "I feel bad about the error."), catch the student's eye, and give the student a reassuring smile and a nod of the head that says, "I understand what happened and I know it won't happen again." The music making does not stop.

Everyone in the ensemble knows what happened and who made the mistake, but by choosing the second option, you have helped turn what could have been an embarrassing situation for the student and an uncomfortable feeling for the band into a positive experience. You have gained more respect from your students because you demonstrated not only insight and control but also kindness. A smile has a strength that can far surpass the sneer and look of anger. Use smile muscles frequently, and show the group how enjoyable making music can be.

Leadership through Personality

Throughout the history of mankind we have had men and women with character, competence, integrity, and skill step forward to provide outstanding leadership in every aspect of our society. There are others who have shown only one or two of the attributes mentioned above and failed in leadership. Strength of *leadership through personality* must involve all four of these elements to ensure positive results.

Strong leadership *sees* what needs to be done and *takes action* to ensure success. Conductors must not turn away from tasks that seem below their station. If a task needs to be done to make the program more efficient and you have the means to carry it out, then do it; leaders serve!

Outstanding conductors influence others not because of their position or power but because the quality of their relationships with people has gained their trust and confidence. In the past I have asked students to write down their thoughts addressing the question, "What makes a great leader?" Amazingly to me, many of the answers turn out to be the same time after time. Here are a few of these shared thoughts describing effective leadership: "they supported me," "they had the courage to do the right thing," "they challenged me," "they listened," "they acted as mentors to others," "they recognized outstanding work," "they followed through on commitments," and perhaps the one shared most often, "they exhibited humility at all times." What a tremendous checklist for all of us to gauge the quality of our leadership skills.

Leadership demands that we are *learners*. We live in an ever-changing world. If someone would have told me twenty years ago that I would be doing this kind of work on a word processor small enough to sit on my lap, I would have smiled and, shaking my head in disbelief, said, "I don't think so." It is difficult to remain current with every new development, but we must continue to grow. Without growth comes stagnation. No one ever has enough knowledge, so continue to learn and grow through every form of communication. Teachers and conductors in our profession have a tremendous advantage because everyone is so cooperative and willing to share information. What a great profession we have chosen. I feel sorry for the millions of people who go to work every day wishing they did not have to go.

Conclusion

Bruno Walter states in his book, *Of Music and Music-Making,* "It is far better for a conductor to build their own style and traits through their own character and personality. The more powerful the personality of the conductor, the more they can demand."

Your students need your energy, your creativity, your courage, your vision, and especially your love of music. There is another aspect I have not yet mentioned, which is that the students need you to *stay* in the profession. The profession needs you to *stay in the profession.* At a presentation I was giving a few years ago at the Midwest clinic, I asked to see the hands of people who were about to embark upon a teaching career. It was a good-sized audience, including a large number of young "soon-to-be-graduated" college students, who quickly raised their hands. I continued by inquiring as to how many had been teaching for five years or less. Again a good number of hands flew into the air. As can be expected, as I progressed through the years in five-year increments the number of hands raised at each level declined dramatically as the number of teaching years increased.

Every precaution must be taken to avoid the all-too-familiar "band director burn-out." Pace yourself and your program. So many programs and teachers keep such demanding schedules that both the teachers and the students begin to lose their motivation and vision for the real music making goals. Stay in good health; exercise on a regular basis; and above all else, save time in your busy schedule for yourself and your family. The music profession needs your strength of character, your powerful personality, and your musical maturity.

I have always enjoyed this pointed statement made by William Steinberg when he said, "I think mainly that every conductor develops their own method with which they express themselves after their own nature and that the only factor that counts is the power of their personality."

Through the *power of personality* and the shared love for music, we can exalt, enlighten, and encourage our students in such a manner as to have a positive impact on them and all future generations of music makers.

CHAPTER 4

Making a Difference
with Your Dash

Ray E. Cramer

The word "dash" has many meanings and connotations. It can be constructive or destructive. Positive definitions include such words as *speed*, *drive*, *spice*, *swell*, *energy*, *spirit*, *gift*, and *élan* (which means *exuberance*, *ardor*, or *enthusiasm*). Negative definitions would include words like *bolt*, *hurl*, *pelt*, *ruin*, *slam*, *crush*, *fling*, *spurn*, *throw*, *collide*, or *hurdle*. The title of this chapter and the use of the word 'dash' also have a duel meaning. In addition to the above definitions, it also relates to a punctuation mark indicating a break. In the following pages, I wish to discuss "dash" as it covers the positive and negative implications in day-to-day living and "dash" as it represents the time line of our lives.

Every day we all face responsibilities requiring decisions that may be as far-reaching as choosing a life partner or as simple as to what to wear to work. The fact remains that as we make these decisions, factors come into play that can impact our lives in ways that seem simple and practical on the surface, but when combined with other obligations can create unbelievable stress. That is why it is so important to "see the big picture" as we are so often told. It is an easy statement to make but one that takes a great deal of thought and creative vision. The younger we are, the more difficult the task to be able to recognize who we are and what our role is going to be in life. As we gain experience and confidence in our chosen field, we begin to formulate goals and expectations of what can be attained during a career. As these elements of your life begin to fall into place, other areas will assume new responsibilities, which will ultimately change how you deal with time commitments throughout your working life.

All of us would like a crystal ball to show how our life will unfold. We want to know how important we will be to our family, friends, students, colleagues and, of course, ourselves. However, that is only fantasy, for we all must live life day by day. We need to remember that the important thing is to each day *make a difference in someone's life*.

How Do You Live Your Dash

I read of a man who stood to speak
At the funeral of a friend.
He referred to the dates on her tombstone
From the beginning...to the end.
He noted that first came her date of birth
And spoke the following date with tears,
But said what mattered most of all
Was the dash between those years.

For that dash represents all the time
That she spent alive on earth...
And now only those who loved her
Know what that little line is worth.
For it matters not, how much we own;
The cars...the house...the cash.
What matters is how we live and love
And how we spend our dash.

So think about this long and hard...
Are there things you'd like to change?
For you never know how much time is left
That can still be rearranged.
If we could just slow down enough
To consider what's true and real,
And always try to understand
The way other people feel.

And be less quick to anger,
And show appreciation more
And love the people in our lives
Like we've never loved before.
If we treat each other with respect,
And more often wear a smile...
Remembering that this special dash
Might only last a while.

So when your eulogy's being read
With your life's actions to rehash...
Would you be proud of the things they say
About how you spent your dash?

—Author unknown

Family Obligations

In a lecture early in my teaching career, a speaker said, "Don't major in the minors." This was a catchy and clever statement meant to elicit a chuckle from those listening. However, as I began to assume more responsibilities, the phrase took on a whole new meaning. I fully understand that there are many different kinds of family responsibilities. Some of you are single, some married, and others married with children. Regardless of your personal situation, family obligations, in any form, are part of your daily routine.

The life of a band director, as you well know, can become all-consuming if you let it. What you must do is establish priorities that will allow you to function in a manner conducive to a stable and effective home life and to being an effective teacher. It is possible! Yes, it takes work and cooperation, but more importantly is the decision to *make it work*.

If you are married with family obligations, then you will experience the wide-ranging demands placed on you by your employer and your family. It is quite easy to become so engulfed in your job that everything else becomes less important. Of course, this can be devastating to your marriage and family. Your family obligations demand as much work and energy as your job to be successful.

Your wife or husband, along with your children, needs to connect with you each day. I personally believe you cannot be effective in your job without a strong and loving home environment. As your children grow up, their requirements change, and with that comes serious decision-making on your part.

Our children are now grown, married, and have careers of their own, but I clearly remember their middle and high school years. They became quite involved in music and sports events, which involved a lot of weekend activities. I was very involved in weekend work myself with professional obligations I felt important to my developing career. I realized my children were only going to be in the house for a limited number of years before they went to college and on to their own careers. If I wanted to truly invest in their lives, then I had to decide which weekend events were the most important to attend.

My teaching career would extend well past the school-age years of my children, so for me the decision was easy to make. I wanted to be able to attend as many of their functions as possible, knowing full well that if I did not, many special moments would only be afforded me vicariously through my wife or related to me secondhand by my children. Even with all the fantastic audio and video equipment available today, none of those recorded events would have the same impact as my being there. Therefore, I wrote my children's events into my calendar first, thus avoiding the temptation to accept professional engagements that would mean missing any event in which my children were involved. While I fully understood I would miss many professional engagements, I was never sorry for being present at our children's activities. Later, they both expressed how much they appreciated our support, interest, and presence at these events during their school years.

Setting Priorities

What it boils down to is setting priorities that you know and believe will make a difference in the lives of your spouse, children, or other family members. It is a little frightening to think what I would have missed had I not decided to become immersed in my family life rather than become someone who only showed up to eat, sleep, or occasionally engage in some form of conversation. Please do not misunderstand me; there are times when job requirements unavoidably demand our undivided attention and energy. However, when you are with your family, make the time you share quality time. Give them your full attention and support. The *quality* of time spent with your family is more important than the *amount* of time…that means give them your undivided attention. If you are lounging in your favorite chair reading the paper or watching TV while your children attempt to get your attention, then even though you are in the same room, you are not making a connection.

Role Models

Perhaps you did not grow up in a home where family life was a top priority. Then it is very important that you identify role models who do place this kind of priority in their lives. My wife and I were fortunate to grow up in homes with parents who were supportive and interested in what we were doing during our school years. There were times, I am sure, when we felt like our parents were being too involved by not allowing our participation in some of the "fun" things we felt our friends were being allowed to do. But in retrospect, we know our parents only had our best interest at heart and wanted to protect us from those things that would be damaging to our personal well being.

Only through love and trust does this kind of connection develop within the family. Love is an ingredient that contains such power and inspiration that lives can be transformed in a way unparalleled by any other emotion. A home without love is a home likely destined for pain, stress, conflict and, usually, failure. I am saddened by the number of fractured lives created by a home environment devoid of love. For as Paul says in I Corinthians:

If I speak in the tongues of men and of angels, but have not love, I am only a resounding gong or a clanging cymbal. Love is patient, love is kind. It does not envy, it does not boast, it is not proud. It is not rude, it is not self-seeking, it is not easily angered, it keeps no record of wrongs. It always protects, always trusts, always hopes, always perseveres. And now these three things remain: faith, hope, and love. But the greatest of these is love.

Probably most of us have former teachers to thank for exciting and motivating us to seek a similar career. What was it about this person who turned us on so we just had to pursue a similar field of endeavor to find personal happiness and satisfaction? Perhaps we saw fame, fortune, glory, prestige, honor, or other attractive benefits that we felt only would come through a similar experience for ourselves. All of these could be a factor, but I can assure you it usually is not fortune. I know of few people in our profession who have become rich, but then again, being rich is relative, and personally speaking, the experiences I have had in teaching far outweigh the monetary rewards I may have missed by not being in a more lucrative profession.

So what did these people have in common that we all wanted to emulate? Assuredly, all included several of the following: enthusiasm about their work and profession, energy, vision, creativeness, passion, desire to share thoughts and feelings, knowledge of subject, sensitivity, positive attitudes, the ability to bring others into the glow of music-making. Most teachers I have known over the years want nothing more than to try to inspire in students their love for music. If you are lucky, perhaps you have had contact with one or more of these teachers during your school years. When this occurs, then you are never the same. We are so moved by the magnetism of these special people that our lives are changed in dramatic and positive ways forever. I can think of no greater way to say thank you to a former teacher who influenced your life than doing your best to become one yourself.

For us to be able to accomplish our goals, we have to make sure we do those things that will allow us to establish positive relationships on a daily basis with our families and with other people. This, of course, involves making correct decisions—decisions that influence how others perceive our existence.

1: Don't be a "loner"!

Most successful people in any profession grow in effectiveness by involving others in their work. If we become self-absorbed, we begin to think that our way is the only way. We are then on the path to ineffective work. Those around us strengthen us in a sharing, collaborative effort that benefits all concerned.

2: Don't try to be someone you are not!

Young students—and people in general—are quite perceptive when it comes to "seeing who we really are." Our society tends to place a high priority on helping individuals become someone they are not. Too often young people are sold a bill of goods, being told they are not good enough, smart enough, pretty or handsome enough to become "popular." All sorts of mechanisms are devised to "assist" them in establishing a different image. Adults are very good at this also. Why is it that who or what we are is not good enough? Who makes those distinctions? Certainly our culture and the media, in all forms, help to create these doubts in our minds. Our most effective manner of establishing good relationships with people is to be ourselves. Be real! We are who we are, and to try and make ourselves into something or someone else only compounds the problems involved in building strong personal relationships.

3: There are no shortcuts!

We see all the time in advertising how important it is to have something now. My wife and I have discussed on several occasions how it seems the younger generation has this fixation on having to have everything now. It is made so easy for us with time payments, long-term loans, or no money down—the pay-later syndrome. This is fine, but in the end we all have to pay, and if we cannot, then we lose all of those things we felt were so important. Most tasks or goals will take time and effort to come to successful conclusions. Patience is a wonderful thing, for with it comes the pleasure of expectation, anticipation, and realization. Don't try to hurry the process, for usually the result is far less satisfying than if we just exercised patience.

4: Avoid the lingering feeling of contentedness!

During any period of our lives, we can quickly become complacent if we fall into a pattern of familiarity and routine. Nothing ever stays the same. So we must be flexible enough to identify those things in our work and daily routine that inhibit our growth and effectiveness. Most people are afraid of change because it represents the unknown or unfamiliar. However, truly outstanding educators establish their effectiveness with their ability to change and their creativity. One of my favorite quotes of the late Will Rogers simply states, "Even if you are on the right track, you'll still get run over if you just sit there." So don't fear change; it can be the vehicle to even greater rewards as we press forward in our teaching career.

Professional Responsibilities

Most people are constantly searching for the perfect job, which means all the pegs in the right holes and the wrinkles carefully ironed out. As a colleague of mine once said, "There is no Mecca" (referring to finding the perfect job). Every job, regardless of the level, has drawbacks and flaws that, on first inspection, may be hidden from view. Only when we are on the job do we find the imperfections. The immediate question, of course, is how to deal with those problems. Usually what one discovers is that most of the difficulties can be overcome with thorough planning and a cooperative attitude. If, over a period of time, it is impossible to solve or remedy the difficulties, then a decision must be made regarding professional goals and the ability to achieve them in this situation.

When considering a job, make sure to find out as much about the responsibilities as humanly possible. That may mean investigating the job beyond the publicized listing. The important element is that you feel your strengths and abilities match those expected by the employer. A team of oxen only works together if they are equally yoked.

As you become more and more involved in the music field, you soon discover how easy it is to become inflicted with the "of course I will do it" disease. This can cause all sorts of pain and strain. There are certainly activities and responsibilities that we want to and must become involved with professionally. However, when the activities outside your regular job become too consuming of time and energy, then it is time to re-evaluate your professional obligations. It is important to be involved in the profession, but not at the expense of job and family stability.

Stress Management

The amount of money spent dealing with stress-related issues in our society today is truly astounding. Stress creates such damage to our health that we need to do everything in our power to alleviate its harmful effects. Just what is stress? People have differing views and opinions on this topic ranging from simple to complex answers. The dictionary defines stress as "a strain or straining force, mental or physical tension, a reaction to resisting such a force." Throughout time, human beings have learned to defend themselves against all kinds of stress assaults. These "assaults" create changes that may include increased heart rate, blood pressure, rate of breathing, muscular tension, and general metabolic rate. It is important to identify the stress in our life and decide if that stress is excessive. If it is, we must learn how to reduce the rate of "wear and tear" being experienced by decreasing the load being carried or increase our ability to carry it. We often need to do both.

How do you handle stress? In general, most people find their own best method to deal with stressful situations. However, some people either do not realize what is causing stress in their life or do not understand the symptoms. Do any of the following questions pertain to how you feel or what you do to deal with stress?

- Is it hard for you to unwind during your free time?
- Do you need a drink or tranquilizer to relax?
- If you're upset about something, do you find that your thoughts race through your mind so you can't sleep?
- When tense or anxious, do you feel the need to smoke or eat?
- Do you often get so worried that you have indigestion, diarrhea, or nausea?
- Are there people or situations in life that make you feel uptight just by thinking about them?
- Do you feel that you're always racing against the clock?

If you answered yes to one or more of these questions, then you ought to think about making some changes in your lifestyle to deal with the situation and your stress level. I will discuss practical ways to help release stress levels and improve your overall health.

Time Management

Work! Work! Work! Go! Go! Go! Hurry! Hurry! Hurry! Does this sound familiar? How many people do you know that remind you of a dog chasing his tail? Round and round they go, and in the end, what did they accomplish? I believe that some people can exist only if they are constantly busy. Perhaps frantic is a better description of their routine. They believe that unless they live a life in frenzy they must be wasting their time. Hurry becomes a way of life. I often get tired just thinking about the hectic pace that some people seem to enjoy. Or do they really? Perhaps the important question is what are they accomplishing? Some folks just have to be busy, because if they're not, then they must be lazy. If you are anything like me, I become uncomfortable around such people. Often, busy people are not accomplishing nearly as much as the illusion they create. All that seems to be accomplished is physical and mental fatigue. After all, if people are not worn to a frazzle, they must not be dedicated to their profession. I do not think we are called to live like this and still be effective in our work and personal relationships. The world would have us believe that being busy, fatigued, and stressed out is a normal lifestyle. Tim Hansel in his book *When I Relax I Feel Guilty* puts it well:

We are called to be faithful, not frantic. If we are to meet the challenges of today, there must be integrity between our words and our lives, and more reliance on the source of our purpose.

We live in a workaholic society. There never seems to be enough time to do the things we really desire to do. We are too busy living as fast as we can. Studies show that the average American household works many more hours per week than twenty years ago. Advanced technology has not helped in this matter; it has only added to the problem. We need to make sure we maintain control of how we use our time. I have taken an excerpt from a poem I read in the monthly publication *Guidepost,* which made great sense to me and maybe to you also.

"Take Time..."

Take time for friends...they are the source of happiness.
Take time for work...it is the price of success.
Take time to think...it is the source of power.
Take time to read...it is the foundation of knowledge.
Take time to laugh...it is the singing that helps with life's loads.
Take time to love...it is the one sacrament of life.
Take time to play...it is the secret of youth.

—Author Unknown

Some people are blessed with more energy than others. I happen to be a person who has always enjoyed the ability to sustain a high energy level for prolonged periods of time. However, that does not mean I do not enjoy those times of quiet relaxation. I also know people who cannot relax anytime, even while on vacation. None of us wish to experience the displeasure of a personal power failure. However, without adequate time to refresh and rejuvenate, we soon begin to fade in the stress of day-to-day existence. What "refills" your tank? I will later share a few ideas for maintaining one's energy and physical stamina.

Our constant battle is that of balancing personal and professional commitments. It is a difficult task. Unfortunately, our society usually recognizes success only as it pertains to our work. However, be aware that any habit or activity that promises short-term satisfaction can be costly in the long run, as we all too often trade the things that are most important for those that are least important. Define early in your career what is important. Make lists with professional goals on one side and personal relationship goals on the other. If one side or the other becomes unbalanced, then you should probably take careful stock of what is going to be the dominant priority in your life. This takes constant personal evaluation and examination. Now just to make certain we understand each other, it is important to work and work hard. We are expected to work and to be productive. However, this should not be at the expense of maintaining a healthy lifestyle.

To gain another perspective on this subject, I would like to refer to a couple of paragraphs taken from a book titled *Your Work Matters to God*, by Doug Sherman and William Hendricks. They are discussing Rocky Balboa, who as a fighter embodies the careerist vision and articulates its ultimate slogan: "Go for it!" The "it" means what? A boxing championship? Lasting fifteen rounds, "going the distance"? The adulation of an adoring public? Defiance—a refusal to "throw" the fight? All this and more for Rocky. His battle, like ours, is to authenticate himself: "It" means whatever it takes to make certain that "self" really does matter. "It" requires determination ("There are many starters, but few finishers"), discipline ("Creativity is two percent inspiration and ninety-eight percent perspiration"), the right goals ("If you aim at nothing, you'll hit it every time"), savvy ("Success in life comes not from holding a good hand, but in playing a poor hand well"), perseverance ("Tough times never last; tough people do"), and vision ("Some people dream dreams and ask, Why? I dream dreams and ask, Why not?"). There is no end to the qualities that supposedly account for success. But all of them reflect human power to somehow "go for it" and get the job done: "Our rewards in life will depend on the quality of the contributions we make."

Developing a Healthful Lifestyle

To achieve positive results in work and life, we must discipline ourselves to develop minds and bodies that will be able to carry out the responsibilities required of our jobs and our families. Without planning and prioritizing these elements of our lives, then we are nothing more than a vessel without a GPS to guide us—of course, I am talking about a Global Positioning System. Aircraft and ships have enjoyed this technology for years, but now we are finding this guidance system in every kind of vehicle. I am amused by watching this system in cars as the system guides you through the most distressing array of streets in the most crowded cities. If you begin to make a wrong turn, a voice will tell you not to turn just yet and to please wait for further instruction. Perhaps as educators we need such a device we can strap on our backs that can tell us when we should say no, yes, right, left, up, down, or give other helpful hints to avoid the traffic jam of over-commitment.

For me, it is important to respect and rely on my faith to guide my decisions. This is my GPS, and it does not require batteries or any other contrived power source. Also, all my life I have tried to stay in good physical condition. It takes time and a consistent effort to maintain a relatively healthy conditioning routine. The effort is well worth the result in how I feel on a day-to-day basis. There are many exercise routines you may choose to follow to assist in keeping you on a regular routine. The one I have used for over thirty years takes little time and does a marvelous job in maintaining fitness and muscle tone. It is the exercise manual developed for the Royal Canadian Air Force. These exercises can be completed in twelve minutes for women and eleven minutes for men. They are simple to do and progress at a rate through charts from 1 (being the easiest) to 6 (usually for advanced athletes only). I believe in this exercise program wholeheartedly. Here are a few passages taken directly from this exercise manual.

Why should you be concerned about physical fitness?

Mechanization, automation, and work-saving devices to make life easy are depriving us of desirable physical activity. As a result, we are in danger of deteriorating physically.

Here are the pertinent facts.

Muscles, unless adequately exercised or used, will become weak and inefficient. Let's look at some of the evidence, which shows why regular vigorous exercise is so essential to physical well-being.

Weak back muscles are associated, in many cases, with lower back pain. It has been estimated that increasing the strength of the back muscles through exercise may eliminate 90 percent of these backaches.

A bulging, sagging abdomen resulting from weakened abdominal muscles is detrimental to good posture.

The efficiency and capacity of your heart, lungs, and other organs can be improved by regular vigorous exercise.

A fit person is less susceptible to common injuries, and, if injured, recovers more rapidly.

The incidence of degenerative heart diseases may be greater in those who have not followed a physically active life.

Regular vigorous exercise plays an important role in controlling your weight.

You are never too old to begin and follow a regular exercise program.

Why You Should Be Fit

Research has shown that:

- The physically fit person is able to withstand fatigue for longer periods than the unfit;

- The physically fit person is better equipped to tolerate physical stress;

- The physically fit person has a stronger and more efficient heart; and

- There is a relationship between good mental alertness, absence of nervous tension (stress), and physical fitness. Physical fitness makes us work better, look better, and feel better.

As I stated earlier, in addition to good physical health through exercise, there are other equally effective ways to relieve stress in our lives. Hobbies and recreational activities can be important in stress management. They take your mind off your worries and give you outlets for your energy. Make a list of the stresses in your life. Cross out the ones out of your control and let go of them. If they are out of your control, don't waste energy on them. Do what you can to reduce the stress in the items left. Here are some additional suggestions to help you reduce the stress levels in your life.

1. Adjust your attitudes and goals. Decide that you're not going to let unimportant things or situations beyond your control bother you. Set realistic short-term and long-term goals. Discuss these goals with others you trust to see if they agree that your goals are realistic and obtainable.

2. Rehearse stressful situations. Visualizing a situation might help you to organize your time, identify what you want, and reduce your anxiety. Even if the situation goes differently than the way you rehearsed, you will be more relaxed about it.

3. Avoid stressful situations. When possible, avoid situations that are likely to make you tense or uptight.

4. Manage your time carefully. Use a planning book, a two- or three-year calendar, or other popular electronic devices to help organize your schedule.

5. Make a "to do" list of the things you want to accomplish everyday.

6. If you are on a tight schedule, allow time for unexpected problems, phone calls, student consultations, and e-mail.

Sometimes the best way to reduce stress is to take a short walk and listen to the wonderful sounds being produced in the great outdoors. In fact, my wife and I find walking one of the very best exercises to keep in shape, release stress, allow for meaningful conversation, and keep life in perspective.

To conclude this section on stress and physical well-being, I would like to quote a few statements from the book *Is It Worth Dying For?*, by Robert B. Eliot, M.D., and Dennis L. Breo. I quote:

Follow your feelings. If you are dissatisfied or want to improve your situation, recognizing that is the first step toward understanding what you do want and moving toward a new goal.

Visualize the future. Dream a little; see yourself where you would like to be (but be realistic, don't make it an impossible dream). Think about what you would like to have written on your tombstone. Define attainable goals, the kind that are achievable and realistic but still require you to stretch. As the poet Robert Browning said, "A man's reach should exceed his grasp." But be practical enough that you can take hold of something.

Concentrate on the few key areas that are most important to you. Don't undermine your efforts by trying to be all things to all people at all times.

In retrospect, look to where you have been to determine your strengths and weaknesses.

Use your time wisely. Make a thorough study of how you spend your time and ruthlessly eliminate the things that you need not be doing. Remember, though, time spent doing "nothing" is often time well spent.

Learn how to delegate. Consider the value of this motto: "Much can be accomplished if you don't care who gets the credit."

Simplify, simplify, simplify. Thoreau said it, "Our lives are too often mired in detail." More true today than in his time. Less really is more.

Take time to plan. Set aside one week or more a year to assess where you've been where you'd like to go, and how you're going to get there.

Conclusion

All of us want to be the best we can be in whatever we do. This is a wonderfully positive attitude and goal. Here are a few other areas that will help us expand our effectiveness as teachers, conductors, fathers, mothers, brothers, and sisters.

Broaden your vision.

It is so easy to become burdened with tunnel vision. We must see around us in all directions. When I was taking flying lessons many years ago, one of my least favorite requirements was to practice flying the aircraft and executing various maneuvers "under the hood." This was a device the instructor placed over your head, which allowed you to only see the instrument panel. The purpose of this exercise was to develop confidence and trust in flying the plane based only on what the instruments were telling me to do. Without the ability to see the horizon, I often felt like the plane was doing something other than what the instruments were reading. My instructor said I was "flying by the seat of your pants." I often found myself "correcting" a problem that did not exist. Of course, when I made a correcting maneuver, then a real problem was created. How often do we do this in real-life situations? We perceive many things incorrectly "flying by the seat of our pants" and only create a more troubling situation by overcorrecting. Trust those things that you have grown to rely on and found to be steady and true. Those tried-and-tested instruments of sensitive communication will keep you flying straight, level.

Involve yourself in as many multi-cultural experiences as you can.

When we see, experience, and understand other cultures, there is renewal, vitality, and freshness in our teaching and music that stretches us to new levels of understanding and competence. Our own personal experience of working with our friends in Japan has brought about a new sensitivity in communicating and expressing thoughts and ideas.

Establish friendships "outside the field."

In each location we have lived, we have worked diligently to develop friendships with people from every walk of life. You get an entirely different perspective on your work by sharing your life with people who have nothing to do with your profession. I have grown personally by observing and understanding the vision and perspective of others.

View the students with whom you work as people, not a name on the class list.

Consider how much time is spent with students over a given length of time in their school career. We may well spend as much quality time with them as will their parents in many situations. While it is important to maintain a student/teacher relationship, there is absolutely nothing wrong with the students seeing that you truly care about them as people and musicians. Respect is a street that clearly runs in two directions. We can only gain the respect of our students by respecting them first. One of the great benefits of any teaching career is the student who returns after graduation to express his/her gratitude for the experience he/she had under your leadership.

Evaluate your "gifts" and search for the most effective ways in which you can share them with the people in your life that mean the most to you, your family, your students, and your colleagues. All of us have been given special gifts. The only way to perpetuate these gifts is to give them away, as this quote of Waite Phillips so aptly states: "The only things we keep permanently are the things we give away."

I would imagine most of you reading this book are involved in a job related to music in some fashion. What a marvelous profession it is. I am now beginning my fortieth year in teaching. Many people ask me what I like most about teaching. It really is quite simple. I love music and the kind of people I have had the pleasure of being associated with all these years. I have been blessed with a wonderful wife who is also my best friend. I am thankful for our children and the wonderful relationship we were able to establish with them at every phase of their formative years. We continue to enjoy them even more as adults with lives and careers of their own. Finally, I am thankful for all the outstanding students whose paths have crossed mine for whatever length of time. We are all impacted by the closeness, intimacy, and passion of music as it is shared by human contact. As David, the writer of Psalms, says, "Praise Him with the sounding of the trumpet, praise Him with the harp and lyre, praise Him with tambourine and dancing, praise Him with the strings and flute, praise Him with the clash of cymbals, praise Him with resounding cymbals."

Day by day strive to make a difference in the lives of the people with whom you come in contact. It is not easy. It is a task that is most difficult and demanding as we attempt to maintain that tenuous balance between faith, home, and work. We must not allow our own schedules, professional engagements, family obligations, job demands, and the time crunch we all feel to become our own worst enemies. Like the ship at sea or the airplane in flight, we must stay straight and level to be effective. There is nothing wrong with "going the extra mile." But when the extra mile begins to disrupt our effectiveness in teaching and life, then it is time for careful and honest personal evaluation. I love this simple thought of Albert Einstein: "There are two ways to live your life. One is as though *nothing* is a miracle. The other is as though *everything* is a miracle."

In the end, we want to be remembered not only as an outstanding educator but also as a person who was well rounded, cooperative, concerned about others feelings, and a loving individual.

So once again—just what is it you want people to remember about **how you spent your dash?**

CHAPTER 5

Live Your Dreams, Not Your Nightmares: An Opus for Life

Ray E. Cramer

Introduction

Growing up in rural Illinois on a small farm, I dreamed of becoming a farmer like my father, brother, and sisters. It was all I knew, it was all I dreamed about, and it was what I envisioned myself becoming. In that rather protected environment, this life seemed to me almost perfect. My vision of a future life was probably similar to that of many young folks. They dreamed of becoming firemen, policemen, teachers, businessmen, movie stars, salespeople, or any other occupation that was ingrained as desirable through familiarity in their lives. We dream of following in the footsteps of those people we are closest to in our early, impressionable years. This has been true from time immemorial.

There was little realization in my dreams of the nightmares associated with striving to make a living on that small farm. Crop production was only as good as the weather allowed: a potentially outstanding crop could be wiped out by a hail storm or grasshoppers could eat the beans. The corn yield might be diminished because of corn borers, or in the worst case, some type of disease could devastate the livestock herd. These were only a few of the nightmares my parents faced.

All I knew was that food was always on the table, and the clothes were always clean and well taken care of (even though most of them were "hand me downs" from my older brother and cousins). We seemed to be able to travel from one place to another in old but reliable vehicles. I even remember two rather extensive trips we took in my youth to visit relatives in California in 1947 and British Columbia in 1952, in a 1939 and 1948 Chevrolet, respectively. I can still recall vivid images from those trips. Perhaps in my recollection some of those images have become mixed with imagination and dreams I had both before and after those trips. What I was *not* aware of were the sacrifices my parents made to make these trips feasible. For them, the reality of the expense and taking the time away from the farm was a nightmare both in planning and execution. The fulfillment of dreams on every level demands the same planning and execution.

During my high school years I had two passions: trombone and football. I was motivated and inspired by my music teacher and my coach, both of whom became role models. I dreamed of coaching a winning football team and conducting my own band. Near the end of my senior year, when it was time to make a decision about which career I wanted to pursue, music or athletics, my dream became a nightmare. Knowing full well that I was not big enough to play football in college and that I had been offered a music scholarship, the decision was easy because I had to pay my own way through college. While I had a lot of success both on the football field and playing trombone, I'm sorry to say that I did not apply myself as passionately in the classroom. I was just having too much fun in sports, music, and life on the farm in general. I was not a poor student and always made good grades, but my priority was not high academic achievement. I quickly found out that if my thinking did not change, it would cause a nightmare beyond the boundaries of recovery.

"A" Theme: Dreams and Nightmares

Dreams and nightmares have been part of our natural experiences from the beginning of time. For example, there are numerous Bible stories referring to dreams and nightmares. In the Book of Genesis, Joseph had a series of extraordinary dreams. When he shared his dreams with his brothers, they were infuriated and threw him into a pit to die. So what started out as a very wonderful dream turned into a nightmare for Joseph. I'm sure most of you have seen or heard the music from *Joseph and the Amazing Technicolor Dreamcoat*, which portrays the events surrounding Joseph and his ability to interpret his dreams. Joseph's dreams dramatically changed people's lives, and our dreams can influence other people's dreams just as easily.

In modern times, we have heard countless stories of people from every walk of life who have experienced dreams and nightmares only to see them later become a reality. We all have dreams, almost every night.

Dreams are described as a series of images, ideas, or wild fancy that occur in certain stages of sleep. While dreams seem so realistic, most of us can't remember them, even shortly after waking up. It has been proven that if you tell someone your dream as soon as you wake up or write your recollections down right away, you stand a pretty good chance of recalling the events of the dream. The Senoi people of Malaysia, during their family breakfast time, would discuss their dreams and nightmares from the preceding night. This gave the parents an opportunity to talk with their children about their dreams and nightmares. They taught their children how to capitalize on the good dreams and change the nightmares into positive experiences. Understanding the events in our dreams can help us direct our actions by establishing hope, envisioning solutions to persistent problems, or making intelligent decisions. Or they can simply allow us to have "flights of fancy" that are pleasant and joyful experiences.

Nightmares, on the other hand, can be very distressing. We may feel a wide range of emotions during a nightmare, such as intense anger, extreme guilt, melancholy, or serious depression. In the worst-case scenario, they can cause us to wake up shaking in a cold sweat with an increased heart rate, which usually makes getting back to sleep difficult. Experiencing these frightening, horrifying, and often traumatic nightmares can shatter our dreams. No matter how intense the nightmare, it can only dictate one's life if one allows it to become a reality.

"B" Theme: Formulating Your Dreams

As I headed off to college, I was still having some doubts about the decision I had made to pursue a degree in music education. Other than my ability to play the trombone, there was little else in my background that would enhance my work in this field. I had no piano training, knew nothing of theory, and sight-singing was totally foreign to me; but I could play "I'm Getting Sentimental Over You" like Tommy Dorsey (my trombone idol) and move the slide with a technique that would make butter melt.

Nightmares became a nightly occurrence prior to my arrival on campus. My music participation in high school was limited to concert band and orchestra as well as playing trombone solos and being in small ensembles at contests. The advantage of attending a small college afforded me the opportunity to be involved in many different kinds of music-making organizations. However, after a short time on campus, a dream began to take shape in my mind that helped me focus on just what it was I wanted to do in life. Getting the degree, however, was not all glitter and gold. There were nightmares, including music history, piano lessons, theory assignments, and term papers. In addition, I plunged headfirst into the world of composition.

When I applied for graduate school at the University of Iowa, I entered as a composition major. Just as I had done in undergraduate school, I continued to play in every ensemble possible including the Hawkeye Marching Band (as a graduate student), knowing it would be my only opportunity to march in a Big 10 marching band. I quickly found out that in a school the size of the University of Iowa, it was unrealistic to think I could play in the marching band, the symphonic band, the brass choir, and the faculty brass quintet as well as take private lessons from William Gower and be a composition major at the same time. It was not going to work. So my dream of doing everything quickly became a huge nightmare, struggling in music history class and completing "X" measures of new music every week for my composition teacher. My nightmare shifted to "survivor mode" when I decided to concentrate on an area in which I could find a job and pay the bills. Having a career as a composer was no longer part of my dream. Nightmares can evolve into pleasant dreams when you allow your attitude to change the outcome of the nightmare.

As I was nearing the end of my graduate work at the University of Iowa, many of my peers, as well as faculty, were sure I would proceed directly into a performance career playing trombone. I guess they had a higher regard for my ability on the instrument than I did. A dream has to be realistic, and it takes an honest assessment of personal attributes to formulate a dream that can come true. I knew the direction I wanted my career to go—and that was into teaching and being involved in the musical lives of young people. I dreamed about what and where I wanted my career to take me in the music education profession.

Development: Realizing Your Dreams

My decision to enter the teaching profession was based on many things, but the overriding reason was because I was fortunate enough to have had many outstanding teachers during my student years. Your assumption would be that these were music teachers. It is true that there were several who influenced my life in positive ways, but I also had knowledgeable, inspirational teachers at every grade level and from many subject areas who were instrumental (no pun intended) in making their dreams become my aspirations.

Realizing our dreams takes concentrated, focused, and energetic work. Nothing happens by accident in our profession; we have to make things happen. Knowing that our dreams can help shape the dreams of others means we have to accept that responsibility with a positive attitude. Too often, dreams can fade because obstacles and setbacks erode our confidence. Don't allow other people's dreams and expectations to change yours. Negative attitudes, perceptions, and situations can become your own worst nightmare.

A few years ago, an orchestra from the West Coast was invited to perform at the annual Midwest Clinic in Chicago. Being selected is an honor for any group, and the anticipation of this performance demands months of careful preparation. The group arrived safely in Chicago—but some of their instruments and music did not. The missing items were nowhere to be found. Somehow the group's luggage had been transferred to a different flight and would not arrive in time for the performance. Their once-in-a-lifetime dream became a huge nightmare for everyone concerned. Worry, disappointment, anger, questioning, and finger pointing could have destroyed not only their dream but also their *esprit de corps*.

But the director kept a level head, and many people stepped in to lend a helping hand. Within a few hours, schools and publishers had located the music they needed. The orchestra borrowed instruments from companies exhibiting at the convention as well as other local directors. So before anyone could get totally absorbed in negativity or depressed, their dream had been fulfilled through a wonderful display of cooperation. Thus, their unbelievable nightmare was turned into a dream beyond reasonable conclusion. So when you hit a dead-end street, don't park; it's a good place to turn around.

Let's face it, some days just aren't as much fun as others. If you let them, these negative challenges can take over your dreams. Confront them as the Senoi people of Malaysia did, and work through them, focusing on the positives of your dreams.

Transition: Allowing Others to Help Shape Our Dreams

I was not far into my teaching career when a new dream began to take shape in the back of my mind. Thanks to the role models I had in Forrest Suycott at Western Illinois University and Frederick C. Ebbs at the University of Iowa, the desire to one day teach and conduct at the university level began to loom large in my dreams.

I was not sure just how this would all transpire, but it wasn't because I disliked my work at the high school level. I made the best possible choice for me at the time, which was to keep working hard, relish the time I had with eager and dedicated students, continue to learn from others, and *not* worry about what my next job would be. Unfortunately, our culture promotes the attitude that to be "successful," we must keep striving for the next advancement: teach the next grade level higher or move from junior high school to high school, classroom teacher to principal, salesperson to CEO, governor to President, and on and on. I have tremendous respect and admiration for teachers who love working with students at their chosen level and enjoy the rewards and satisfaction that come through dedication and hard work. Others shape and formulate our dreams. We must do the same thing for our students—help them honestly access their capabilities and understand how they can help or hinder the accomplishment of their dreams.

Unrealistic dreams, if not carefully analyzed, may quickly become nightmares. Having a realistic dream does not guarantee that it will come true. There must be clear direction and a plan to achieve the goals we envision.

I often tell students who are trying to make decisions about different jobs to sit down and write out the positives and negatives about each situation.

There is something about seeing these points on paper that helps us focus on the real issues. Few people just out of college or early in their teaching careers have formulated just what they want to achieve in their lives. As we strive to make our dreams become reality, it is necessary to write out a clear plan that will lead to a successful conclusion. Once you have a plan in place, take care not to allow family and friends, who may not fully understand your dream, to impose their plan on you. If you are motivated to attain your dreams and enjoy your chosen path, hard work will come easily. Since dreams require choices, you have to choose your path. But remember: You can reach as far as your vision, character, and integrity will take you.

Recapitulation: Avoid Turning Your Dreams into Nightmares

Be like a duck on a pond, calm on the surface,
but always paddling like the dickens underneath.
—Michael Caine

While living your dream, falling asleep can quickly turn it into a nightmare! There are many ways we can "go to sleep" if we are not careful. Becoming complacent about our work is one sure way of allowing our work to become less effective. Once a person achieves success in any line of work, it is very easy for that person to become bigger than the result of his or her work. Inflated egos and self-importance can lead to professional turbulence and loss of respect in short order. A humble person is a picture of quiet strength and depth of character.

I have witnessed wonderful teachers become stuck in their proverbial tracks because they are unwilling to try new things, and they stop growing professionally as a result. Likewise, a propensity for organizational dysfunction will create nightmares with untold consequences. Creativity and forward momentum go hand in hand. Our society today demands flexibility, which is extremely important to successful teaching. If we are too rigid or demand perfection beyond the potential of our group's ability levels, everyone becomes totally frustrated and discouraged. Ultimately, our dreams burn away like morning fog, and our nightmares become real-time events. Self-evaluation and outside mentoring will help to prevent these potentially devastating pitfalls.

Coda: Dreaming Must Include Having Fun

Are we having fun yet? This is a question we are all familiar with, and we usually ask it in a situation that *isn't* very fun. Perhaps a student will whisper this question to a stand partner in the middle of a very intense and stressful rehearsal. (The director is probably not having much fun either!) It is not intended for us to go through life without having fun. Granted, every moment of our life is not going to be fun, but to survive, mentally intact, fun must find a niche in our daily routine.

A simple Google search revealed more than three million references to "having fun." No, I didn't check them all out, but the sheer number of entries indicates that this topic is important for us to maintain some balance in our lives. Maybe you know people who seem to lack fun or enjoyment in their lives. Fun can be defined in many ways: enjoyment, pleasure, glee, delight, or just plain merriment. For us to effectively balance our lives between work and pleasure, we need to have fun. Preferably, we want to have fun in our occupation, in our personal lives, and with the students under our tutelage. Having fun is a cultivated art. Here are some "fun"-related thoughts to help us focus on this important aspect of our lives. They certainly work for me.

- Having fun should be contagious; others can catch it from you.

- Having fun should carry over into every area of your life.

- If you are only having fun at leisure activities and not at work, or at work and not at home, then evaluate why this is true.

- Fun has to be shared to be genuine.

- The art of having fun should be mutual, never at the expense of others being made fun of or humiliated.

- We need to take ourselves less seriously so we can at times make fun of ourselves.

As a conductor, fun can come with that sense of satisfaction in having achieved worthy rehearsal and performance goals. We're not going to hit a home run in every rehearsal, but if we finish well, a sense of pride and accomplishment will prevail among all who participate.

Balancing work and fun is a tedious task in keeping our "real world" responsibilities and "fun" experiences on an even keel. This is a somewhat daunting mission given the pace and demands of the twenty-first century. For this to happen, perhaps we need to actually plan to have fun. Following are some suggestions for inexpensive activities that can help you "enjoy" a change of pace and explore ways to enhance your "fun."

- Explore natural settings: woods, streams, mountains, seasides, clouds—and don't just look; actually feel, smell, and listen.

- Do physical work in your yard or garden, or something that will cause you to become physically exhausted.

- Take a short break outdoors where you can breathe fresh air; a colleague of mine used to say, "It's time to go out and blow the stink off."

- Eat a meal without gulping it down to meet the next scheduled demand.

- Make a point to share time with people who have fun and enjoy life.

- Listen to music outside of your focus area. I listen to a wide variety of music that I find refreshing, freeing, and cleansing.

- Find time for regular exercise, even if it is nothing more than walking for a half-hour four times a week. Not only will your stress level go down, but you will be healthier, lose weight, and have fun.

- Smile and say "hello" to everyone you meet on your walk. You will help make their day.

- Finally, when the opportunity avails itself, take a half day or even a full day to do something you always thought about doing but never felt you had the time to do. If you don't, the opportunity may not avail itself again.

I truly look forward to going to work every day. Sadly speaking, not everyone can make that statement. I love working with students in the collaborative effort of making music and watching them grow individually and collectively as an ensemble. Don't forget to have fun; life is just too short not to. Smiles shared bring joy to those on the receiving end.

Fine: Living Your Dream

*Celebrate what you've accomplished but raise
the bar a little higher each time you succeed.*
—Mia Hamm

Never stop dreaming. Dreams are the vehicles that can get us going, keep us going, and transport us to the most unexpected places. I have always felt fortunate to have the opportunities to move from one type and size of job to another. When I began my teaching career, which was my initial dream, it was in the very small community of Bardolph, Illinois (with seventeen students in my high school band—and no clarinets). There was no dream on my horizon for a job as the director of bands at Indiana University. Dreaming of a position such as that was not anywhere on the radar screen. There is a valuable lesson here—while living one dream, be aware that others may be taking root. So always be willing to expand and reshape your dreams.

At the end of our careers, each of us should be able to outline and chart our musical journey. Framing this outline would be the dreams and nightmares we experienced as part of our growth. Could we have predicted our path from the beginning? No, of course not, but through our willingness to dream, establish goals, and devise (and revise) a plan for achieving them, magical things can happen. To paraphrase a quote by Judith Orloff in *Guidepost* (September 2004): "Dreaming is not about pretending . . . it's what gets you going and then following it."

When nightmares cause you to lose sight of your dream, trust your original goals and your plan to reestablish faith in your choices. Don't let outside situations control your dreams. You maintain control of those circumstances. We all have either read or heard the phrase, "When it's all said and done, there is more said than done." We all need to be "doers" and not just "sayers."

Finally, our dreams and their fulfillment are inherently entwined with our students. They are the lifeblood of our existence. My mentor, Frederick C. Ebbs, had a phrase I always enjoyed for its humor and truth: "You can't have a zoo without animals." How true! Without our students' energy, talent, enthusiasm, dedication, commitment, creativity, and cooperation, what could we do? Nothing, I'm afraid. Certainly without them our dreams would be nothing more than just dreams. The fantastic opportunity we have in being able to share our dreams with them produces new generations who will be influenced to carry their own dreams into the future.

As I approach retirement, many students and colleagues have asked me what I am going to do. First, I tell them I am not going to retire; I'm just going to change jobs! Second, I have no intention of not being involved with teaching and conducting young people for as long as the Lord is willing to let me remain upright. Finally, there are other dreams to pursue, and as long as I live, I will continue to pursue them.

Enjoy the pursuit of your dreams, always keeping them in sight. Don't be timid, go forward with confidence, and compose your own **Opus for Life**.

CHAPTER 6

Soundings:
Developing Beautiful Tone

Ray E. Cramer

Introduction

But words are things; and a small drop of ink,
Falling like dew upon a thought, produces
That which makes thousands, perhaps millions think.
        —Lord Byron (1788–1824) from *Don Juan*

I have no illusion that thousands or even millions of people will read this chapter. My hope and desire is to invoke positive thinking and perhaps reevaluation by directors and teachers of all ages, to encourage them to consider the impact a prioritized thought process and plan of action might have on the musical sounds and souls of their students and ensembles. Developing a beautiful tone has been a point of emphasis and musical passion of mine for forty-five years of active teaching and conducting.

In this hectic, high-tech twenty-first century, we are surrounded by various implications of sound. The word *sound* is an integral and active part of our lives. We hear the word used in our culture daily—*sound* advice, *sound* investment, *sound* dollar, *sound* bite, *sound* decision, *sound* system, *sound* mind, *sound* body, *sound* thinking, and, most significantly, a *sound* engineer. In a sense, we are all "*sound* engineers," and I cannot think of a more demanding and rewarding occupation. The word *sound* is defined as being "well founded." My goal is to encourage you to focus on the well-founded precepts of this important aspect in musical development.

When I first decided to play an instrument, my teacher immediately emphasized to me the importance of developing a beautiful sound. As I gained technique, my teacher realized dexterity was becoming my top priority. My mentor quickly admonished me in no uncertain terms: "No matter how high, fast, and loud you can play, Ray, no one will be interested in seriously listening to you without the beauty of outstanding tone production." This early training and focus in my music making carried over into my years teaching and conducting bands. Playing with a great sound is simply the most important aspect of any musician's success. I ask you to focus your attention and maintain an open mind as you read this chapter.

I have asked outstanding conductors and musicians at every level to contribute thoughts and observations on this subject. Some are former students who played under my leadership during my high school tenure or my thirty-six years at Indiana University. Their comments are not intended as testimonials to my position as their conductor, but highlight my sincere desire, focus, and passion to produce the best sounding ensembles possible, within my knowledge and experience.

History

I will not provide a detailed history lesson on the development of beautiful band tone as there are fine books on wind band history, including *The American Wind Band: A Cultural History* by Richard K. Hansen (GIA Publications). Nonetheless, it is worthwhile to consider a few historical perspectives on good ensemble sound.

The quality of musical sound has been a concern for musicians since the very beginnings of organized music making. Finding just the right stone, hollow log, or the best hides to stretch over handmade bowls to produce sounds that would resonate clearly was of vital importance in daily musical life.

When wood turning became more accurate, early woodwind instruments produced more pleasing sounds and improved intonation over previous models. Early European military and town bands went through various transformations involving instrumentation and size.

Adolphe Sax (1814–1894) must be recognized for the innovative instruments he invented, constructed, and interjected into military band instrumentation. His bands had a deeper, more sonorous projection due to the powerful sound of his instruments. Several of those instruments can be found in any modern ensemble today. Most band historians agree that the first "modern" band was the Band of the National Guard, formed during the French Revolution. This was a band that, for the first time, carried a more balanced instrumentation between woodwinds, brass, and percussion.

Wilhelm Friedrich Wieprecht (1802–1872), a Prussian military bandmaster, also studied acoustics to correct the deficiencies in military musical instruments. As a result, he improved the valves of brass instruments and succeeded in constructing them on sounder acoustical principles, greatly increasing the volume and purity of their tone. He invented the bass tuba, or bombardon, to give greater richness and power to the bass parts. Wieprecht profoundly affected band sound throughout Europe with the invention of these instruments and a new concept—the acoustical pyramid—the very concept of building band sound from the foundations on up, which we use today. Wieprecht took European band contests by storm, winning virtually every one he entered with his fine, dark-sounding Prussian Army Bands.

The sound and tonal concepts of early bands, except for those of a few ensembles in early American military bands, dictated our understanding of band sound well into the twentieth century. After the professional band era, school band and orchestra programs exploded, and the American Bandmasters Association, the College Band Directors National Association, the National Band Association, and many other professional organizations were founded. These factors increased the standards of band performance and encouraged the writing of original literature for the band.

During the 1940s through the 1970s, instrumentation and sound concepts were associated with the large "symphonic" band. Depending on the high school or university, the size of the band could range anywhere from ninety to one hundred and twenty. Imagine the sound of this size band with five or six tubas, four bass clarinets, two contrabass clarinets, four bassoons, eleven flutes, three or four oboes, eighteen to twenty-one B-flat clarinets, four alto saxophones, a tenor and a baritone, six cornets, four trumpets, eight horns, eight trombones, four euphoniums, and a percussion section of six. Bands of this size under the batons of A. A. Harding, Mark Hindsley, Ray Dvorak, Glenn Cliffe Bainum, William Revelli, Frederick C. Ebbs, John P. Paynter, and Harry Begian, to name but a few, produced beautifully rich, dark, and powerfully sonorous sounds. Many high school and university bands during this period did their best to emulate these outstanding bands in both instrumentation and sound.

In 1952, the band world rocketed in a totally new direction, when Frederick Fennell founded the Eastman Wind Ensemble. His original idea was to keep the instrumentation to one on a part, representing the wind section of the orchestra, with the addition of saxophone and euphonium color to the ensemble. While this innovation proved to be a dramatic departure from the large symphonic band, it quickly gained popularity for many reasons.

In retrospect, the invention of the wind ensemble created a totally new focus in the band development in terms of size, tone color, clarity, and sound. Furthermore, it had a positive impact on the compositional output by leading composers around the world, whose new works established a different spectrum of instrumental color possibilities in the wind ensemble, revolutionizing the overall sound of the wind band.

Whether you conduct a large symphonic band, a wind ensemble, a wind symphony, or a wind orchestra, the tenets of producing great ensemble sounds remain steadfast. Producing beautiful, musical, sensitive sounds in your band, no matter what name you attach to the group, is simply the most basic foundation to expressive music making.

Silence Is Golden

It may seem out of place that a chapter devoted to sound has a discussion on silence. Still, no matter where we go or what we do today, our ears are bombarded with sounds of all kinds. We live, work, and play in a noisy society that daily continues to contribute to sound pollution, dulling our senses and impairing our hearing and concentration. When was the last time you enjoyed true silence? I do not mean quiet; I am referring to the kind of silence where you can hear your blood coursing through your veins!

There are few places we can actually experience this silence. Most rooms in which we live all produce some kind of buzz, hum, or ring. That is true for our rehearsal rooms as well. Few rooms are without some kind of noise pollution that interferes with the concentration of the musicians and causes frustration when working in extremely soft passages. This problem, while irritating for conductors, is equally difficult for performers. Composer Libby Larsen has taken significant steps to soundproof her home in order to compose in a silent environment. Should we not take the same great care for establishing a quiet environment in which our students create musical sounds as well or, more importantly, to study our scores?

Sound can have both a beneficial and a harmful effect on people. Philosophers and composers alike, from Ancient Greece to present day have written on the Doctrine of Ethos or variants on the doctrine and the uplifting impact of music on our lives. The Mozart Effect has been talked and written about extensively. Music therapists have documented cases of the positive, healthy effects music has on people since the 1930s.

In contrast, the negative, dark side of sound is well documented too. The American Medical Association recently published an article in their journal recommending that doctors immediately inquire about listening habits whenever teens come to them with nervous disorders. With the invention of the i-Pod, we have potentially become the "most listening" society in the history of the world. In Japan, I rarely see a teenager walking, riding a bike, or taking a train or a bus who does not have some type of listening device in their ears attached to an i-Pod. The volume they habitually experience will in time damage their hearing. The same is true for American teenagers.

When an artist begins a new painting, he or she begins with a blank canvas; musicians begin with a room of silence. The artist typically has no predetermined or limited assortment of colors, but creates what the imagination and inner sense inspires using traditional colors and equipment. Such is the case with music and musicians. All music making must begin from silence. From that silence or blank canvas, we use notation, instruments, expressive indications, and tone production skills equipped with our collective, collaborative musical perceptions and imaginations to create musical sounds.

Tone Production

As stated earlier, a beautiful-sounding ensemble can be achieved through rehearsal techniques, but perhaps the most important way to achieve great ensemble sound is through the tone quality generated by each member. Observe the similarities of the following two statements.

John Rommel, professor of trumpet, Indiana University:

> Playing with a great sound is simply the most important aspect of any musician's success. It is the first thing I listen for when I hear someone perform, and it is the cornerstone of great music making. The sound should be clear and focused, with energy that matches the musical phrase. Our goal is to play with the exact sound required to make the musical phrase that we conceive in our mind.

M. Dee Stewart, professor of trombone, Indiana University:

> Tone quality is the first thing one notices in a musical presentation. If the sound is not pleasing, no one wants to hear the performance no matter how amazing the technique might be. The musical message is lost. On the other hand, if the tone is beautiful, the audience listens and can be touched by the music.

Their statements are quite revealing in their approach to reaching great musicianship. It all centers on the ability to make beautiful sounds and the importance of a vibrant, singing tone, which allows for much better blend, balance, and intonation. Dee Stewart further states:

> It is very difficult to separate those aspects of ensemble sound. Often, if balance is improved, intonation gets better, or if blend is addressed, balance follows. However, if a vibrant sound is addressed, blend, balance, and intonation all are always much improved.

Professor Stephen W. Pratt, director of bands and wind conducting at Indiana University, writes concerning ensemble tone:

> The tone of an ensemble is one of the most important and yet difficult to describe aspects of musical performance. Since it is a complex issue that is difficult to deal with, it is often neglected by conductors and players in favor of working on note correction, style, or tempo. An aspiring conductor should listen intently to recordings and attend live performances of great ensembles to decide on a quality tonal concept to emulate. The sound of a group will be no better than the idealized sound that is in the conductor's imagination.

Another consideration in building ensemble sound is something seldom discussed in clinics or workshops, the people behind the instrument and the human qualities they bring to music making. Richard K. Hansen, director of bands and professor of conducting and musicology at St. Cloud State University, shares the following comments on this topic.

> Great sounds produced by musicians are full of human warmth. Many ensembles play in tune with a good sense of characteristic tone, accurate pitch, and fine balance. In short, they sound nice and pleasing to the ear. Nonetheless, a sound that lacks in the vital dimension of human warmth that communicates leaves the listener unfulfilled. Musicians who are constantly aware they are playing music created "by people, for people" tend to play with warm sounds. Their sounds vibrate and communicate. Warm, communicative musical sounds are much more than pleasant to listen to—they are compelling. The humanity of soul-to-soul communication vibrating in our sounds transcends music making to a higher plane.

A fantastic sounding ensemble heightens our senses and takes the audience to a new level of listening. We can literally draw our listeners into the musical experience with great, warm sounds.

There are literally as many techniques and ideas for building tone as one can imagine. It has always seemed to me that successful, well-established music educators at every level and in every part of the country have their own systems for improving tone production individually and with a full ensemble. Undoubtedly, most people reading this chapter have been creative in helping students produce satisfactory tonal results as well.

Here is a novel idea for building tone shared by M. Dee Stewart:

> So how does a player go about creating this efficient, pleasant sounding tone on a brass instrument? In order for the lips to freely vibrate, the flow of air needs to be addressed. The lips can do nothing without the air. If the air flows freely, the lips will respond. We often "train" ourselves so extremely that we lose the ability to naturally and easily move air.
>
> Many students at all levels come to study with me for a variety of time periods, from one quick lesson to years. I have had great success with all of them by using "pinwheel pedagogy." Each year, I buy out our local stores of their supply of pinwheels. My students each get one at their first lesson. You should see the looks on their faces when I present them with this high-quality diagnostic remedial tool. However, after just a very few minutes, they are amazed at their tremendous tone quality and the ease of their production. Over the years, I have developed an approach, which is neither childish nor highly intellectual, just common sense and having fun as the process progresses.

The pinwheel is just a toy. Yet it gives the player a target and displays the visual action of the air. Those are two areas that the brass instrument does not offer. The focus of the player then is adapted to a lighthearted approach aimed at a bull's-eye at a distance with the goal being to make the wheel spin. When done, as any child knows how, the air flows freely and the wheel flies.

The next step is to apply that approach to blowing into the horn. The "training" may need to be erased in order to make that happen. I have the student put the pinwheel in one hand and the horn in the other. The player can then comfortably blow the pinwheel two or three times, quickly drop it to the floor so as to not lose time, immediately bring the horn into playing position, and blow it in the same way as the pinwheel.

The result is like magic! We have played a little trick on the body/mind, and the student is now blowing freely into the horn in the same way that [he or she] blew the pinwheel. It is the freedom of the air, not the quantity, that is important. The lips are now free to vibrate, and a great sound is produced.

This approach has been used on occasion with ensembles of many sizes. Of course, a pinwheel does not have to be used. Blowing on one's hand, a tissue, or a piece of paper works pretty well. I have done this with groups while conducting them and having the players breathe in on the upbeat and blow out on the downbeat. We do that a few times and then apply the same approach to the instrument. It is always startling how not only the sound of the group is much better, but the blend, balance, and intonation are greatly improved as well. Most importantly, the players notice it immediately in improved performance and ease of playing. See if you can create your own magic. Try it; I am sure you will like it!

Sensitizing the Ears

The old adage "you are what you eat" can be expressed in a similar manner for musicians: You are what you listen to. I cannot emphasize strongly enough the importance of listening to outstanding ensembles, large and small and soloists of every genre, instrumental and vocal, both live and on recordings. However, choose carefully what you listen for, with today's advanced technological recording equipment, it is easy to be fooled into thinking you're hearing true balance, blend, transparency, and, to some extent, tone color. Regardless of the size of the ensemble, with careful microphone placement (sometimes for each individual player) the balance of the ensemble can be manipulated so that hearing any part, regardless of the dynamic level or the instrumentation, is not a problem with knowledgeable engineering. We live very much in an age of produced sound.

My own concept of sound is based on listening to and performing in outstanding ensembles and listening to great individual performers. There is nothing like sitting in a live concert, being drawn into the musical passion and drama delivered from the stage by competent musicians led by an expressive conductor. For many years I have told students, parents, and administrators about the one-of-a-kind experience of sitting in an ensemble creating the beauty of great music in collaboration with fellow musicians. No CD, earphones, or speakers, regardless of the size and power, can create the human atmosphere and feelings generated in live performance.

Earlier I mentioned the importance of listening to music from other genres to help sensitize and expand the ears. My first lessons on trombone were dedicated to attempting to reproduce the beautiful sound of my teacher, who had one of the sweetest sounds on trombone I have ever heard. Yes, even the lyrical sounds of Tommy Dorsey captured my attention as I stood out in our front yard at night, trying my best to emulate his "I'm Getting Sentimental over You." Our high school band in a small rural community in Illinois had an outstanding concert band, which my trombone teacher led. I vividly remember the rich, dark sounds this band was able to produce through careful training and practical applications to tone production.

My later influences came from playing in the outstanding Symphony Band at the University of Iowa under the baton of Frederick C. Ebbs. I have learned more guiding principles through careful listening to live performances of the University of Illinois band under Mark Hindsley, Northwestern University under John P. Paynter, the fabulous Cass Tech High School Band under the guidance of Harry Begian, and numerous other junior and high school bands at the Midwest Clinic from 1960 to the present. These outstanding ensembles helped me establish an expectation during my first years of teaching I had not imagined possible until hearing those concerts.

I also listened to early recordings of the University of Michigan Symphony Band under William Revelli. While I did not have the opportunity to hear the Eastman Wind Ensemble conducted by Frederick Fennell live in the 1950s, I did listen to the first Mercury recordings, and my ears took on a new understanding of band sound. Another influence came from listening to the Chicago Symphony, and, while teaching in Cleveland at Parma Senior High School, I had the opportunity to observe rehearsals and listen to live performances of the Cleveland Symphony under George Szell. That was an advanced degree in itself, as I watched this master of sound manipulation take the leading musicians in the world through their paces, focusing intently on tone, balance, blend and the total orchestral sound production.

Stephen Pratt had this to contribute about sensitizing the ears through carefully selected listening:

First, we have to decide what we want. Many of the biographies of famous conductors of the past waxed eloquently on the "sound" the conductor produced. We hear about the "Stokowski sound" of the Philadelphia Orchestra. Leopold Stokowski manipulated the sound effectively of many orchestras with great success. Listening to recordings, you can hear the difference Leonard Bernstein made with the New York Philharmonic very shortly after he became the music director. These changes were made by individuals who knew exactly the sound [they] wanted. We cannot think in superficial terms here. "I want the sound to be pretty. I do not want the sound of the group to be so harsh." Instead, we must decide exactly the tone quality we desire and then find ways to get that sound.

I particularly like these comments from John Rommel concerning listening habits:

> The only way to truly develop a beautiful concept of sound is by developing our musicianship. It is crucial that aspiring musicians listen to the great masters of music. While it is important to listen to great trumpeters when developing our sound concept, it is equally important to listen to great artists of other instruments as well. The human voice is the most natural of all instruments, and we are essentially copying the human voice when we play the trumpet (or any instrument for that matter). Therefore, I recommend considerable time be spent listening to great singers. This will help us develop a vocal quality to our playing that will greatly enhance our musicianship.

I encourage you to find groups and artists to listen to that will help you be more intent on recognizing great pitch, great tone, and great sounds. Here are a few of my personal favorite non-band, non-orchestral listening treats, all fantastic examples of tuning, tonal control, musical passion, and sound vibrancy: Yo-Yo Ma, The Anonymous Four, any recording of Joshua Bell, Eva Cassidy, or Robert Shaw's choral ensembles. I have many others, but the important point is to heighten our senses to the beautiful sounds in the world of music and strive to bring the beauty of those sounds to our ensembles.

Establishing Expectations

In order to achieve maximum results with minimum rehearsal time, certain priorities and expectations need to be established. We should ask ourselves a few questions about the beginning of our rehearsal procedure.

1. Does the rehearsal begin on time with all of the equipment in place, proper chair and stand placement, and rehearsal order displayed?
2. Will the first few minutes of the rehearsal set the tone for the day?
3. What is the focus of the warm-up time?
4. Do you establish a routine in which musicians respond to the conductor, or is the warm-up "by the numbers" (using a metronome)?
5. What do your face and body language communicate to the ensemble during the warm-up time?
6. Does the warm-up time include balance, blend, sound production, articulation, and stylistic concerns of the pieces you will rehearse later?

I want students to understand from the start of the rehearsal that I take "ensemble sensitizing time" (I use this term rather than warm-up because my university students came to rehearsals warmed up) very seriously. They know there are specific goals to attain during this time. Here are a few comments from former wind ensemble players about my approach to the "ensemble sensitizing time."

Jonathan Whitaker, professor of trombone at Henderson State University had this to share:

> From my first rehearsal in the IU Wind Ensemble I could tell that making sure the balance, blend, intonation and ensemble sound was the most important aspect of what we were doing. The thing that surprises most people is the amount of time we spent in Lip Benders and playing long tones and unison passages. Time was spent each and every day the ensemble rehearsed to make sure this standard was always present. The resonance the group achieved with this focus of quality, balance and pitch in place is a sound and feeling I will never forget.

Will Petersen, assistant director of bands at Virginia Tech, contributed the following about expectations during the warm-up:

> As a former principal tuba player in the IU Wind Ensemble, I felt there were cornerstones to Mr. Cramer's approach that ensured that the ensemble sound appeared in a short amount of time. First was the enthusiasm that accompanied the work for producing the best tone quality at all times. Each rehearsal began with sound fundamentals of ensemble playing, never aimless drill, but rather focused ensemble warm-ups. Through these, players focused on producing a rich tone; achieving ensemble clarity through attacks, releases, note length, ensemble pitch, and tone control.

Have a plan, prepare a plan, and execute that plan for achieving the success you desire for your ensemble's sound product. Do not relent; strive to establish the best sound you can with your ensemble, regardless of the age level or instrumentation. My first high school band only had seventeen players (and soon I had only sixteen—I excused a trombone player from being in the group when he decided he did not have to attend rehearsals on a regular basis). None of the players had a mature sound. However, we began from day one to build individual tone quality and ensemble sound. We had no clarinets and five drummers, but by the end of the first semester we achieved a decent and well-balanced sound (even with five drummers) as any ensemble could with that limited instrumentation.

It is all about expectations, focused goals for tonal production and convincing students that even with sixteen players they can improve their sound with diligent work and concentration on tone-building fundamentals. Do not let your students decide what they are going to sound like; you must establish the parameters and give them the tools and inspiration to attain your expectations.

Practical Pedagogy

My father used to tell me,
"OK, it's time to hitch the horse to the plow."
In other words, it is time to get to work and attend to the practical side
    of what really is involved in getting the job accomplished.
It is much easier to write and talk about the "hitching" rather than
    actually "hitching up the horse."
In the process of compiling information and comments pertaining to this chapter, I asked several colleagues to share some practical procedures and techniques that have worked well for them. After all, there is a lot of great teaching that goes on in our profession. What makes this profession so stimulating and wonderful, I might add, is the willingness of people to be so giving. Each of these contributors is recognized by name as I impart his or her techniques and suggestions. Thank you, each and every one!

In addition, I will suggest some methods in the "Performers' Perceptions" section that have worked for me over the years in both the IU Wind Ensemble as well as with honor bands around the United States, in Europe, and in Japan. Even with a language barrier, using clear conducting techniques, facial expression, and body language, you can communicate strong feelings about the production of ensemble sound. I can tell you, however, it is much easier to share concepts when everyone speaks the same language.

Very important components in establishing a good warm-up/ensemble sensitizing time are the choice of material and how they are used. There are many outstanding publications available that make suggestions concerning how to use your warm-up time. The main point is that, regardless of the warm-up material you choose to put in front of your ensemble, how you use that material must be musically motivated. No matter how difficult the technical challenges of the day are, the group must know they are contributing to the sensitivity and musicality of every rehearsal. Even if you are just playing a beautiful phrase of Grainger or Bach, provide the vehicle for the ensemble to produce great sounds and singing musical phrases.

Seating

Richard Miles, coauthor and editor of this publication, wrote a wonderful chapter in Volume 5 that includes valuable information on the various ways of seating the ensemble. I will not attempt to rewrite his excellent diagrams but would like to add a few thoughts to go along with his suggestions and observations.

One of the main criticisms one hears about many bands is the seeming lack of attention to good balance and blend. Over the years, I have heard my share of band concerts at every level and must agree that ensembles oftentimes have a difficult time achieving satisfactory balance and blend.

While much of this problem has to do with a poor perception of balance, many times I feel a change in the seating could easily assist in helping to correct this problem. Where are the woodwinds located? Are the brass and percussion on elevated platforms? What is the ratio between the woodwinds and brass? Are the trumpets and trombone bells playing straight at the audience and elevated? Do you experiment with different seating arrangements to gain the best results with your particular instrumentation? Do you modify your seating to enhance the sound of the group due to limited instrumentation in one section, while another section has too many players?

Be creative; there is no hard and fast rule that says it has to be done in a certain way. Avoid falling into the "seven last words" trap: "It's never been done that way before." I know directors who use a rather unorthodox procedure of having students leave their chairs and move to any location they choose in the band room (some have rooms big enough to do this). While the students are standing all around the room with the instrumentation all mixed up, they play a memorized chorale, non-conducted, working to achieve great balance and blend. Immediately, the ears and musical sensitivity of each player elevates to a new level of concentration and listening. The next time you are rehearsing in a large enough room or an auditorium, try this. You may be surprised by the increased attention students have for one another and the musical phrase.

There are few directors, at any level, who have the luxury of knowing that their personnel and instrumentation will be exactly the same from one semester to another. Even if you have that luxury, perhaps you still face the problem of having sections of unequal strength. These kinds of "opportunities" can be addressed and corrected through creative seating.

Balance and Blend

Those of you who have taken your bands to play at competitive festivals or contests could certainly fill several pages of a dissertation called *Adjudicators Say the Darndest Things* with comments pertaining to balance and blend. This aspect of performance, combined with intonation, considerably reduces the supply of lead and ink in the world, as judges (excuse me, adjudicators) express their displeasure of the sound your band produces in a flurry of clichés. As is to be expected, I received some valuable insights and creative rehearsal techniques that address this problem.

Richard Strange, emeritus director of bands from Arizona State University provided these comments on the subject:

> Effective band balance must exist in the mind of the conductor before it is projected by musicians to the ears of the audience. If the conductor has not originated a stable concept of "ideal" balance in his head, the result is musical happenstance. However, it is not by chance that the finest bands, orchestras, and choruses "sing" the music to their respective audiences with clarity and excellent balance. It is invariably because the conductor guided the ensemble to this enviable goal.
>
> When listening to some groups in concert, it is not clear that their conductors understand the implications of the term balance, the word musicians use to describe the relative loudness of the instruments in relationship to each other. If a firm concept of balance exists in the ear (mind) of every conductor, why are the results from one maestro to another so drastically different? But musicians, no matter how good, cannot know whether specific sounds blend with the group as a whole (especially large groups). That must be the province of the conductor, the only person who is in the central position necessary to hear and compare the relative strength of all parts. Therefore, it stands to reason that the conductor is the one who has the responsibility to create "perfect" balance between all the different parts that are competing for the attention of the audience.

Mark Kelly, emeritus director of bands at Bowling Green State University, has this to add pertaining to balance and blend:

> We must first assume that fundamental tone production is secure!
>
> Balance: Make your tone part of the section or ensemble. All lines need to be heard clearly.
>
> Blend: Poor tone quality will not blend with others. Adjust the embouchure, breath support, or posture. If you are playing softly and you still hear only yourself, perhaps you are playing with poor tone quality or just plain old too loud. Blend involves the mixing of

individual sounds into the conductor's desired combination of color/ texture. You cannot get a good sound from a band unless you have the sound in your head before you start.

Balance and blend, which results in color, has to do with the players being able to hear their part…and listening to everybody else's part. Frequent overscoring often results in a sameness or gray sound where melodies and moving parts get lost…call it a brown sound…or a bland band sound. There are many ways to enhance the band's color, density, and transparency. Find them, and you will soon understand how color affects emotion.

Richard Hansen further explains concepts of color:

The key to achieving a wide spectrum of individual or ensemble tone color is the development of a characteristic, centered, dark, singing sound. When all of these qualities can be achieved, a wide spectrum of tone color can be explored through tending toward more brilliance in certain moments of the music, or changing the rate of the singing vibrato. The amount of tension or "de-tension" (relaxation) in the musical expression dictates what is desirable in coloration.

Every musical style, composition, and moment within a composition may demand a different sound from us. The differences may be subtle, but in reality the basic sound required for a Mozart *Horn Concerto,* for example, is worlds apart from the tone production desired for the Beethoven Horn Sonata, even though the two pieces were written at approximately the same time and in the same place for the same instrument.

James Keene, director of bands at the University of Illinois, adds these observations on this important topic:

Too often band directors focus on "covering flaws" as opposed to *creating* sounds and colors based on the composer's intent. Many band conductors employ a one-size-fits-all formula for ensemble sound.

Too often, directors strive for a homogenized sound that lacks the *separate* characteristic concepts of blend, balance, and sonority. This can only be realized if one possesses the "concepts" that only come to fruition through conscientious score study, a history of quality experiences, and practical knowledge and application of solid fundamental instrumental pedagogy.

I have always admired and respected the work of Roy Holder, director of bands at Lake Braddock High School in Virginia. I have heard his band live on several occasions. While the individual musicians are outstanding in their own right, the sound Holder is able to produce with his young players is obviously the result of sound concepts he has successfully taught for years. I asked him to share how he works to attain the beautiful sound his bands always seem to achieve, and this was his response:

> The "band sound" is, in my mind, a combination of several things. Like everyone else, I use many words to encourage the production of the type [of] sounds I wish to hear—warm, dark, rich, resonate, lush, etc.—and discourage the type [of] sounds I do not wish to hear— harsh, bright, pointed, nasal, directional, etc. We try to apply this to individual sounds first, then attempt to create a band sound that is more than just those individuals playing together. We first discuss "blending" individual sounds. By this I mean you should hear the same amount of your sound as you hear of the person on either side of you. No individual should dominate the sound in his or her area of the ensemble.
>
> Next, we describe balance, which to me means having the right amount of each voice in the ensemble. We use a lot of standard aids, like the band pyramid, that show the bass voice as supporting the sound and the highest sounding treble voice as minimal. I draw a large circle on the board and say, "This is the tuba sound." Inside that circle I draw a slightly smaller circle and say, "This is the low wood-wind sound." I continue drawing circles, assigning voices ascending through the range of the band until there is a very small circle for the flute/piccolo.
>
> We then visit the concept of staying inside the sound of the band. Sometimes I use the term "disappear into the sound." (Disappearing into the sound should not be interpreted as meaning playing a wimpy or puny sound, just that one must produce a good sound with respect for what is happening around you.) However, if we can agree on the "sound of the band" on this type playing, it is much easier to adjust to other scorings, as we now have a common point of departure. I think that what is essential is to convince students to listen to what is going on around them and function in relation to what they hear. They are very smart, and if they learn what to listen for, they can fix most things themselves.

These are wise words and creative techniques that work amazingly well for Roy Holder and his band, for their performances always sound super and are musically satisfying.

Matt Vaughn, co-principal trombone of the Philadelphia Orchestra, commented on his perception of how we achieved successful results in the IU Wind Ensemble pertaining to the ever-present balance and blend issues.

I recall very well the attention you gave to the sound concept you wanted to create in the ensemble. I remember your emphasis on a sound pyramid, with the low instruments providing a solid fundamental base and the rest of the ensemble "sitting on top," fitting into the sounds below. You taught us how to listen and understand how we fit as individuals and as sections within the complete ensemble and how that would change depending on the dynamics, orchestration, style, etc.—when it was important to blend and when to predominate.

It is no secret that anyone who played in my ensembles understood that my approach to establishing a full, rich, dark band sound was bass driven. Without a proper "footing," the rest of the ensemble sounds thin and bright. This was apparent during my first teaching experiences at the junior and senior high school level. Richard Hansen, whom I quoted earlier, recalls his days as a contrabass clarinet player in our Harlan (Iowa) High School Band, where a "bass-driven" sound and tonal control of dynamics provided a solid sound framework for the band.

The concept of a harmonically bass-driven tone and musicality is much more than "tuning chords from the foundation on up." Although that process is certainly one that should never be neglected, it is more a matter of developing bass-voiced musicians in both their sound and the way they shape their sounds. It is developing low-instrument people to think and phrase lines and to possess the tonal control to whisper sounds in and out of silences as well as to resonate (vibrate) their instruments to their full capacity.

Professor Hansen further describes a pedagogical process we used to teach the Harlan students tonal control:

I can recall several lessons and practice sessions (during practice room study halls) doing an exercise on contrabass clarinet, where we would work on *crescendos* and *diminuendos* "by the numbers." Each click of a second (mm = 60) marked an arrival of the next number and a stronger or weaker dynamic level, during which the sound would need to remain "in-tone, full and beautiful." We would attain the arrivals in very gradual increments; the smaller unit clicks would allow us to think in the amount of detail we needed to conceive and achieve even *crescendos*.

At first we did so in front of a strobe tuner, where we could see and hear changes of pitch, as we would increase and decrease volume intensity. Later, as we developed our air and embouchure flexibility and sense of intonation, we used only our ears. Band members would then coach each other on the intonation tendencies. *Crescendos* and diminishes would sustain from eight counts to sixteen or twenty (on good air days). There was always an emphasis on starting the tone seamlessly from silence and releasing the tone seamlessly into silence.

The tone production approach you gave us during practice room study halls in Harlan was very similar to what the late Wayne Rapier provided WASBE members during the 2003 Eleventh International Congress in Jönköping, Sweden. (Mr. Rapier was oboist for the Boston Symphony Orchestra for two decades and taught oboe at the New England Conservatory of Music and the Longy School of Music in Boston with positions prior to that in the Philadelphia Orchestra, the Kansas City Orchestra, and the Indianapolis Symphony).

This is an approach that he and other Boston Symphony Orchestra members employed in increasing and decreasing tonal intensity "by the numbers" together in their private, partnership and sectional rehearsals. They also exercised this process in tutti rehearsals. These professional musicians did so in order to achieve perfect balance, matching tone color, intonation, and nuance of expression in the music. I was stunned that I had been trained at an early age in a small Midwestern farming town to strive for the same results with the same methods major symphony orchestral musicians used.

This kind of foundational work can reap maximum benefits for your ensemble, as musicians learn to control and express themselves with beautiful sounds that sing. This may be the greatest long-term gift we can provide our students.

Tuning

Where does one begin when discussing this most important, relevant, difficult and urgent topic? So much has been written on this subject, so much equipment is available, and mountains of imaginative techniques for tuning have been suggested. Yet, it can be as simple as the single-word tuning instruction Frederick Fennell posted on the rehearsal room wall at Eastman—LISTEN! Or, perhaps you employ the mindset I read on a young musician's t-shirt while conducting a rehearsal with his high school band: TUNE IT OR DIE! That may be extreme, but it does emphasize the importance of the issue. Bands must play in tune if they are going to achieve the greatest possible sound potential.

Edward Lisk, former director of bands at Oswego High School in New York, developed one of the great high school instrumental programs in the country. Since his retirement, he has published excellent material, sharing valuable information on the techniques he used to develop sensitive listening, balance, blend, and tonal success with his fine ensemble. He travels around the country, giving clinics and workshops on how to use his material to help make the ensemble equally successful. He shares the following about "In-Line Tuning" which has advice about training in sound for young musicians.

When the principal players in each section use the fundamental pitch as the "law of sound," there is an aural target rather than a visual one (a strobe picture). Without established tuning "targets," an ensemble will struggle throughout an entire performance or rehearsal trying to play in tune or ignoring tuning altogether. When two or more players try to play in tune without identifying a target player, it is nearly impossible to resolve the pitch discrepancies (similar to chasing someone in a circle and never catching them). This is because the players are attempting to get in tune with someone who, in turn, is trying to tune to someone else.

The target tuning process establishes the principal player as playing the correct or in-tune pitch. (There is usually a more advanced player in this position). Using this process, it is the section player's responsibility to play in tune with the section leader, the target.

For musical excellence, a student must have opportunities to exercise listening just as much as any other required skill. Unfortunately, strategies that go beyond the conventional tuning methods are often limited to a pattern that very seldom exceeds the one- or two-note tuning process via a strobe followed by some type of warm-up chorale. Such patterns do very little considering how a musician's mind and ear must be exercised to recognize a variety of settings, including pitch, chord qualities, melodic patterns and tutti playing. We cannot assume that this will naturally happen when playing in an ensemble.

The tuning line is the only straight line in music. If this pitch line is jagged, the ensemble suffers. Tuning is a three-part process. First, playing in tune begins as an individual decision, when each player matches the target pitch to make a straight line of sound. Second, the individual's in-tune pitch must be perfectly matched and in tune with the section when it plays a straight-line unison with the section leader. (Individuals lose their identity.)

Finally, how section listening and decisions contribute to the full ensemble's in-tuneness and tone quality must be understood. The quality of listening exercised when playing as a section determines the overall quality of the ensemble. Students control the musical quality of the organization through what they have been taught. If one individual is not attuned to the specifics of section listening and how it contributes to the total ensemble, the overall ensemble quality suffers. Moreover, excessive rehearsal time is wasted trying to achieve ensemble balance, blend, and intonation.

This is valuable information and a formula that has proven to be successful on a national level. One of my mentors, Frederick C. Ebbs, used to say, "Intonation is a *daily* fact and responsibility of every musician, whether you're sitting in the ensemble or standing on the podium; it has to be addressed each and every time you play or conduct."

I know there are conductors who expound that it is the responsibility of the player, not theirs, to control intonation. That is basically true, but just as players in the ensemble cannot always hear correct balance and blend from their listening perspective, the conductor must respond and react to pitch inconsistencies as they are determined in the course of the rehearsal. If not attended to, they will remain unfixed. The longer a player or conductor accepts incorrect pitches, over the course of time they get used to hearing pitch inaccuracies as no problem. No matter what material you use in your warm-up time, the students will become complacent and lack concentration by playing the warm-up drill in the *same* way every day. There is truth in the saying "variety is the spice of life." You will get the troop's attention from the get-go if you vary your routine.

Here is a tuning technique I used with our IU Wind Ensemble and currently use with honor bands around the country. Have the entire clarinet section play the C below the staff (concert B-flat) with a nice rich, full tone at least *forte*. As the pitch begins to settle add tubas playing their B-flat, making sure they can still hear the clarinet sound. Then add all the low reeds, euphoniums, and trombones, making certain everyone can still hear the clarinets. Next, add the trumpets, horns, oboes, and flutes on their concert F. Add trumpets on their G4, and let the sound of the fifth resonate fully.

Have students sing those two pitches, and then play, matching the better intonation they achieved while they were singing. Move these two pitches in a slurred, downward motion (Remington-style warm-up) down a half step, back, then down a whole step, and back, continuing as you desire. The ensemble will soon begin to establish a warm, resonant sound. Always insist that everyone still be able to hear the clarinet sound.

Next, I start with the two pitches, concert B-flat and concert F, and while the concert B-flat players remain on their pitch, I conduct the F-concert players up the scale to the concert B-flat. I caution them it is very natural to raise the pitch of the seventh and octave, as the B-flat pitch is usually too high. After a couple of times, they soon hear the octave more clearly, and the pitch begins to find a true key center, establishing a beautiful in-tone concept.

I also like to do a lot with chromatic scales using various kinds of articulation patterns, all slurred, all tongued or two slurred, two tongued, or four slurred or tongued in both directions. To have the ensemble focus on intervallic pitch, I will ask the players to begin on F-sharp concert. All low voices descend by half steps, and high voices ascend by half steps. After each note (up and down) everyone goes back to the unison F-sharp. This continues until they arrive on a B-natural octave. This creates various intervals within the octave structure that help train their ears.

I used another interesting teaching technique while conducting "Brass Theatre" and, later, "Blast." We warmed up in a circle, playing chords until the pitch center and overtones were ringing beautifully with a great resulting sense of balance, blend, and intonation. I then asked players to push or pull their tuning slides one way or another (their choice), play the same chord or chords, and play them with the same sensitivity of balance, blend, and pitch control. Even with the slides askew, they soon learned to trust their ears and adjust their individual pitches with embouchure and breath control to reestablish the same level of intonation. After a few trials and careful listening, I was truly amazed at how quickly they were able to "lock in" on pitch and tonal control. You should try this method with your ensemble sometime; you will soon find out if your students are truly listening or just watching the needle.

Professor Hansen made some pithy statements during his clinic presentation "Tenets on Tone Production" that concludes this section on teaching techniques well.

Tenets on Tone Production

1. Pursuing perfect intonation heightens our senses and is one of the greatest powers in music making.
2. Hearing the tone in your imagination before playing the tone is the single most important factor in achieving good intonation.
3. Musicians must first experience good intonation to truly know what good intonation is.
4. The instruction "play in tone" with good air, characteristic sound, center, balance, fullness, [and] matching color means much more than the phrase "play in tune," which implies only good pitch.
5. A common problem encountered in trying to achieve good intonation is caused by not adhering to a standard pitch (A 440). Have a wind musician (oboist, clarinetist) establish A 440 as the source pitch.
6. The tuning note is merely the tone of departure, not the end result of being intone.
7. Pushing and pulling tuning slides, venting, and cheating should be final resorts to aid in the achievement of good intonation. First, work on the foundations: air, ear, embouchure, and a characteristic sound that sings. Each musician must know what his or her specific tendencies of pitch and tone production are in order to achieve good ensemble intonation. Charting these tendencies on a daily/weekly basis can improve this process.

8. Ensemble intonation involves players eliminating all beats or distortions of sound. Possess an accurate, steady, "source tone" from your pool of players and have all other players match that tone, eliminating all beats.

10. Good and poor intonation amongst a few players has infectious results for many players in a large ensemble setting.

11. Most musicians (according to a pitch perception test published in JRME) are pitch confused (most of us do not have perfect pitch). Therefore, do not burden students too much about being sharp or flat. Rather, sensitize them to the concept of beat elimination. Oftentimes professional ensembles will play a bit high at the close of an exciting movement or brilliant moment in the music. The key is that they all rise slightly in pitch and brilliance together.

12. "Tune down" is a more appropriate instruction than "tune up" since we listen and tune from the fundamental bass voice so often and since so much music is harmonically bass driven.

13. Poor intonation in the upper woodwinds is caused (more often than not) by poor intonation in the low reeds and low brass. Therefore, focus on tuning the low voices first, making certain the foundation is an accurate in-tone guide from which upper-part players can listen.

14. *Crescendos* disturb intonation in the following ways: Flute pitch tendency is sharp. Brass and reed pitch tendency is flat. A louder note is perceived by the ear to be lower. When low-frequency instruments *crescendo,* the ear perceives the pitch as going up.

15. Being in tone is not only hearing the pitch; it is also a physical feel. Individual intonation is the result of a balance between air pressure and embouchure muscle placement. Group in tone-ness results in undertones and overtones being heard and felt in the body and the instrument.

My greatest desire is that this section of the chapter will be the most read and underlined, prompting tremendous experimentation, evaluation, inspiration, and sound/tone fulfillment for you and your ensemble.

The Performer's Perception

In previous chapters for this series, I discussed topics that have great influence on the "performer's perception" about what happens in rehearsals, and of course, the performance. The two topics to which I am referring are the power of the podium and podium personality. These ingredients are the essence of who we are and what we do as conductors. Over the course of my teaching experience, I made it a practice to constantly evaluate my effectiveness while on the podium. From the beginning of my career, I recorded rehearsals on a regular basis. This was not only to really 'hear' what the ensemble was playing during rehearsals, but also to evaluate teaching effectiveness.

So often, we fall into verbal traps and waste valuable time. I found I was doing entirely too much talking. Students are there to rehearse with purpose and direction, not to listen to me talk them to success. The saying "when it's all said and done, there is more said than done," is so true in so many rehearsals. When I was teaching undergraduate students, I would ask them just prior to their student teaching experience to make rehearsal observations at the middle school, high school, and university level, taking specific notes on topics. One of these topics was to keep track of the actual talking and playing time done in the course of the rehearsal. Not surprisingly, they found in almost each case that the percentage of talking vs. playing time was unusually high.

On another level, I found myself in the "beating a dead horse" trap. There are some passages during rehearsals you can only engage students in for so long. So rehearse until you feel positive forward progress has been gained, and then move ahead to the next part of your rehearsal plan. Otherwise, you waste a lot of time on passages that may not get better until students practice on their own or in sections.

An even greater concern to me, personally, involves band members' perception about what takes place in the ensemble experience both in rehearsals and in performances. A conductor's responsibility is vast and varied. For any ensemble to feel comfortable and secure, players must trust the conductor, have confidence in his or her musical sensitivity, know the conductor is a decision maker, is technically competent, creates an atmosphere of cooperation among the members, and, above all, know the conductor cares about them as individuals. A mutual respect must be present.

Conductors and parents are similar in so many ways. Both have a responsibility to train, guide, prepare, instill character and integrity, demonstrate humanness, and always show love for them in everything students or children do. My goal was always to communicate these feelings to each student if it was within my grasp. In completely effective performances, there can be no "musical jealousy." When you work in a situation with a lot of "star" talent, this can be difficult to attain.

Attitude, Ego, and Group Dynamics

A close friend who plays in a major professional organization shared that a great frustration in the professional world is that the sound of the ensemble is often determined by the abilities and the egos of individual members and sections rather than by the conductor. Unfortunately, I have witnessed similar situations with nonprofessional ensembles as well. Attitude and ego play major roles in what happens during a musical performance. They dictate group dynamics to the point where the audience can readily perceive the negative impact this has on the overall performance. The conductor must intercede and exhibit strength from the podium to insure that this kind of attitude and performance practice within the ensemble do not inhibit the musicality of the performance.

On a personal note, I had an experience while teaching at the high school level that may happen to any of you during your career. I truly hope it does not, for it causes a lot of undesired stress. A player in my ensemble, who was perhaps one of the finest high school musicians I had heard up to that point in my career, had an attitude and ego that would not allow him to participate with the effectiveness expected of a musical leader in the ensemble. This became a stumbling block for other members in the band. The individual let down others by not fulfilling obligations to the ensemble, ultimately to the point of undependability.

As I observed the negative attitude and stress this was creating within the entire group, there was little recourse other than to ask this musician to leave the program. This was a most difficult decision for me, but because the whole band was being adversely affected, there was no other choice. Once the student left the band, the attitude, sense of relief, and the positive work ethic that replaced the frustration in the ensemble was like turning on a light in a dark room. The positive results were immediate and dramatic.

Yes, we are required to make decisions of all kinds, not just about balance and blend and making "sound" choices. Occasionally, we must deal with attitudes and personal egos, which can be more difficult to handle than balance and blend but are also important responsibilities.

Does It Work?

Returning to the topic of sound/tone development, the following are some further observations of former students pertaining to the kinds of things we did in rehearsals to achieve what the students referred to as the "Cramer Sound." For any student at any level to "buy into" a philosophy on sound, they have to be able to hear the difference in what you are trying to attain with sound/tonal control. For the Indiana University Wind Ensemble, this sound philosophy made a difference; students could readily hear the sound concept at work in practical, musical ways.

Grady McGrannahan, a doctoral student in trombone and wind conducting at Florida State University, contributed the following:

> The "Cramer Sound" as students used to call it, was always a well-balanced, in-tune, transparent sound with a huge, resonant bottom. We spent much time on *Lip Benders*. I believe those unison studies of Arban-like exercises, along with the #10 and #11 chorales, helped

us achieve a beautiful ensemble sound. He was unrelenting about our precision on these warm-ups, leading us to a focused rehearsal. Despite a band filled with all-stars who wanted to be heard, you kept us under control and reiterated your concepts of ensemble playing that has stuck with me ever since.

Jon Whitaker, professor of trombone at Henderson State University, adds this:

We would at times have some of the most challenging literature programmed, but we would always spend several minutes on getting balance, blend, and intonation, even [in] the days leading up to the concert.

The balance and blend of the full ensemble [were] achieved through this process. He would have the clarinets play a unison B-flat concert (low). Once the pitch and balance were obtained within the section, he would begin to add instruments to the color, keeping in mind that the clarinet sound should always be present. Next would be the low reeds (bass clarinet, bassoon, tenor and baritone saxophone) and the tubas, again making sure that the reed color from the clarinet [was] present in the sound. Next would be the euphonium and trombone. This collection of instruments (clarinets, low reed, low brass) is the basis of the "Cramer Sound."

The resonance and overtones this group of instruments creates when it is perfectly in tune and balanced [are] remarkable. There were many days I was sure someone in the low reed section was playing a fifth above the group because the overtones were that loud. The overtones were not just a result of good pitch. Good intonation has just as much to do with balance and blend as the actual pitch.

Kelly Cooper, instrumental music director in London, England, was a contrabass clarinet player in the ensemble, and she sent me these comments:

I think a large contributing factor to the "Cramer Sound" was the emphasis on balancing the woodwinds. From the first note of each rehearsal, you stressed the importance of always being able to hear the clarinets. One exercise that seemed to work well was having the B-flat clarinets sustain their concert B-flat just below the staff while the remainder of the ensemble ascended the B-flat major scale. While they ascended, you asked the group to make sure they could still hear the clarinet pitch.

This type of sound focus helped the group lock into a center that established proper tone production, balance, and blend. You also made sure we understood the compositional structure of the score so we could perform each piece with an understanding of how our part fit into the whole, and, in turn, each part within the score could be heard.

Susan Rider, a former first trumpeter in the wind ensemble for seven years, has been a member of "The President's Own" United States Marine Band, Orchestra, and Chamber Players since 1997. Perhaps more than any other player, she has contributed and observed much to the band during her years of participation.

I firmly believe Ray Cramer's *Lip Benders* exercises are one of the key elements to developing the sound of his ensemble. Each of the drills serves different purposes—for articulation, listening to chordal structures for tuning, or playing hymn tunes for balance, to name a few. For the performer in his band this reinforces the sound of the ensemble as the most important goal. One is a soloist only when the music calls for it. Even when compositions that require one on a part are performed, the group is still an ensemble. By using the *Lip Benders*, the musicians learn how to listen across the group in every aspect of their sound. The balance learned from playing these exercises was essential in developing the success of the team and individual musician.

Another significant aspect of the "Cramer Sound" is the idea of the pyramid effect—low and middle voices dominate, as the upper voices "sit" on their sound. I feel this ultimately creates a more equal balance between the woodwinds, brass, and percussion. Higher pitched instruments are not too glaring or bright. He never let the brass sound dominate in an unattractive fashion (as can be heard in many orchestral and wind groups), and when he wants to emphasize this particular color, he demands the sound be full, rich, and round.

Most importantly, performances are always about the musical product and never about the individual musician. However, Ray's personal interest in each of his performers creates a loyalty and bond that is unique among so many who share a similar position. Though concerts are never note perfect, I firmly believe he creates an environment in his groups that produce[s] energetic and passionate performances, a more important aspect in my opinion. Ray consistently demands the very best from his players—no matter their level of development—and in this way each concert is unique. Players always feel like it has a broader purpose. For my own individual development, he truly taught me how to be a successful ensemble player.

Kelly Rogers Niiyama, a solo clarinetist in the wind ensemble, shared these comments pertaining to "podium personality" and its impact on sound production.

> I think the sound you were able to produce is about more than the technical process of putting together the layers of color that comprise any wind ensemble. There was an honesty about it that is not at all self-serving. You were able to interpret the composer's wishes without involving your ego, which is very rare. On par with honesty is your incredible energy. Your energy alone made me work as hard as I could to achieve what you asked—and sometimes demanded—through your conducting.
>
> Few conductors I have worked with are able to achieve the kinds of sounds you did without spending a lot of time talking about color, balance, etc. You were able to show what you wanted clearly. Essentially, it comes down to communication. I think the sound we were able to make came about because you were a true communicator. You actually connected with the people that you were leading.

Niiyama's final comment prompts a brief explanation on why I took so much time with these "ensemble sensitivity training" procedures. The way the ensemble system works at Indiana requires students to audition for ensembles every semester. Thus, I knew every semester I would be looking at a turnover rate of at least 50 to 60 percent. With the first concert in each semester coming only two and one half weeks from the start of rehearsals, this method of "ensemble sensitizing" helped establish ensemble concepts and "sound indoctrination" in a short period.

Score Study and Making Sound Decisions

No director can begin to transfer any warm-up material used into a comprehensive performance without diligent score study relative to the kind of sound he or she wishes to produce in each composition, even in each phrase. This chapter is not about score study per se, as this has been covered in previous *Teaching Music through Performance in Band* chapters. However, it is important to mention the necessity of conductors making sound decisions pertaining to selected repertoire.

Professor Pratt shares this practical advice:

> The conductor will also want to analyze the piece to produce the tone quality appropriate to the composer and the era. Every piece should not sound the same. Every piece should sound good, but appropriate to the repertoire. A chorale-based piece will have a different tone quality than a very transparent piece with light

instrumentation. A work composed by a contemporary composer will produce a different ensemble tone than a transcription of a work from the orchestral repertoire.

I try to evaluate the group quickly to make major changes in balance as necessary. This often involves asking for more bass sound and less treble sound. It often also means asking for better blend in the middle parts (most often horns and saxophones). Many of our groups simply have too many treble players and not enough bass players. At times it also means insisting on less overall volume—particularly from individual players who are accustomed to leading.

This all assumes I have studied the score and know what I want. It is my desire to go into the first rehearsal with an idealized sound in my head and then work to produce it as soon as possible.

The importance of transferring what you see in the score to the sound you wish to have your ensemble produce must be a major focus when you study. One of the first things I look for is the dynamic distribution of the work. Where are the high and low points emotionally? What solo voices are there, what are their accompanying voices? In what tessitura are the solos scored? Where is the *true* climax of the piece? If you look at most scores, there are always several points in the music where the scoring looks the same and has the same dynamic marking, but it is necessary that you decide where the ultimate climax is going to be and the kind of sound you wish to produce.

William Petersen, associate director of bands at Virginia Tech, graciously contributed these comments about score study prior to rehearsal:

> Another important aspect of the "Cramer Sound" is thorough score study. I have never seen Mr. Cramer unprepared for a rehearsal. As a result, his ensembles have a quiet confidence that the entire rehearsal will be concise, thoughtful, and productive. We were always convinced there was a vision for each work. As a result, there was never a moment of aimless repetition or wasted time rehearsing to achieve a sound that the conductor had not developed in his head.
>
> Mr. Cramer often talks about the aural image of how he desires a work to be played. That image is conveyed through his comments to the group, many of which concern the type of sound he envisions. I strongly believe Mr. Cramer achieves his sound because he has already heard the music in his mind *before* he steps on the podium.

When we contemplate the great conductors of bands, orchestras, and choirs, past and present, we must appreciate the complex nature of the conductor's responsibilities and have tremendous respect for their accomplishments. Respect is what each of us desires from our ensembles. Hopefully they see the love and devotion we have for our art and for our commitment to musical excellence.

The Audience's Perception

One of the often-overlooked aspects of working with ensemble sound in rehearsals is focusing on exactly what the audience is going to hear. There are few rehearsal facilities that provide the same acoustical properties as the performance site will produce. During my years at Indiana, I rehearsed in a facility that could not have been further from our normal concert hall. This posed problems for me each and every rehearsal. I had to rehearse with the acoustics of the concert hall in my ear. It was not possible to let the brass and percussion play too loudly because the room was so loud. As a result, it was very difficult to find a balance in the rehearsal room that would work in the concert site.

Many conductors have shared that they face the same problem in their own situations. Advanced players can adjust to new acoustical surroundings more quickly than younger players can. However, changing balance requirements in rehearsals does not necessarily mean you should change your sound concepts. If you find you have to rehearse in a similar situation, try to find inexpensive solutions to the room. Add drapes, egg cartons, carpet on a hard-surface floor, or a combination of these suggestions for sound absorption.

It is ultimately important to rehearse at the concert site prior to a performance in order for the group to become acclimated to different listening requirements. I was fortunate in that most times we were able to rehearse at least twice in the concert hall before performances. Not only does this give the ensemble the much needed opportunity to hear themselves in the performance environment, but it also gives you and your colleagues the opportunity to position yourselves in different places around the auditorium to hear the group as the audience will. In doing this, I heard the ensemble balance in a very different perspective than in the rehearsal room. So, during rehearsals I often walk about the room while the band is playing, to more clearly hear just what the students are hearing.

Another rehearsal format I use to combat poor rehearsal room acoustics and to focus on smaller groups within the ensemble is to hold regular sectional rehearsals. I found these to be extremely fruitful. Members feel that much is accomplished in a positive manner by the conclusion of these rehearsals. Sectionals help balance instrumental families. Players gain confidence in individual playing, and they listen to vertical alignment and understand musical roles. Sectionals can also help students understand how their parts fit into their instrument family as well as in the full ensemble, resulting in a more accurate placing of musical and emotional interpretations.

Richard Strange, emeritus director of bands at Arizona State University, shared these thoughts concerning audience perception:

> Dynamic markings are for the audience, not necessarily for the performer. Play the music so that any musically knowledgeable member of the audience could describe the major dynamic markings in the score if asked to do so. The conductor must put himself mentally in the place of the audience and see that the composer's intentions are imparted to the listener, i.e., the audience must be able to always hear and follow the ideas of the composer, whatever they are. What the conductor sees in the score should be clearly heard by the audience if scored correctly by the composer.

I find myself manipulating dynamic levels as the need arises for the balance I believe the composer intends the audience to hear. If you are conducting an ensemble with an incomplete or improperly balanced instrumentation, re-scoring may be necessary. Most composers will not have a problem with this as long as the musical integrity is maintained. The most important fact to remember is that the audience desires, expects, and deserves to experience a performance that is musically satisfying.

Observations and Comments

I hope by this point in the chapter you have found concepts and teaching techniques that will benefit your ensemble. Perhaps you have discovered or rekindled thoughts on some aspect of sound production, tonal concepts, tuning, breath control, philosophy, practicality, attitude, score awareness, conductor responsibilities or any other ideas that were offered. I firmly believe we desire to work with our bands (no matter the size or age) to create an atmosphere of emotional involvement with the music. The *sound* of the performing ensemble greatly impacts the emotional listening experience of both the performers and audience.

I have no way of knowing how many performances I have been involved with playing, listening, or conducting over the past fifty-six years. I started playing trombone in grade five, then, fairly soon, gave it up because it was inhibiting my enjoyment of baseball, swimming, fishing and almost every other fun thing there was to do on a farm at age ten. Fortunately for me, a new music director moved into our district, saw my name on a list of beginners from the previous year, got directions to our farm, showed up in our driveway (with his trombone) and inquired why I had decided to drop out of the instrumental program. After I gave him a litany of rather lame excuses, he unpacked his trombone and proceeded to play for my parents and me.

Frankly, I had no idea a trombone could sound so fantastic. I told him I had been disillusioned by how badly I had sounded; mainly, I did not like to practice! He asked if I still had my old trombone, which I did have stuck in a closet. So, I retrieved it and wiped the dust off, and he proceeded to give me a thirty-minute lesson. When the lesson was finished, I sounded better than I had at any time in my previous playing experience. In that short time, his personality, warmth, brilliant playing, and fantastic sound inspired me. From that point on, I think my parents were amazed by my commitment to practicing, which was a good thing, but my Dad got tired of hearing the same things (and I might have been a bit loud) because I recall one time he asked me, "to go practice in the barn."

If Don Zimmerman had not taken an interest and extended himself, then my story would have a very different ending. All my life I have thanked that talented and dedicated teacher for his influence. It was while playing in Mr. Zimmerman's band and orchestra that I learned to appreciate the fun of making music and placing the beauty of great sounding ensembles in my ear. An important teaching philosophy I learned from Mr. Zimmerman is that good things happen when we go the extra mile and personally reach out to our students.

Over the years there have been concerts in which I have forgotten the literature performed but remembered the *sound* of the group because it left such an astounding impression on me; I can still hear those sounds in my head today. Those sounds somehow have been imprinted into my internal aural sensory mechanism without my having to load a CD, push a play button, or download it from the Internet. I hear those sounds vividly in my mind and apply them to my own interpretative decisions every rehearsal.

As conductors we have to ask ourselves the question: What can we do to dictate the kind of sound the group produces? While I have purposely avoided delving into a conducting clinic exposé, there are specific techniques we need to be aware of as conductors to enable our ensembles to achieve the best possible sound. When you give the prep beat for your ensemble to breathe, what is your body language? What are your arms doing? Where is the focus of your eyes?

Breath is a most vital element in creating a steady, characteristic tone that sings. *Breath* is how we deliver the sound and is the most important physical aspect of playing an instrument. The breath must always be loose and free with the concept of the sound riding on top of the breath. We must practice producing sound in a relaxed manner to play with the great sound we desire.

Professor Craig Kirchhoff, director of bands at the University of Minnesota, illustrated the importance of this in a session on rehearsal techniques given at the Midwest Clinic in 2005.

I firmly believe the facet of music making we, as conductors, have the most control over is *breath*—even more so than tempo. After all, students can keep pulse together on their own. However, we must show them *breath* in the music.

When a conductor sets up with a relaxed, high torso frame and takes a deep preparatory breath, the musicians before us will more likely take the same kind of breath. In a very real sense, we become models for the kind of breath we require players to take. Key factors in this regard are: 1) Our torsos must remain open to the players, and 2) We must use a good amount of space in our gesture, so players have room to take deep breaths.

Professor Pratt also shared these thoughts on how gesture can impact the sound of an ensemble.

The conductor must first realize how much his or her physical movement affects the ensemble tone. A tense conductor will produce a different ensemble sound than a more relaxed conductor. A conductor who has excellent clarity of beat will produce a different ensemble tone than one who is unclear or indecisive. A cheerleader-type conductor will produce a different sound than a traffic cop–type conductor. If we are aware of how much our physical motions and personalities affect our ensemble tone, we can learn to modify ourselves, if necessary.

Professor Hansen suggests breath connected to emblematic conducting gestures can build a strong base of sound and an unlimited spectrum of tone.

To generate darker sounds from the ensemble, a conductor can do any combination or all of these emblematic gestures dependent upon the music and how dark the tone color is that you desire.
- Anchor your feet more widely, moving the weight to the heels.
- Take in big tanks of breath, as if you are playing a wind instrument.
- Open your mouth slightly in an "O" formation to show openness for the players and a relaxed airstream.
- Use a marcato grip to show the appearance of weight.
- Point the tip of the stick slightly downward to display the illusion of weight and resistance.
- Conduct slightly below the normal ictus table.
- Furrow the brow.

In contrast, to generate lighter sounds conductors can:
- Narrow the feet base and move weight to toes.
- Take in big tanks of breath.

- Keep the mouth open for a relaxed airstream but in a more normal position.
- Use a *leggiero* grip to show lightness.
- Elevate the ictus table to display the illusion of lightness.
- Heighten the brow.

Naturally, there is an "ebb and flow" to music. Almost always there are potentials for fluid, unlimited changes in color (if even very slight). Likewise, we must fluently change our gestures, always stimulating musicians to explore these varying colors in sound and the emotions involved with them. The connection of breath to our altering gestures and the resultant colors is the single most important aspect of achieving beautiful, colorful sounds.

A personal visual check of all the above-stated suggestions can be quickly accomplished by standing in front of a mirror to evaluate what we do and how we look. This is a very important step in helping our ensembles take in the kind of breath necessary to produce the kind of sounds we hear in our minds. With concentrated practice on particular conducting gestures to help frame our approach to ensemble breath, you will train your bands to develop a natural and relaxed breath. I must also add here the importance of doing these prep beats in rhythm with a solid visual reference for musical style and pulse.

Closing Thoughts

I hope you all realize how special the work is you have chosen. Making music with terrific young people, who want to be challenged, motivated, and encouraged to reach higher levels has to be one of the most rewarding occupations in the world. When students recall my time with them, I truly hope they recognize how much I appreciated their talent, dedication, and cooperation and understand how much I loved making music with all of them. They made the *joy* of my career possible.

Everyone is busy, but when it is time to rehearse our ensembles, there can be only one focus on our minds. Do not think of your band as a group, but rather, as a gathering of individuals who desire to be led into the magical world of ensemble performance. Never underestimate the high levels of success young people can attain when led with musical insight, knowledge, and enthusiasm. Be a conductor who has and maintains high expectations. We can be demanding without allowing our demeanors to become nasty or condescending. As Dee Stewart shares, "Aspire to inspire before you expire!"

We are there to lead and guide, not to win a popularity contest. Mutual respect for one another allows us to exist on a very different plane than the rest of our society. Achieving outstanding ensemble sound should always be a work in progress. There is always room for improvement. We must remain focused with a "sound goal," and let students know when they are making progress in a positive direction to achieve that goal. Celebrate in their victories and let them know you are proud of their efforts.

Perhaps the ultimate final thought and possibly the most important is to maintain a *positive attitude*. A smile and a sincere passion for sharing our musical journey will give us pleasure and lifetime satisfaction. Putting music together is like putting together a 5,000-piece jigsaw puzzle. Just when you think you have found the right piece of the puzzle, you look about and see there are still 4,999 more to go! The manipulation of sound is but one piece, but oh, such an important piece of this musical puzzle. Enjoy putting it all together.

> After silence, that comes nearest to expressing the inexpressible
> is music.
>
> —Aldous Leonard Huxley

CHAPTER 7

Exploring the Japanese Band Culture

A Personal Journey from Delong to Tokyo

Ray E. Cramer

So long as the human spirit thrives on this planet, music in some living form will accompany and sustain it and give it expressive meaning.

—Aaron Copland

Introduction

After reading the title of this chapter, you must be thinking, "Where in the heck is Delong?" That would be a good question, as few people in this world have heard of Delong, unless of course you lived in Knoxville, Abington, or even Maquon, Illinois. I wouldn't bet on many in those towns having heard of Delong, either.

If you care to google Delong, Illinois, you will be amazed (I was) that it actually comes up. It is in Knox County (home of the Lincoln/Douglas debate) and the map of Delong shows three north-south streets and two east-west streets. The railroad track that shows on the map has not been in existence since the 1930s. However, that happens to be the town closest to where I grew up. Notice I said *closest* to where I grew up.

My father used to tell people we lived at "Eleventh and Plum—eleven miles plum out in the country." Delong was a very nice, small (very small) rural town. I'm not sure "town" would be the correct description, either, but it did have a grocery store, gas station, post office, hardware store, soda fountain, drug store, and clothing store—all in the same thirty-by-fifty-foot building. The owners were way ahead of their time (a.k.a. strip mall), but in Delong, it was just the general store.

The town did have a two-room schoolhouse, with one room housing grades 1 through 3 and the other 4 through 6. There was one church, the Delong Congregational Church, which housed one of the five existing pianos in town and a very large garage in which Sam Cline housed his fertilizer business. On Thursday night, Sam would park all of his fertilizer trucks outside, sweep the floor (if he had time), hang up a big white sheet, set-up folding chairs, and show movies with an admission price of twenty-five cents for adults and ten cents for children under twelve. This only took place in warmer weather, as the garage was not heated.

One of the small houses in town contained the local telephone switchboard. Every residence in the community had crank telephones hanging on a wall of their home. When someone wanted to call you, the switchboard operator would plug into your party line and dial—no, crank your number. Ours was two shorts and three longs. There were few secrets in the community, for everyone on your line knew your ring and would often listen in just to catch up on the latest gossip in the community. Delong probably had a population of ninety when I was growing up, including family pets.

I did not live in town, but grew up on a farm one mile from town (and I use the word loosely in Delong's case). It was just close enough that when you earned twenty-five cents for some odd job or mowing a yard, you could bike to the general store and buy a pop and a bag of salty peanuts for fifteen cents and still have a dime left over for the piggy bank, which in my case, was an old sock I kept in my dresser drawer.

There was no piano in our house, nor a record player or TV, but I did listen faithfully to my favorite radio programs, where I heard my first classical music (even though I didn't know it at the time) on shows like *The Lone Ranger* and *Sergeant Preston of the Yukon*. Other than the radio there was no other music in our home.

Occasionally I would hear my older sisters hum or sing some popular music they knew, but that certainly did not inspire me to pursue a music profession. That inspiration actually did not begin until sometime during my sixth-grade year in our local two-room school.

A music teacher from the city (population 1,672) visited our class carrying several different wind instruments that I had never seen or heard. After a short demonstration of these instruments, he asked the students which instrument they would like to play. The most popular choices were the trumpet, clarinet, saxophone, flute, and of course, percussion.

No one had chosen trombone, and I thought it was the most interesting one of all because it looked cool, and he played these really neat glissandos during the demonstration. (I had no idea what a glissando was, but it sounded like it would be fun to play.) As I surveyed the situation, no one else had picked the trombone, so right away I thought to myself, "That would make me the first chair player!"

This same logic served me well when I decided to go out for football. Everyone wanted to play one of the skill positions because of the honor and visibility; no one wanted to play center or linebacker, so as a result I was always a starter from then until I graduated.

I convinced my parents I *really* wanted to play the trombone, so my father finally agreed and sold a couple of hogs so we could by a Pan American trombone. I was so happy, and from the very first lesson I could play glissandos like a pro. My parents tired of this very quickly and my dad deemed that the best practice area for me would be the in barn. Better for my parents, but egg and milk production dropped off dramatically in the next few weeks.

As the weeks progressed, I found out there was an expectation to *practice* in order to learn real notes and rhythms. The glissandos became increasingly less fun, and the practice time was cutting into my fishing, football, baseball, bike-riding, and in general, having fun time. So, like so many disillusioned young musicians at that age, I quit. This did not sit well with my parents, especially my dad, because it cost him two hogs, and the trombone was not sturdy enough to patch a hole in the fence.

Had it not been for a new music teacher who moved into our school district, I would have missed out on the most fantastic career one could imagine. Somehow this new teacher, Mr. Zimmerman, found my name on a list and saw I had not signed up for junior high instrumental music. Mr. Zimmerman just showed up at our farm (at Eleventh and Plum) one afternoon, questioning why I had not signed up for band. I told him it was quite simple: "I was a terrible player, did not enjoy playing the trombone, didn't like to practice, and the only thing I did learn to do fairly well was play glissandos."

He proceeded to get his own trombone out of the car and played some of the most beautiful sounds I had ever heard that did not involve a glissando. Even my father smiled and thought it had potential as a musical instrument rather than using it as farm equipment, like a water pump for the horse tank. He asked me to get out my trombone (I was hoping it was still in my closet and that my dad had not flattened it out to patch a hole in the grain bin) and proceeded to give me a lesson right then and there.

Within thirty minutes I was playing better than I had ever sounded before without playing a single glissando. Mr. Zimmerman convinced me I was a natural, blessed with a great embouchure, a nice, focused sound, and that I would really enjoy the experience of playing in his band. He also offered to give me lessons each week, at no cost (can you believe that?) if my parents would just bring me to town (not Delong, but the city of population 1,672) once a week for a lesson.

I had no idea at this young age where this new perception of music making would take me. Never underestimate *your* power to motivate and inspire young people. Mr. Zimmerman, and others along the way, did just that, and it changed my life and propelled me into the great profession of teaching and a life-long joy of conducting bands.

I have been blessed with the opportunity to have experiences in our profession at every level. I spent my first seven years teaching in public school instrumental music programs ranging from my first job, where the high school enrollment was 53 students (in the whole school, only 16 in band) to a program with an enrollment of 3,600 students in three grades at my last public school job at Parma Senior High School, just outside of Cleveland.

At Parma Senior High School, every student in the top band of ninety players and most of the second band, also studied privately with top professional musicians in the Cleveland area, including members of the Cleveland Orchestra. Those seven years involved four different schools before I accepted a position as the Assistant Director of Bands at Indiana University. Little did I know I would spend the next thirty-six years of my life (the last twenty-four as Director of Bands) at this fantastic institution, teaching and conducting in one of the nation's great schools of music, the Jacobs School of Music. This position presented to me the great pleasure of working with some of the most talented young musicians in the country and without question, a world-renowned faculty.

Japan, the Land of the Rising Sun and Lots of Outstanding Bands

My first time to experience the country of Japan and to hear Japanese bands was in 1984 when the IU Symphonic Band was invited to perform at the joint ABA/JBA convention in Tokyo. I was in my second year as the Director of Bands, and taking a trip like this was a challenge, a thrill, and frightening, all at the same time. During our sixteen-day tour, the band performed seven concerts in cities around Japan, providing the opportunity to hear several outstanding Japanese bands in the various locations. At the ABA/JBA convention, we were able to hear the Kosei Wind Ensemble (the group's name at that time) under the direction of their newly-appointed music director and conductor, Frederick Fennell.

On the same program we heard two of the top military bands from Japan along with two outstanding high school bands. Needless to say, they were impressive performances, and opened our eyes to the performance level of Japanese bands ranging from school to professional bands.

After our arrival in Tokyo, our first rehearsal took place at the Musashino Academy of Music. This was the largest music school in Japan, with approximately 4,000 music majors in the program. Of the 4,000, there were 2,000 piano majors. Can you imagine that? There was no way of knowing then that six years later I would be invited to conduct their top wind ensemble for a semester, thus beginning a professional relationship that has now extended to eighteen years.

These experiences have given me the opportunity to enjoy extended tenures with two major institutions in two different cultures. These two universities have provided a framework in which I could continue to grow professionally, participate, experience, and investigate the impact each culture has had on the other. I will relate more about the Musashino Academy of Music and its influences on the Japanese band culture later in this chapter.

Historical Foundations

In 1853, United States Navy Admiral Perry broke the policy of no foreign contact with Japan when he sailed into Tokyo Bay with a fleet of nine ships. On board this fleet was a small military band that performed the first band music in Japan. There is no record of the instrumentation of that band, but we can assume it mirrored the accepted size and instrumentation found in other U. S. military bands of the period.

The Meiji Period began in 1868, and there were English and French bands stationed in Yokohama that performed on a regular basis. It wasn't until 1871 that the first Japanese Navy Band was formed, comprised of thirty-six instrumentalists. Much like the French model of the time, the band was woodwind-dominated. One year later the first Japanese Army Band was established with a French Bandmaster as the teacher/conductor. Throughout the remainder of the nineteenth century, Japanese bands continued to grow and were mainly influenced by foreign teachers and conductors.

A retired Japanese army bandmaster led the first Japanese high school band, organized in 1903 in Kyoto. The first band association was formed in 1934, and the following year saw the first local band contest established in Nagoya and Tokyo. In 1939 the All-Japan Band Association was formed, resulting in the first All-Japan Band Contest held in Osaka. This major contest continued for three years, but it was discontinued in 1943 due to World War II. This contest did not resume again until 1956. After World War II, Japan adopted the American Educational System of 6–3–3.

The 6–3 system was compulsory, but the last three years of high school were not because of the need for a larger work force following the war. Almost all of the schools were co-educational, except for some technical high schools, traditional all-girl high schools, and a few private schools. Band activities resumed very slowly.

It is common knowledge that the person most influential in helping re-ignite the Japanese band movement after the war was Toshio Akiyama. However, being the humble person that he is, he asked me to acknowledge others he felt deserve equal notice. Here is Toshio's list of additional movers and shakers in this rebuilding effort.

Pioneer and Leading Band Directors in Japan 1950-1960

1. Kansai Area (Osaka)
   Ichitaro Tujii (1910–1986), Director of Osaka City Concert Band
      (professional)
   Kiyoshi Yano (1902–1973), Director of Tenri HS Band
   Takeshi Tokutsu (1917–1982), Director of Imazu JH Band
   Masamori Matsudaira (1925–2008), Director of Kureha Elementary
   School Band
   Takeo Suzuki (1923–2005) Director of Hankyu Department Store
   Band (Pioneer of Marching Band, especially Stage Show)

2. Chubu Area (Nagoya)
   Terumi Jinno (1899–1987), Director of Toho HS Band
   Susumu Yamamoto (1907–1989), Director of Gamagori Junior
      HS Band

3. Kanto Area (Tokyo)
   Masato Yamamoto (1916–1986), Director of Tokyo University
      of Fine Arts Symphonic Band
   Yoshio Hiroka (1898–1988), Director of Ochanomizu JH Band
      (author of an individual instrumental method)
   Tetsuya Hiroka (1930–), Director of Kanto Gakuen HS Marching
      Band (pioneer of marching band in Japan, son of Yoshio)
   Tomoaki Mito (1901–1987), President of Music Publishing
      Company, author and conductor
   Toshio Akiyama (1929–), Band Director, Sakuragi JH, Omiya Tech
      HS; in 1958, he founded the Sony Concert Band

4. Influential American Band Directors
   George Howard, Director of USAF Band, visited Japan in 1956
      leading the first foreign band to perform in Japan after the war
   Paul Yoder, encouraged Japanese directors to establish the Japanese
      Band Directors Association
   Clarence Sawhill, Director of Bands at ULCA, who gave the
      very first band clinics in Japan following the war

5. Later influences from 1960 to the present
   Francis McBeth, with his book Effective Performance of Band Music
   Fred Fennell, Conductor of Tokyo Kosei Wind Orchestra (1984)
   Alfred Reed, Visiting Professor at Senzoku School of Music
   All visiting professors at Musashino Academy of Music

Harold Walters was a visiting clinician for Rubank Publishing Company presenting new teaching materials and methods for young musicians. Paul Yoder, American composer, conductor, and educator, was a frequent visitor and became a very popular and often-performed composer in the country. In 1951 Akiyama started the Sakuragi Junior High School Band in Omiya City, Saitama Prefecture with twenty-five members. Toshio shared that they used all second-hand instruments (that was all they could find and afford) except for drums.

Within a short time the band became one of the premier young bands in the country. Following his outstanding work with his junior high band he directed the Omiya Technical HS band to a lofty national status. In 1958 Akiyama founded the Sony Concert Band and was the conductor of that outstanding corporation band for the next forty-two years.

To get a better understanding of American bands, Akiyama became the first Japanese band director to visit the United States in 1963 to observe band activities and to study at the Eastman School of Music. Following that year he invited many American band directors to Japan and introduced new band music and method books to Japanese directors. American bands became the model for Japanese bands in size, tonal production, and literature performed. It seems, however, in recent years Japanese bands have become a model for bands around the world as they exhibit their outstanding performance standards.

The Japanese Educational System

Japan is a relatively small country in terms of land area—about the size of California—but with a population of 127,433,494, according to a 2007 census. School education is under the supervision of the national government. The Ministry of Education has total control for hiring teachers and decisions on curriculum offerings. There are approximately 24,000 elementary schools, 10,000 junior high schools and 5,000 high schools in the country. As mentioned earlier, the present system adopted (for the most part) after World War II remains largely intact today. As opposed to the philosophy after the war, when high school was optional, today over ninety-five percent of junior high school graduates enter high school.

Music in the Schools

Classes begin daily at 8:30 AM and continue in almost every school until 3:30 or 4:00 PM. Saturday mornings are also utilized for the purpose of academic classes, except on the second and fourth Saturdays of the month. The school term is much different than in American schools. In Japan, the academic year is divided into three terms, with the first beginning in April, the second in

September and the third in January, with summer vacation falling between July 20 and August 31.

Generally speaking, there are two elementary music classes a week with the classroom teacher in charge. During these classes the focus is on rhythm instruments, singing, and the use of recorder-type instruments to learn note reading. They also listen to many recordings to instill sensitivity to music. I have listened to some elementary classes sing, and I am very impressed with their ability to sing in tune, producing a very pleasing sound.

Fifth- and sixth-grade students who wish to learn a wind or percussion instrument do this exclusively after school hours in what is a club activity. Many of these instrumental classes are taught by what Akiyama calls a "hobby teacher"—a person interested in band and who is willing to take on this assignment, but not necessarily musically trained to teach.

Junior high music classes continue with the same schedule, with music classes meeting twice a week. These classes provide the same basic emphasis as the elementary classes, but include a music laboratory system with multiple keyboards for advanced study in music theory, technical training, and even composition.

For those students who continue with their instrumental music training, the schedule is much more intense, with daily rehearsals, especially if the band wishes to compete in various contests. Once a student reaches high school, music courses are no longer offered. Due to intense testing in order to get into better universities, many students choose a more academic course of study. Unfortunately, much the same occurs in the United States.

Band Activities

Concert band offerings in the schools, regardless if they are public or private, take place almost exclusively after the school day, continuing as a club activity. As such, it is important to note that almost all clubs require students to pay a fee to participate.

The monthly fee for participation in band clubs normally runs in the neighborhood of 2,000 Yen ($20 USD). These funds go toward the purchase of new music, instrument repair, some travel costs, and administrative expenditures.

Teachers who have a keen desire to see these ensembles flourish direct these organizations, including orchestras and choirs. According to information supplied by Toshio Akiyama, there are approximately 1,000 elementary concert bands in Japan, ranging is size from forty to sixty members.

Junior High School concert bands probably comprise the largest segment of band activity in Japan. There are about 7,000 bands at this level, with probably half being strongly competitive, which requires students to be present for rehearsal at least two hours every day after school, including Saturday and Sunday. Some bands rehearse even longer periods of time, especially if they desire to reach the coveted position of inclusion in the All-Japan Band Contest held each October and November in Tokyo.

High school concert bands number around 3,800, and are organized in much the same manner as junior high ensembles. The main reason there are not more high school bands is, once again, related to the pressure students feel for academic excellence. This results in fewer ensembles and with fewer upperclassmen taking part. By the time students reach their senior year they are focusing on the all-important college entrance exams and do not have the time to participate in these activities.

Another thing I have noticed during the past fifteen years in my visits to Japan is the fewer number of boys participating in bands. Just as in America, athletics, other club activities, and the need to work part-time jobs to earn extra money in particular leads boys away from band participation. For those bands that wish to seriously compete in the All-Japan Band Contest, the time demand for rehearsal is even more extreme than for junior high ensembles. For the high school ensembles that make the final contest, rehearsal requirements can be over thirty hours a week, all of which occur after school and on Saturday and Sunday. I will share more about the specifics of this incredible contest later in the chapter.

The performance capability of Japanese bands has increased dramatically in the past twenty-five years. There are many contributing factors to this but here are a few perspectives.

- Education of the directors has improved significantly with school of music training
- A great enthusiasm for bands and band literature
- The popularity and significance of the contest system
- The influence of visiting American conductors, clinicians, and composers
- Developing better tonal and pitch concepts based on American trends
- Greater understanding and support from schools and parents
- Improved instrumentation and a better focus on tonal concepts, balance, and blend
- More emphasis on performing quality original compositions for wind band
- The increase of beautiful concert venues throughout the country

Contest

The All-Japan Band Contest is one of the most fascinating events I have ever witnessed. The process and intense competition that permeates the atmosphere of this contest season dominates the thoughts and efforts of students and directors alike. Literally every director in the country takes interest in the event, and many attend even if their own ensembles are not involved. Without question, this competitive atmosphere has contributed more significantly to raising the performance standard of Japanese bands than any other individual factor. School bands rehearse intensely for months leading up to the contest season. In my own estimation, perhaps too many hours are focused on the two pieces they will perform. The contest is not just for junior and senior high school bands. There are five categories in which bands may participate.

- Junior high school
- Senior high school
- College or university
- Industrial or corporation
- Community

I am not sure of the total number of bands participating in 2006, as I only attended the senior high contest day. However, for the three-day event, I am sure there were nearly ninety bands selected from Japan's ten districts, with all of the above categories represented. The junior- and senior-high contests are held separately, with the other three categories occurring on a separate day; they change from city to city each year. Over 10,000 bands begin the process with the first prefecture-level contest (like American state-level events) held in August. District-level contest is held in September, with the final contest taking place in October and November in Tokyo, held in the largest concert hall in Japan—Fumonkan Hall—which seats approximately 5,500.

The junior- and senior-high contest is held on two consecutive days with twenty-eight bands each day. These fifty-six bands represent the top winners in each of the districts. Some districts have more than one representative because of the population of that district. Competing bands must limit the size of the ensemble to fifty members.

Each year the Japan Band Association commissions five Japanese composers to write a required composition for the contest. These compositions vary in difficulty, representing junior high to university level. However, any group, in any category may select any of the five pieces to play for their required selection. It is not unusual for a junior high ensemble to perform the more advanced selections. The performance time of these commissioned numbers is between three to five minutes.

The ensemble then performs a showcase number of their own choosing in the remaining time. Since total performance time allowed is only twelve minutes, the audience is instructed to applaud only following the final number as the band is leaving the stage in order not to take any performance time away from the band. Each ensemble has a fifteen-minute stage time, but that includes time to enter and exit. If a competing band goes over their time limit even by one second, the band is excluded from the evaluation.

Bands compete for a Gold, Silver, or Copper rating. The adjudication panel is comprised of nine people representing every level of teaching and conducting as well as specialists in winds, brass, and percussion. During the three days of the contest there will be twenty-seven different adjudicators, nine for each day.

There is no recording of adjudicators made, and scores are not provided to adjudicators. Adjudicators watch and listen only. Following a performance, they write very brief comments, and indicate their rating on a form provided by the All-Japan Band Directors Association.

When the morning or afternoon session is finished (fourteen bands in each session), scoring sheets are collected by an officer of the AJBA so that all adjudicator scores may be calculated. Then the Board of Directors of the AJBA discuss where the lines will be drawn to establish Gold, Silver, and Copper ratings. Following this procedure, the President of the AJBA will show adjudicators this result to get their agreement. There are rarely any changes made by adjudicators. A public awards ceremony then takes place announcing the final results to the audience and all fourteen bands. You have never heard such loud cheers when the Gold medal winners are announced.

Another astounding fact of this event is the size of the audience. I mentioned earlier the concert hall seats 5,500. There is standing room only. After the morning session, the hall is cleared and another 5,500 attend the afternoon session. Tickets for each session are $20. Many people purchase tickets for both sessions. It would seemingly unnerve the young people participating, but they seem to take it all in stride, always exhibiting great poise and professionalism.

I have discussed the contest in detail, as is deserving of this huge event, but I would like to share one last observation involving the stage change between bands. Every band has its own particular set-up and uses their own percussion equipment. As a band is leaving the stage, every person has a piece of equipment assigned to them to take offstage while the next band enters, carrying, pushing, or pulling their own equipment.

At the same time bands are leaving and entering, a stage crew is re-adjusting chairs for the next group. They allow forty-five seconds between bands, and the amazing thing is that they stay within this time frame. The entire event is truly mind-boggling.

Each year several American directors travel to Tokyo in order to visit schools and attend the two-day junior- and senior-high contest. Their response mirrors what I have said many times: "You have to see it and hear it to believe it!"

Directors have asked me if there is any opportunity for those students who wish to participate in some form of solo and ensemble contest. The short answer is, "Yes!" There are many options for this kind of contest, depending on the location of the school district. Otaki, Director of Bands at Saitama-Sakae High School, shared the following information:

> There are a lot of ensemble contests held nationally each year. In Saitama prefecture, we are allowed to enter two ensemble groups from each school. There are try-outs prior to the contests in order to choose those two entries. So, most students experience ensemble performance. There are numerous contests named "for Jr. and Sr. High School Students" organized by different associations and companies (such as AJBC, each instrumental association, instrument and music shops, and Shobi Music College and Toho Music College) and we let students know about them as we receive announcements.

Rehearsal Technique/Procedure

Before launching into rehearsal techniques, it might be interesting to know a little bit about the general instrumentation of these competitive ensembles. In the past few years I have seen a general trend to smaller ensembles at both the high school and university level. Some instrumental departments with large numbers of students in the total program will generally use a larger ensemble for their regular concerts. As I mentioned earlier, bands that compete in the All-Japan Band Contest have a fifty-member limit for their performance. It might be interesting to see a typical fifty-member instrumentation, with minor alterations, depending on personnel and literature being performed:

1	Piccolo	4	Saxophones (2–1–1)
4	Flutes (2–2)	5	Horns
2	Oboes (one doubling EH as needed)	6	Trumpets
2	Bassoons	4	Trombones
9	B-flat clarinets (1 doubles on E-flat as needed)	2	Euphoniums
		2	Tubas
2	Bass clarinets (1 doubles on contrabass clarinet as needed)	2	Double basses
		5	Percussion

This instrumentation has the capacity to play with power, depth, and richness of sound, and yet the ability to be wonderfully transparent and light.

For the top fifty-six junior and senior high school bands reaching the final contest, there is a rehearsal style and procedure employed in order to achieve their goal. I most certainly have not observed all of these schools, but I have visited several that do make the finals to witness firsthand what happens in the course of a rehearsal.

Keep in mind that most of these ensembles rehearse daily, including weekends, for a lengthy period of time. A typical weekly schedule for these top bands is to meet daily after school (4:00 PM) for four hours, six hours on Saturday, and four hours on Sunday afternoon. I can hear your question burning through the page right now: "How do they get students to commit and adhere to such a schedule? I could never get my students to agree to such a demanding rehearsal schedule."

I hear you, and agree that it would be difficult to get most American students to see the benefits of such a demanding schedule. This is where you must understand the cultural differences between the two countries. Japanese tradition, going back century upon century, relishes the concept of group identity. There is a sense of commitment, pride, and confidence that comes from group activities. As such, the time commitment is not as important as the *result* of the time spent together in any type of ensemble experience. (I firmly believe this previous statement should be a fact in *any* rehearsal, even if it only lasts an hour!) If at the end of a four-hour rehearsal the students feel *rewarded* by seeing *improvement* in their performance level, then the time is justified.

My wife and I often take early morning walks or bikes rides in our Tokyo neighborhood and observe business, fire station, office workers or police station personnel doing group exercises together in the parking lot before beginning their daily responsibilities. The exercise is important, but the real thrust is pulling together thoughts and focus for the work that is ahead, knowing the group is beginning on the same page.

Looking specifically at these lengthy rehearsals: There is a procedural routine, carefully outlined rehearsal objectives, and a breakdown of specified times of when various parts of the rehearsal will take place. I can assure you that in most of the top programs, there will be some personnel change from one musical selection to another. If you do not adhere to the schedule, students will either be early or late for their segment of the rehearsal.

Rehearsal begins with students standing and bowing to the director as a group asking to be taught. The director responds with, *"Yoi rehearsal ni si ma shou"* (Let's have a good rehearsal). The director then makes specific announcements, focusing on rehearsal goals.

The director launches into the warm-up and tuning segment. In the rehearsals I have attended, this portion is extremely important, and a significant amount of time is devoted to these fundamentals. In almost every situation, this portion of the rehearsal is not conducted by the director, but rather by the concertmaster, a band officer, or other designated student leader.

During this warm-up, the leader carefully monitors the pitch and tone production of each individual and section. Sometimes a listening device is used, but more often than not students rely on careful listening and matching pitches to their section leader. As the process proceeds, when a new section is to begin the tuning process, the section leader must match pitch with the previous section leader. The most commonly used technique is to begin with the lowest voices in the ensemble and work to the top, each time checking the pitch level with the lower voice.

After the designated leader feels the individual pitch level has been attained, they proceed to full ensemble warm-ups. This usually involves unison and chorale exercises. Also as part of this warm-up process the group does some solfege and chorale singing, and I mean belt-it-out singing. The singing of Japanese band students would make most symphonic choirs proud. There is strong belief that if you can't sing it in tune, you can't play it in tune. I know many outstanding American programs that employ the same philosophy.

The materials used for these warm-ups are both manuscript and some of the most commonly-published materials one would find in American band rooms. This warm-up period will last up to one hour or more. The ensemble will then take a short break and begin the pre-set rehearsal order. The director now takes the podium and initiates the rehearsal of the specific segments to rehearse.

In every rehearsal room I have visited, an electric piano stands next to the director's podium. If the director detects a pitch problem she turns to the keyboard and asks the students to refocus the chord, or listen to the melody as it fits into the chord structure, or if a partial of the chord is out of tune, have those with just that part of the chord play with the keyboard to attain the proper pitch.

For example, if the third of the chord is out of tune, the director will play the root and fifth and have students play the third until it fits properly with the root and fifth. The emphasis is on individual listening.

In some American band rooms, I have observed all members of the band with their own listening device attached to their instrument to monitor their own pitch level. This can work well and is practical in a shorter rehearsal time frame, but when the device is removed, do students listen more carefully than before? While electronic pitch devices are quick and practical, I would much rather see students rely on their ears to make pitch adjustment. Don't forget, the only pitch adjustment device in the Eastman rehearsal hall when Fennell was the conductor was a sign in the front of the room that just said, **LISTEN.** This is a little subtler than the sign I saw in an American high school band hall that read, **TUNE IT OR DIE!** That would be seriously stressful!

The other aspect of these long rehearsals that impresses me is student attentiveness and concentration level. I have sat in on several of these long rehearsals, and have conducted a few of that length as well. The conductor never has to say a thing about talking during rehearsal. Golden silence. Again, this is a cultural thing, but I have always been tremendously impressed by the ability of the Japanese bands to sit still without any talking for such long periods of time. And to top it off, they stand at the end of the rehearsal, bow to the conductor and say "thank you" for teaching them. With that many hours of focused rehearsal in a week's time, it is no wonder that these top bands achieve such a high performance standard.

There are some negative aspects to this type of rehearsal. In some schools students and directors rely too much on rote teaching, which leads to a more mechanical performance and poor sight-reading skills. Students taught this way also do not learn to read well, so more individual practice time is required to learn a new piece of music.

Not so much today, but some early directors used pretty severe discipline in order to achieve satisfactory results. But, was that not the case in the United States as well a few generations ago? I am happy to share that this practice is not very common any longer in Japan or in the United States. Just as in the States, when students are subjected to extra, long hours of out-of-school rehearsals, there is a burn-out that takes place, to the point where students do not wish to participate in any kind of ensemble after high school. This is one of the reasons why most of the music schools in Japan have witnessed a decline in enrollment in the past few years.

The other two reasons for a drop in enrollment at most universities is a declining national population and the economy. Once instrumental students attain a certain proficiency level through club activity and wish to improve, they begin private lessons with an approved teacher. Most high-attaining school programs have a list of recommended teachers that has been assembled by the director.

There is another philosophy that is effectively utilized by some directors, involving older students teaching the younger students in the program. Otaki who conducts the Saitama-Sakae high school band (one of the outstanding programs in the country, I believe), utilizes this system to great success. Following is what he explained to me about this system.

> When the new students start the band, they form groups of a couple of new students for one older student. This is called Senpai-Kohai method. *Senpai* are the older students, and younger are called *kohai*. Senpai teaches kohai every little thing, not only about the instrument and performance technique but also band club rules, principles and everyday life in high school. So, Senpai looks after kohai and his behavior. Learning communication skills through the band is very important. It influences everyday life in high school.

When I asked Otaki how he goes about choosing leaders in this system, this is what he shared.

> We select a leader by elections. Each student has numerous sides to them, and the students themselves know each other better than I or other teachers do. That is why students elect their own leader, and the quality of that selection determines their seriousness in choosing as well as the band club's future.

On the surface this seems dangerous, as one would assume that personalities and personal feelings could cause friction between students. Here is where cultural differences come into play again. It is the *respect* factor that is such a deeply ingrained concept in the country. You see it at every level, in every kind of relationship or personal transaction. It can be observed daily, as people meet for the first time, in the manner and depth of the bow.

While handshakes are taking place more and more due to foreign influences, the bow in Japanese society is still most important. For example, if a younger person meets an older person, then the bow must be lower. Music students from elementary to professional level refer to their teachers and ensemble conductors as *sensei*. This is an honorific expression showing the highest level of respect, regardless of the profession. So younger students respond well to the leadership of older music students and appreciate the time and energy they share so they might improve.

This is so excellent to observe. Directors examine leaders carefully to make sure they have the personality, skill, and desire to make a difference in younger students' lives. Where I see this form of instruction taking place, I see a program that is progressive, focused, and musically savvy. Students exhibit a fantastic attitude and have a deep respect for each other and the overall program.

The history of current Japanese bands is relatively short, beginning only in the mid-1950s. This methodology and pedagogy of rehearsal technique goes back to the time when many bands were led by teachers who were not formally trained as musicians in a university or school of music, but who directed the band because they were interested and available to spend the time. However, without the proper training, they relied on repetitive techniques. Today, more and more of the outstanding young conductors are well trained. Many have visited and studied in America, and learned that achieving musical excellence can occur without lengthy and repetitive rehearsals. I am delighted to see this style of preparation taking place more and more.

College, University, and Schools of Music

Colleges and universities are numerous in Japan, and while I do not have an exact number, I can assure you there are well over a thousand. This does not include the many private institutions or music schools also present in Japan. However, within the college and university systems, there are probably only 350 that include band programs.

Once again, the stress on academics is so strong in most of these institutions that there is not time for these extra musical organizations. The institutions that do have band programs are generally not considered as having the top ensembles at the university level. However, the All-Japan Band Contest does provide a category where these bands can compete if they desire. This goal provides these better university bands an outlet and a goal for high achievement.

In addition to college and universities, there are over a hundred schools of music of varying sizes in the country. Probably half of these schools offer some type of music education course of study. This in itself is having a positive impact on the training of future band directors. It is generally agreed among Japanese directors that there are eleven or twelve top schools of music in Japan with outstanding symphonic bands and wind ensembles. Seven of these top schools of music reside within the city of Tokyo.

At one time or another I have heard the bands from these institutions, and can attest to the high quality of their music making. The size of these bands and the kind of literature performed has changed pretty dramatically in the past ten to fifteen years. While most of these schools now embrace the wind ensemble concept, a few still make use of the concert band format popular in the United States from 1950 to the mid-1980s, with groups of 90–130 members or more, depending on the school.

The literature of choice in most of these bands was transcriptions of famous orchestral works. At the All-Japan Band Contest, transcriptions are still a fairly common choice for the showcase selection, even with the fifty-member limit.

In the past few years, schools of music that have traditionally had very large symphonic bands are now changing to wind ensembles and inviting guest conductors to help them achieve satisfactory results with wind ensemble literature selection and performance practice.

One school of music that adopted the wind ensemble concept early on is the Musashino Academia of Musicae. This large and very fine school of music in Tokyo began the wind ensemble concept in 1954, only two years after the Eastman Wind Ensemble was formed.

The Musashino Academia of Musicae

Naoaki Fukui founded the Musashino Academy of Music in 1929 with a focus on promoting western classical music in Japan. World harmony through music has always been a principal goal of the school. Guest teachers, conductors, and performers from all parts of the world have played a significant role in creating the international flavor and awareness of the school.

Musashino Academia has three campuses: the Iruma campus for freshmen, sophomores, the new music environment management class, and students studying for a doctorate; the Ekoda campus for juniors, seniors, the virtuoso class, and graduates studying for a master's degree; and the Parnassos Tama campus, which focuses primarily on child and adult training.

In keeping with its international philosophy and with facilities and a curriculum comparable to the world's finest music schools and conservatories, Musashino has one of the finest collections of original music manuscripts and a major instrument museum. The collection of world instruments consists of some 5,000 pieces. There is also a collection of Japanese instruments, both folk and traditional.

Membership in the Musashino wind ensemble is selected every year from the best junior and senior wind and percussion students, and usually rehearses twice a week in two-hour sessions. Since its inception, the ensemble has given great thought to the content of its programs, accepting ideas and advice both from within Japan and internationally.

The main focus of the ensemble's study has been American wind ensembles, well known for its high-level programs, the richness of compositions by American composers, and conductors. The school feels a great sense of honor and gratitude for the opportunity to perform in 1995 and 2006 at the Midwest Clinic.

The Musashino wind ensemble has recorded fourteen CDs under the Sony label. In keeping with their philosophy, there have been nine American guest conductors, and one each from Czechoslovakia and Bulgaria since 1971. Most of the American conductors have been there multiple times. Working with these outstanding young people is a rich and rewarding experience. A guest conductor spends an entire semester with the ensemble, which allows for a wonderful bond to take place between the conductor and students.

Like most ensembles within Japanese schools of music, performance standards are very high and expectation for outstanding performances is assumed. Lending to the aesthetic satisfaction in these performances is the concert halls in which most of these ensembles perform. While major cities in America may boast of one or two great concert halls, Tokyo probably has ten or twelve major concert venues that are beautiful and acoustically exquisite, and most concerts are sold out. (This last statement was a big surprise to me since, most university concerts in the United States struggle to assemble a modest audience at best.) Not only are the concert halls filled to capacity, but ensembles need to be prepared to play at least three or four encores.

Another fact about concerts in Japan is the huge number of young students who attend these programs. I love looking out in the audience and see the age range in attendance. The Japanese people love bands, and they love to hear new music. During the summer, when most of the junior and senior high bands are diligently preparing their contest music, it is appropriate to include on the program one or two of the required numbers. Just before these numbers are performed, young musicians in the audience will pull their music out of their backpack so they can follow their part while the music is being performed. You can tell by their smiles if you played the music to their satisfaction. In my conclusion I will include some observations and additional comments from a few of the other American guest conductors.

The Midwest Clinic and the International Connection

The Midwest Clinic (an international band and orchestra convention) has long promoted ensembles and clinicians from other countries. This outreach only helps to strengthen music education, performance standards, and music industry and philosophical collaboration around the world.

Not only is every American state represented at the convention, but also there are additionally over forty different countries in attendance each year. This is very pleasing to the Midwest Clinic, which plans to continue the importance of this collaboration for the foreseeable future. With travel costs continuing to spiral upward everyday, the Clinic truly hopes it can continue to attract outstanding ensembles from around the world.

Until 1991, the country that had performed the most concerts at the Midwest Clinic was Canada, having presented groups on five different occasions dating back to the first performance in 1952. There have been fifteen different countries featured in performances in the last seventeen years. Since 2000, Japanese bands have regularly been featured at the convention. These groups represent almost every category of wind ensemble in Japan, specifically, professional, corporation, university, and high school groups.

A few years ago the Midwest Clinic offered an invitation to a Japanese elementary band to perform, but the community determined they would not be able to raise the necessary finances to make the trip to Chicago. I know there are many outstanding elementary bands that would love to perform at this international convention. We hope it will take place in the future.

The first Japanese band to perform at the Midwest Clinic was the Fukuoka Technical University High School Concert Band under the direction of Takayoshi Suzuki in 1987. Many American directors know the conductor as Tad. He has been on the faculty at the University of Nevada in Las Vegas for several years. I well remember his performance at Midwest. Sitting as close to the front as I could get (a practice that goes all the way back to my first Midwest Clinic in 1960), the thrill I got from the fantastic sound, musical expression, and flawless technique still resonates in my musical memory. That performance was the talk of the convention, and even today many directors, including myself, remember with clarity the impact it had on the audience. Midwest attendees from that performance on have fallen in love with Japanese bands.

Following that first performance, there have now been ten other presentations by Japanese bands, including the Ensemble Liberte Wind Orchestra that will perform in December 2008.

I believe the first Japanese band director to attend the Midwest Clinic was Toshio Akiyama. I do not know the year he first attended, but I do know he has not missed a clinic since. This happens to many people. Over the years, Toshio single-handedly encouraged other directors to attend the Midwest

Clinic. He recognized from the beginning what directors could learn by attending performances, clinics, and the exhibits. For several years now, the number of directors from Japan registering at Midwest Clinic far surpasses that of any other foreign country. However, in the past two or three years, it has been encouraging and rewarding to see groups of directors attending for the first time from China and Russia. It is the Midwest Clinic's goal to continue the pursuit of attracting international attendees and performing ensembles from around the globe.

Other Japanese Band Activity

I have, as accurately as possible, shared information related to bands ranging from elementary through the university level. Thus far I have mainly focused on the top ensembles, exploring their activities, methodology, and philosophies. However, there are thousands of bands which, for one reason or another, choose to not compete at the All-Japan Contest level. Among these non-competitive bands there are still many outstanding ensembles that wish to focus on student development through performance in band to encourage participation at some level of music throughout their lives. In the following paragraphs you will see the impact this is having by the number of community bands that now function in Japan.

There are many superior military bands in Japan, representing the Army, Navy, and Air Force. There are thirty in all within the country, but the Army (Japan Ground Self Defense Band) claims the majority with nineteen groups. As in the United States, these bands provide a wonderful source of musical fulfillment and security for student musicians who graduate from one of the universities or schools of music and wish to pursue a professional playing career. I have heard several of these ensembles in concert, and their performances have been highly rewarding, both musically and technically.

Corporation bands in Japan have been an integral part of band activity for many years. I was informed that, twenty-five years ago, there were nearly 300 corporation bands throughout the country. Recently, the difficult Japanese economy has caused many corporations to discontinue their bands due to financial concerns. I understand this scenario, but feel bad for the musicians, as they had a tremendous sense of pride and commitment to these ensembles. Even with the economy forcing the termination of many of these groups, there still is a significant number of corporation bands in the country—nearly 100.

These groups rehearse weekly and present formal concerts three or four times a year in beautiful concert venues. For example, the Yamaha Symphonic Band (which performed at the Midwest Clinic in 2005) rehearses twice a week for two hours. Membership consists entirely of musicians who work daily in the Yamaha plant in Hamamatsu. Devoting two hours twice a week for rehearsal is quite a commitment after putting in a full day's work. If you heard their concert in Chicago, then you will understand that the members feel the time is well spent in order to achieve the performance level they enjoy.

Company and corporation bands are prevalent in Japan, but the number of community bands is staggering, and keeps growing each year. Nearly 1,800 of these bands are active in Japan. This is exciting and encouraging, for it gives the impression that musicians understand and realize that participation in a music group helps reduce stress levels (and believe me they need this) and helps provide a more fulfilling life. Playing in an organization like a community band can change one's perspective on life. One Japanese statistic that makes me very sad is the incredibly high suicide rate. The old saying, "music soothes the savage beast" must contain significance for the thousands of people who participate in community bands.

There are also a large number of police and fire department that function throughout the country. These groups perform *many* concerts throughout the year and present clinics and concerts in schools throughout their prefecture.

There are five professional bands in Japan: the Tokyo Wind Orchestra, Osaka City Symphonic Band, Tokyo Symphonic Band, Siena Wind Orchestra, and the Philharmonic Winds Osakan. Only the Tokyo Kosei Wind Orchestra and Osaka Symphonic Band offer full-time employment for musicians. While the other groups pay their members, it is only on a concert-to-concert basis and not full-time employment.

If you have kept track of the numbers presented in this chapter, you can easily ascertain that band activity at every level is exceedingly popular. Once again, Toshio Akiyama told me last summer there are probably close to 14,250 active bands in Japan. Is band important and popular in Japan? A rhetorical question, I believe!

Literature

I briefly commented earlier that many of the top bands at the university and high school levels perform transcriptions on a pretty regular basis. These transcriptions are standards that have been popular in the United States as well, the Mark Hindsley transcriptions being the most-often performed.

A problem occurs at the All-Japan Band Contest, as ensembles have ten minutes or less to perform a showcase number. So directors make major cuts in the music or hire a composer or arranger to make alterations in order to fit the time allowed. More often than not, directors of the top ensembles commission special arrangements of either classic orchestral repertoire or to alter original major works for wind band to fit their time limitations.

At the first All-Japan Band Contest I attended in 1990, there were few original works for band performed as a showcase selection. Most bands performed transcriptions. When I attended the contest in 2006, I was delighted to see that over half of the showcase numbers were major, original works for band. However, the problem of length remains. So these original works often require selective cuts to stay within the time limit.

One particular work stands out, as it was a major work that I knew was nearly thirty-five minutes in length. The band played the major themes very skillfully knit together into one satisfying ten-minute work. It was very cleverly done and did not leave me musically unsatisfied. The composer might not have thought it was so great, but it received a flawless performance and was enthusiastically received by the 5,500 in attendance. I think any composer would like to have his compositions so beautifully performed and received by so many people at one hearing. I am sure it prompted many directors to buy the music, and their performances would likely be of the entire work.

More and more conductors from America guest-conduct in Japan each year. These conductors are very knowledgeable of the best compositions being written and performed by the top American wind ensembles. They are bringing these fine works to Japan and its wind ensembles, and their regular conductors and audiences are eagerly adopting these new compositions. That being said, I need to unequivocally state I have been impressed by the quality and quantity of band music being written by outstanding Japanese composers.

During my first trip to Japan (now nearly twenty-five years ago), I had the opportunity to hear many bands in concert. I was surprised then to discover very few original works by Japanese composers. Those that I did hear were not of the musical depth that one would hear today. Now there are many outstanding Japanese composers writing exceedingly fine works for wind band. These excellent works are being performed regularly around the world.

In the spring of 2007 I had the opportunity to guest-conduct in a program called Kyo-en. Kyo-en is sponsored by Brain Music Company and features eight different bands. Every number on the afternoon and evening program is a world premier written by a Japanese composer. Some compositions are highly demanding, requiring the most mature and proficient ensemble. Other works are geared for younger ensembles, but still quality pieces for the less-proficient band.

I was very impressed by the quality, creativity, and depth of these compositions. Wind band literature written by Japanese composers is growing by leaps and bounds, as the cliché goes. I would like to have added a representative list of composers at this point in the chapter, but out of fear of forgetting (and upsetting) someone, I defer to your desire to check publisher websites to find many of these outstanding compositions. To keep up with this growing demand and to find a means for distribution, there is an expanding list of music publishers in Japan. Toshio supplied me with a list of thirteen publishers now in operation. That represents quite a shift from twenty-five years ago.

Musashino Academia of Musicae Reprise

Musashino Academia of Musicae is a very unique school. The enrollment numbers have dropped, as is true for most institutions of higher learning in Japan due to the economic downturn and population decline. The school still remains the largest in Japan, and is faithful to the founding principal of exposing their students to guest teachers, conductors, and performers from Europe, America, and within its own country. This focus plays a significant role in creating the international flavor and awareness of the Academia of Musicae.

As I mentioned in the introduction, my journey to Tokyo came out of the proverbial blue. Late one night in the summer of 1990 I received a call from Robert Bergt, chair of the music department at Valparaiso University. I had known Robert for a few years, as we would see each other at various professional meetings. At the time, he was the full-time orchestra director at Musashino, having taken a long-term leave of absence from Valparaiso. In keeping with the school's policy of inviting conductors from America, President Fukui asked him to contact me to see if I would be interested in conducting their wind ensemble in the coming fall.

I had known of this ensemble and heard recordings (LPs at the time) and knew the group was very fine. After discussing this with my wife Molly, and, of course, Dean Webb of the IU School of Music, I decided to take a leave without pay (I had just taken my first sabbatical the previous spring, so without pay was the only way), as this might possibly be my only opportunity to experience a new culture and wind ensemble experience. That late night call was the beginning of a long and rewarding relationship. It has become a second home for us, as we have developed so many close friendships there over the years.

The fact is, we have been able to tour with the wind ensemble throughout Japan and have probably seen more parts of the country than most students in the band or their parents. It is an association I hope will continue for several more years. I harbor a deep love and respect for the administration, faculty, staff, and students—especially the students, for they are extremely bright, diligent, cooperative, friendly, and a joy to conduct. Here are a few brief comments and impressions from other American guest conductors who have worked at Musashino in recent years.

Ken Bloomquist, Director of Bands Emeritus, Michigan State University

It is imperative that we as teachers and conductors create an atmosphere in which the educational process can flourish. My first rehearsal with the Musashino Wind Ensemble was very exciting. I gave the downbeat to what I considered to be a difficult concert opening selection. To my amazement they performed the piece virtually note-perfect. Following rehearsal I went back to my residence and told my wife, "I've got a problem!" I reiterated the rehearsal experience and wondered out loud what in the world I was gong to do for the next three months. Remembering my maxim of creating an atmosphere where the educational process can flourish carried me throughout, and in the process I was able to elevate my expectations to another level. The joy of rehearsing every detail and nuance and never losing the interest and dedication of the performers, most of whom were junior and senior college students, was a dream come true.

We must always pursue perfection. This sounds like an impossible goal and the arrogant raving of a conductor who is ignoring reality. But the work ethic displayed by the Musashino Wind Ensemble is all-encompassing. It is realized out of accomplishing the impossible, a love of making music, satisfying inner needs to learn, and pleasing parents, conductors, teachers, audience, and self. Plain hard work satisfies the old adage that "practice makes perfect!"

Russell Coleman, Director of Bands Emeritus, University of Central Missouri

Before my first trip to Tokyo, I had heard several Japanese bands perform in the United States. I was very impressed with their excellent intonation and technique, but disappointed in their rigid performances and a general lack of musical expression. It was my goal to see if I couldn't improve that with the wind ensemble. It was a very pleasant surprise to learn that when you encouraged and *freed* them to express themselves musically, they played with just as much heart as any group I have ever heard! It was a joy to turn them loose and listen to their wonderful musicianship. In pondering this pleasant occurrence I reached the following conclusions:

1. Japanese culture is very rigid in allowing people to show or express any emotion.
2. People tend to avoid drawing attention to themselves.
3. They grow up in a very structured environment.
4. It is not proper to show emotion.
5. Younger musicians, however, have a desire to put their hearts into the music.

In my subsequent trips as their guest conductor, the ensemble often brought me near to tears as I heard what wonderful music they made as they put their hearts into their performances.

Richard Hansen, Director of Bands, St. Cloud State University

It is rare in today's society that we experience *profound silence*. Surrounded by and steeped in all sorts of electric gadgets and conveniences, and driven into our hectic lifestyles with "noisy wheels," we rarely experience profound silence. We suffer as much or more from noise pollution as we do air pollution. As a boy growing up in Iowa, I sometimes experienced special moments of pure silence in the country. Recently, the only time I have experienced this in America is on treks to northern Minnesota boundary waters. It seems oddly strange then, that the place I have known the phenomenon of profound silence most frequently is in the bustling city of Tokyo, for, as with New York, Tokyo never sleeps. Nonetheless, as I walk through the narrow, little, winding paths into the neighborhoods, I have on numerous occasions known the air to be completely devoid of sound. It is like taking a breath of fresh air.

Directly related to profound silence in Japanese daily life is the extraordinary ability of Japanese musicians to listen (*kiite*). Profound silence has a tremendous impact upon musicians' ability to produce beautiful sounds. Sounds coming out of silence are not only a matter of the physics of sound, but the *feelings* of serenity inside players caused by the calm of silences. This elevates musicians' skills to match teachers, conductors' articulations and singing, and student section leaders. Recorded and live sound models and matching cultivate extraordinary playing skills in Japanese wind band musicians. Musicians tend to grow from student leadership models in Japan most powerfully and accurately. Their listening and matching skills are so keen, that when "model" professional recordings are flawed, students will match even the flaws! The conductor must be *very* careful to sing and articulate accurate models, because what you give is what you will very precisely get!

The influence Musashino Academy of Music has had on Japanese band culture is clear, and perhaps best stated by Naotaka Fukui, President of the school. He precisely states,

I have no doubt that our connection with guest conductors has helped to create what is known as the "Musashino Sound," a sound much admired for its dynamic range and beauty, and a sound seen as a target level by all concerned with wind ensemble work in Japan.

One of the facts I find so exciting is that, of the wind and percussion students in the school, almost seventy-five percent are in the music education curriculum. Each year at the All-Japan Band Contest there are bands whose directors are Musashino Alumni. This speaks well for their education and for the future of music education in Japan.

Hands Across the Sea: a Conclusion

My brother Eddie was stationed in Japan in the early 1950s, and I remember the fascinating stories he shared about his experiences. He brought home exotic gifts, silk kimonos for my sisters, exquisite fans and silk scarves for my mother, and a miniature samurai sword for me, which I loved showing to my grade school buddies. Today I would be arrested for taking this to school—even in Delong. I do not recall what my father received, but I do know he was happy to have his son back in Delong. Oh yes, the journey (sorry, I got wrapped up in nostalgia there for a moment).

In the first program I conducted at Musashino, it seemed obvious that a march I should and needed to play was the great Sousa march, *Hands across the Sea*, thinking it would be politically correct and appropriate. The band performed it with a spirit and bravura that would make the Marine Band proud. The audience responded enthusiastically, making me smile, thinking how smart a move this was. It wasn't until subsequent visits that I realized Japanese audiences *love* American marches, and they are *always a hit!*)

Hands across the Sea portrays the image that collaborative ideas and concepts go both ways. The interpersonal relationship of extended friendship and camaraderie, and enjoying the exhilaration that comes in making exciting and memorable music together are experiences I could not have anticipated growing up in Delong (while playing nasty glissandos on my Pan American trombone). Having the opportunity to spend nearly three months with the students and live in a real Japanese neighborhood, attending a local Japanese Baptist Church (very rare in Japan), shopping and eating at small mom-and-pop stores and restaurants, and buying vegetables on the street where you watch the farmer pick the vegetables, gives one a much more complete picture of what daily life is like in Japan.

Because of the length of the residency, the Musashino engagement offers these kinds of non-musical experiences that contribute tremendously to understanding the culture and how that impacts the musical heart and face of the students. Many guest conductors who visit Japan are generally there for a relatively short time, live in hotels, eat out every meal and have little chance to interact with students and faculty outside of rehearsal. I know the students receive a wonderful musical experience, but the guest does not have the opportunity to feel the culture.

Over my teaching career, one of the tenets of my ensemble experience has been to learn students' names as quickly as possible. I feel this establishes a positive atmosphere and an important relationship with students that helps solidify communication through the music. American names are easy, but I did worry the first time about learning Japanese names quickly. Students in Japan are rarely called by name in class and almost never in a rehearsal situation. However, with my philosophy in this regard, I determined to do my best to learn their names so I could call them by name in rehearsal and around school or even on the street in Ekoda. Once I knew the wind ensemble set-up and the names of students in the set-up, I diligently set about memorizing names before the first rehearsal. At that rehearsal I endeavored to put faces with names. During the second rehearsal I went around the ensemble and called every student by name; they were flabbergasted—they always are. (I'm not sure there is a Japanese translation for *flabbergasted,* and if there is, it might take five minutes to speak.) I follow this format each time I return to the school.

Communicating in rehearsal was another story, for I found out very quickly that even though Japanese students have had several years of English study, none of it embodies verbal communication or conversational skills. Working with an interpreter (which was not an option anyway) takes forever.

You might ask the group to "Please start at number forty-two, and could you play a little softer?" I can say that in three seconds (or less if I am pressed for time), but an interpreter might take a full minute to say the same thing. So I would resort to what most people do when trying to communicate in some other language than their own: I spoke much louder and slower, "Please...start...at...number...forty...two," then raised my arms in preparation for the downbeat. Horns quickly came to playing position, I gave the downbeat and only one person played a very tentative note! So I thought, "Okay, they don't understand, 'Please start at number forty-two.'" That's when I came to the realization that, if I was to have a rehearsal that moved with quickness and pacing, I was going to have to learn how to say "Please start at number forty-two" in Japanese.

I began to make a list of rehearsal phrases I used with my IU wind ensemble and asked for help translating these into Japanese. Like student names, I started to memorize phrases that I knew would be useful in every rehearsal. I did learn very quickly how to say numbers, where to tell the group to start, how many measures before or after, or to play the pick-up, and many other rehearsal necessities. The students are very patient and understanding, and I believe appreciate the fact that I try to communicate in their native tongue. I also have made some embarrassing blunders I will not go into here, but if you want to hear a couple, you will have to—well, never mind.

The Japanese band movement has developed and grown expansively through interaction with American, European, and Japanese conductors, composers, and performing artists. Japanese directors desire to continue our association to delve even deeper into the concepts of sound, literature, and conducting technique. A major goal of mine during each visit to Musashino is to help mold tonal concepts into the sounds I have in my head through the many years of conducting the IU wind ensemble. The exposure of Japanese bands to American conductors and audiences at the Midwest Clinic and other association meetings around the United States has helped to elevate performance expectations. Our methods and procedures may be very different due to educational and cultural differences, but the musical glue that binds us together is the intense power and magnetism in music performance.

Before my final paragraphs, I want to take this opportunity to express my thanks and gratitude to Toshio Akiyama for providing me with the numbers and factoids I used throughout this chapter. They came from two sources: the first from a paper he assembled for the seventh WASBE conference held in Hamamatsu in 1995; the second from an email he sent me following a personal meeting we had this summer in Tokyo, where I asked him several questions pertaining to specific facts about Japan band activity. No director in Japan has a better understanding and knowledge of the Japanese band movement than Toshio.

Akiyama has been a vital part of Japanese band expansion for nearly sixty years. If you go with Toshio anywhere, you had better be prepared to run, for he can move through a congested train station faster than anyone half his age—no, make that two-thirds his age—especially if they have two bad knees. Fortunately, I was tall enough that I could keep track of his full head of white hair among the throng of all-black hair. Thank you, Toshio, for everything you have done in the past and for the impact I know you will continue to have on the band movement in Japan. The respect you have among directors is well deserved. Thank you!

I truly hope you have found this chapter to be informative, interesting, and insightful, and that it has provided a clearer picture of the Japanese band culture and Japanese life in general. For me, a farm boy who grew up at Eleventh and Plum (near Delong), whose musical experience began by letting things slide (sorry about that, but you should hear me play Lassus Trombone), this has been a growing, thrilling, rewarding, and humbling but always joyful experience finding new ways to communicate the magnificence embodied in music-making, regardless of the culture.

Many American directors have the belief that Japanese musicians and ensembles play with fantastic technique but little emotion or expression. As Russ Coleman expressed in his brief comments, this is just not the case. These young people feel deeply and express themselves in many ways that should be visible as well as audible to audiences. I love watching Japanese ensembles perform, the way they move with phrases and accents. This is natural for them. They have grown up feeling the music in this manner. Their movements match the musical character and style.

Karada de Ongaku o hyogen shite (Move with the Music). They know this phrase well and respond to the music, not just the notes.

Ongaku wa kokoro kara dete kuru mono desu (Music comes from the heart!) I have witnessed emotion, tears on stage during a performance responding to a beautiful phrase, backstage hugs and laughter, and congratulating one another on a job well done, just as with our American students.

The title of this book series, *Teaching Music through Performance in Band*, could not be more significant or meaningful than the subject of this chapter. As directors and music educators, we must always make it our goal and mission, regardless of age level or culture, to teach and inspire students to explore the richness of music and help them to fully experience the joy in making music together.

What I have discovered during my forty-seven years in this profession is that if we, the teachers and conductors, are *passionate* about what we do, are *committed* to the music we are conducting, are *compassionate* people and *respect* the people in front of us, our jobs will be incredibly rewarding.

Music can name the unnamable and communicate the unknowable.
—Leonard Bernstein

This can happen in Delong or Tokyo. Well, probably not Delong, as the two-room school and the general store are now family dwellings, and three of the five pianos no longer exist. However, there might be some young farm boy just waiting to discover the joy of playing glissandos.

With Masashino students, I use the phrase "play with heart" more than any other. Our bodies are made up of many different elements and a large percentage of water, but the heart can be one hundred percent musical. *Always play with heart and you will never be musically unfulfilled!*

In Delong we said goodbye with the phrase, "See you later." In Japan they say, *"Sayonara."* When in Japan, I teach students as many cultural collaborations as possible, and ask them to combine the American and Japanese phrases for "goodbye," so I end by saying, *"Sayo-later."*

CHAPTER 8

The iRoads to Inspired Teaching: Ingenuity, Insite, Integrity, and Inspiration

Ray E. Cramer

On June 29, 1956 President Dwight D. Eisenhower signed the Federal Aid Highway Act that established the framework and financial support to begin the process of linking U. S. cities with a population of 50,000 or more with an Interstate System. Many believe the Interstate System could very well be the greatest public works project in history.

I am old enough to fully, and maybe painfully, remember two major trips I took with my parents prior to the Interstate System. One trip was to California in 1947 to visit relatives of my mother in our then eight-year-old Chevrolet. The other extended trip in 1952 was to British Columbia, Canada to again visit relatives of my mother. (Mother had a lot of long-distance relatives.) What I vividly recall about these trips was the very slow pace, no air conditioning, an uncomfortable ride and not even a working radio. My father wasn't necessarily a slow driver, but two-lane roads led to traffic back-ups, limited opportunities to pass, and what seemed like having to pass through the very heart of every small town and major city along our route. The plan was to hopefully travel 250 miles each day leaving very early in the morning and stopping early enough in the afternoon to find a motel with a vacancy. On many days the 250 miles could not be achieved. Car games with my grandmother, reading the Burma Shave signs, keeping a tally of all the different state license plates and trying to guess how many miles it would be to the next grain elevator that you could spot on the horizon (in Kansas that was a long way) occupied my time.

The Interstate System has become part of our daily lives and culture. Our American way of life would be far different today without the presence of this vast system. Each of us has been impacted by it, if not directly as drivers or passengers, then indirectly as almost every item we purchase has at some point been transported over the Interstate System.

President Eisenhower considered the establishment of the Interstate System to be one of the most important achievements of his presidency. Transportation officials of the time knew that to get people from one place to another over the 40,000-plus miles of the system in a safe and efficient manner, numbering would become a crucial element.

The interstate highway numbering system is ingenious and yet simple to follow. East-West routes are all even numbers; the North-South routes are all odd numbers. All East-West routes start with the lowest number in the South and proceed to the highest number in the North (e.g., I-10 to I-90), while all North-South routes begin with the lowest number in the West and proceed to the highest number in the East (e.g., ex. I-5 to I-95).

There are also three-digit numbers designating a route circling around a city, a bypass through a city to the same route, and even specifically assigned numbers if the interstate goes directly through the heart of a city. One of the most interesting facts about the interstate system is that it requires one mile in every five to be straight. These straight sections are usable as airstrips in times of war or other emergencies.

Like many great ideas, the initial concept of a "National Hi-way System" was formulated in 1921. The planning of this vast system continued to develop and grow in scope over the next thirty-five years to the signing of the Federal Aid Highway Act in 1956. It took the next thirty-five years for the project to be completed.

Today it is even easier to get from one location to another with the use of a GPS (Global Positioning System). It is still stunning and awe-inspiring how this small, deck-of-cards-sized instrument can deliver us to a desired destination without fail. (Well, usually without fail, or without a verbal announcement that we made a wrong turn, prompting the voice inside the GPS to say "recalculating").

How often in my teaching career did I wish for well-thought-out and defined routes to guide me through difficult problems, decisions, frustrations and disappointments? Or better yet, a GPS that would pick the absolute *best* road to teaching fulfillment and professional satisfaction. When making a wrong turn or poor decision, I would gently be reminded that the system was "recalculating" to find a more desirable route.

Music education students today are receiving the best education and acquiring more knowledge about their profession than ever before. If they feel they are lacking in knowledge, all they have to do is read any number of outstanding books or attend conferences that provide outstanding clinicians willing to share their professional knowledge to help guide teachers through the challenging aspects of their careers.

Our profession however, involves so many intangible ingredients to success that it is very easy to become disoriented and confused. When that happens, self doubt sets in, delivering an even more crippling barrier to productive work and achievement. For many years I have personally felt that the iRoads I wish to explore in this chapter are some of the most important topics and the most elusive in our quest for quality teaching experiences. Please read on as we examine the characteristics involved in the iRoads of *ingenuity*, *insight*, *integrity* and *inspiration*.

Ingenuity

When faced with a situation that one has never dealt with before, one can easily become frustrated, angry, frozen in place with no place to turn, usually ending in discouragement and failure to make logical decisions. There are no courses that instruct us on how to respond when faced with a circumstance that has no ready solution. That is when our inventive skills and imagination need to kick into high gear to find problem solving solutions. Our ability (or inability) to find ways to achieve immediate results can make the difference between satisfactory conclusions or student frustrations.

A few years ago, a former student invited me to visit his school to rehearse his band. I kept hearing inaccuracies occurring in one particular passage and proceeded to find out just what the basis of the problem was. It only took a minute to locate the offending inaccuracies, and this allowed the rehearsal to continue with little lost time. After the rehearsal, my former student asked me how I was able to locate and fix the problem so quickly. The most important fact was that I knew the score well and had dealt with similar issues before in this particular passage, which enabled me to anticipate just where the problem might be occurring. In our discussion I shared that part of the ability to deal with the problem was experience and in-depth study of the score. I had done this before and had a good idea of not only where the problem was but also drew upon previous rehearsals where ingenuity took over in finding and fixing the errors.

Many directors fear the digging-in process during rehearsal, feeling they do not want to waste time, or more importantly, fearing that they might not be able to find and fix the problem once discovered. I told this young director that a conductor must become a "musical mechanic." To fix a mechanical problem one must be willing to take things apart to find the offending part in order to make the machine once again operate smoothly. Generally speaking, there are no manuals to guide us in this "mechanical" work, but our ingenuity and imagination can flash to the forefront if we approach the problem with fresh eyes, ears and an open mind.

Standing in front of an ensemble and dealing with musical issues is no different. Take it apart, become a confident and consistent "musical mechanic" using your ingenuity, imagination, inventive skill and cleverness.

Is it possible to improve our level of effective ingenuity? Perhaps. Here are some things we can do to stretch our creative ingenuity.

- Don't be afraid to try something and have it fail. The failure is in not attempting to solve the problem.
- Have confidence in your own on-your-feet thinking and ability.
- Embrace mentorship and don't retreat from sound advice.
- Make it a point to observe master teachers in their own environment. If contacted in advance, most will readily welcome you to visit a rehearsal or teaching session.
- Step out of your comfort zone, drawing your students to a new level of attention and response.
- Avoid the "seven last words" syndrome: "It's never been done that way before."

Insight

Insight is the capacity to discern the true nature of a situation and the ability to grasp the inward or hidden nature of things. Another way of defining insight is being able to perceive in an intuitive manner, understanding your own or even others' mental processes.

An old Scottish saying states that "Some things are better felt than telt." It goes without saying that mothers seem to have that special innate, intuitive sense that is hard to explain. That was always true with my mother. How she was able to "know" what was going on with me was baffling and at times upsetting. (Sometimes painful on the "seat" of justice.) Our own daughter, Heather, asked Molly how she always seemed to know everything that was going on in her life. Molly's response was classic, telling her that when she had her own children she would soon learn this secret. What Molly did not tell Heather was that if you just listen carefully to what your children are saying around the house and make careful observations, it is easy to decipher what is going on.

Is it any different with our students? Not really. Perhaps the lesson here is the necessity of really careful *listening and observation* of our students *in and out* of rehearsal situations.

Insight embodies all of the mystery surrounding the combination of intuition, perception, alertness and sensitivity. Like ingenuity, I believe insight is nearly impossible to teach, but I do believe we can become more sensitized to this important phenomenon. Can we nurture it or even expand it? Possibly, but there's no quick and easy process that suddenly makes one insightful. However, I am a firm believer that, although insight is essential in all of life, it is especially true in professions like teaching, counseling, writing or composing. When insight is present, any of those professions jump to life, making simple things profound and the difficult reachable.

My parents used to tell me to "use your common sense." Or, if I had made a poor decision, the same thought would come out like this: "Where was your common sense?" Entrenched in all of us is this basic instinct of common sense. Listen to that small inner voice, and usually decisions will be more easily determined and be in line with appropriate response.

In music circles we often refer to this as having the right *touch*—that special gift of being able to transform those black-and-white notes on the page into colorful and moving performances. It is the difference of transforming a masterwork from skill to craft. A skilled musician can take a score and produce exactly what the composer has written on the page. A musician with the added bonus of *craft* (insight or touch) can produce something that is more elegant and moving than what the notes on the page represent.

A composer friend once told me that if he tried to put everything in the score that a conductor should think about and be aware of, you wouldn't be able to read the page. Besides, that would be taking the musical responsibility *away* from the person who needs to be the *most* responsible, the conductor. The harmony, rhythm and dynamics can always be attainable if played with proper execution, but the musician with *touch* feels it, is moved by it and fully experiences the nuances helping the performers and the audiences become entranced in the musical depth of the performance. It becomes a vital, living experience. Unlike mathematics where four plus four will always equal eight, in music, the result, it seems to me, is *always greater* when given that special *touch* with insightful, and yes, inspired realization of the score. As George Szell said, "In music one must think with the heart and feel with the brain."

A popular saying often heard either in a serious vein or a joking manner is, "If you've got it—flaunt it." Some musicians are blessed with the gift of insight or touch while others feel they have been left high and dry without this rare quality. These two poles can pose a practical problem, leaving some feeling deprived while the egos of others can become inflated to the extent of aloofness.

First Corinthians 4:7 says,

> What do you have that you did not receive? And if you did receive it, why do you boast as if you had not received it?

Let's face it, insight is a gift; and gifts are more precious when shared. Every teacher (really, every person) has gifts to share. It is of utmost importance that we discover our gifts or that others identify them in us. We are *all* gifted with ability, capability, sensibility and insight, and it is our responsibility to share these in the most effective way possible.

Integrity

The word *integrity* stems from the Latin adjective *integer*, meaning whole or complete. In this context, integrity is the inner sense of wholeness derived from qualities such as honesty and consistency of character. We may look at others whom we believe to have integrity and determine whether they behave according to the values, beliefs and principles they claim to hold. It is important for us to not only recognize integrity in others, but also to use it as a measuring stick for our own personal and inward integrity from which flows the outward signs of honesty and fairness.

As I was working on this brief chapter, the United States was in the midst of mid-term elections of government officials. The word *integrity* was thrown about with reckless abandon to the point where our senses and sensibility became clouded in confusion and suspicion. The wicked and vicious campaign ads seen on television as one candidate took verbal potshots at the opposition, with the other candidate immediately retaliating with their own counterattack prompted the question, "Where is the integrity in this style of campaigning?"

The financial crisis in which Americans currently find their nation has been devastating to millions of citizens who have lost retirement income, jobs (certainly our teaching profession has suffered tremendously) and financial security. Yet, we read that many CEOs of huge corporations that received bailouts were paid huge "bonuses." I pose the question once again: "Where is the integrity?"

In musical terms, integrity *resonates* with our students, colleagues, parents and administration. However, our integrity might not resonate the same with everyone. This is normal and does not mean that integrity is not imbedded within our personal character.

If you are a person who operates on and off the podium with integrity, then people who observe your organization from the outside will recognize the integrity *throughout* the width and breadth of your organization. High integrity instills vision, organizational mission, honesty and sincerity. As the cornerstone of the organization, the expectation of your position is one of outstanding moral principle. A program that focuses on high integrity is a program that will be successful.

If students see your integrity, they will be drawn to you like bees to clover. They will want to emulate you and your energy and provide a work ethic that will propel the entire organization toward higher accomplishments (but remember that the higher the accomplishment the greater the satisfaction). Does this mean if we possess or believe we operate with integrity that we are perfect? Not by any means. However, we can, and must, respect ourselves even with the mistakes we make (and we will make mistakes). Just don't be afraid to admit them, as that exhibits integrity. If we don't, then chances are others will not hold us in high esteem, either. This does not mean we display arrogance or the aloofness mentioned above, but should display humility, knowing full well we were given the special gift of integrity.

As the designated leader of your program, are there road signs to help establish integrity throughout your program? Following are a few suggestions that can help along those lines.

- Establish a core of integrity and ethics from the top.
- Establish strong and effective internal leadership.
- Create situations where students have a chance to display and exhibit integrity.
- Provide positive praise when integrity and honesty are displayed.
- In your organization, promote the culture of no musical jealousy.
- Make sure the integrity you portray is clear concerning individual and organizational responsibility and accountability.

We cannot become what we need to be by remaining what we are.

–Max DePree

First learn the meaning of what you say, and then speak.

–Epictetus
Greek-born Roman slave and
Stoic philosopher, 55–135 AD

These two quotes speak directly to the core of the expectation of integrity and personal character. If you are a teacher, and you most likely are if you are reading this book, you know we are viewed differently from others. There is an expectation that we will deal with the students under our responsibility with sincere integrity and accountability to them and to the community as a whole.

In Japan, teachers are referred to as *Sensei,* which means they regard the position of teacher with highest respect and honor. That term is not used in the United States, but a teacher who is known for their sincere integrity will be respected and honored by students and community alike.

Are there ways for us to identify integrity in ourselves as well as others? Here are a few suggestions that can be used as a checklist for ourselves or for identifying integrity in others.

- Accept personal responsibility when called for.
- Lead a balanced life.
- Stay open to professional feedback.
- Maintain a strong support system.
- Act with integrity even when uncomfortable or unpopular.
- Do and say what you mean.

Inspiration

I find the history of the word *inspiration* very interesting. The ancient Hebrew

147

and Greek words for *spirit* were root word that meant *breath.* In other words, our spirit or life is sustained by breathing or inspiration. So if you can breath, you can create inspiration that can move others.

> Aspire to inspire before you expire.
>
> –*Author unknown*

This famous quote is heard often and used by many people. It is, however, so true, for everyone wants *to* inspire and *be* inspired.

Nothing provides more direct input to success and personal fulfillment than inspiration. I am sure almost everyone is familiar with the Thomas Edison quote, "Genius is ninety-nine percent perspiration and one percent inspiration." As an inventor with a world record of 1,093 registered patents, one can surely agree with his words. That being said, I believe the following thought is more firmly grounded in the work of the teacher, artist, composer, and truly, in any work demanding strong leadership.

> If your actions inspire others to dream more, learn more, do more and become more, you are a leader.
>
> –*John Quincy Adams*

The Reality of Inspiration

For one moment, envision G. F. Handel sitting at his desk with limited lighting, a stack of manuscript paper at his elbow and the challenge presented to him by librettist Charles Jennens to write an oratorio based on the life of the messiah as recorded in both the Old and New Testaments. Many historians consider Handel as the founder of the oratorio, which is basically a composition so constructed to teach the Scriptures by setting them to music. He seems to have immediately understood how important this composition might be, and he set to work on it right away.

"Set to work" is a gross understatement. Once again, historians have recorded that using Jennens' libretto, Handel completed the entire musical score in only twenty-four days. Was Handel inspired? In my heart and mind, this accomplishment, this masterpiece would not have been possible to compose in that short a time frame without inspiration. Handel did not write *Messiah* for artists, the elite class of society, or even musicians, but for ordinary people, so that with this masterpiece, this magnificent story unfolds through the language of the inspired heart.

One further illustration of compositional inspiration is Beethoven's Ninth Symphony. Consider the fact that at the time he wrote the Ninth Symphony he was completely deaf. Did he throw up his hands and proclaim his career was over? Absolutely not. He proceeded to write what many agree to be his most powerful and inspiring symphony.

Every time I listen to this monumental work I get chills up and down my spine, particularly in the fourth movement, where Beethoven builds the musical and textural tension to what you know is going to be a fantastic climax in the movement, with a brilliant cadence in A Major. You know it's coming, you begin to anticipate it, you can feel it, your heart is beating faster as you prepare for what you know is going to be the penultimate climax. Only an inspired Beethoven would at *the moment* of cadence, slip an F natural in all the bass voices while the upper voices land on a unison A producing, one of the greatest deceptive cadences to F major of all times. As a listener you are stunned and thrilled all at the same time. Beethoven's Ninth Symphony is recognized throughout the world for its musical power and depth.

One fall while teaching in Japan I attended a concert in one of the large concert halls in Tokyo. In the lobby area there were spaces to advertise upcoming concert events throughout the city. I was shocked to count no less than twenty-nine different performances of Beethoven's Ninth Symphony in a two-week period during the month of December. In Japan, as well as all over the world, this fantastic composition must continue to be performed for the people. Mr. Beethoven, I know you must smile broadly from your heavenly heights following every performance, realizing after all these years that listening to your Ninth Symphony inspires the listener to hope and glory every time.

If you have not had an opportunity to hear a *great*, *live* performance of either *Messiah* or the Ninth Symphony, then plan to do so even if you have to travel a distance and pay whatever the price of admission. I assure you that you will leave the performance changed and inspired in a way not experienced before.

Further, consider a young twenty-year-old, still in undergraduate school, sitting in the third row of his first Midwest Clinic concert, listening to the Cass Technical High School Band under the direction of Harry Begian. Not only is the performance technically brilliant, but also the depth of musicality sent shivers throughout the audience. It is the listener's first realization of what was possible to produce with young, talented musicians who have been so enthusiastically inspired by the leadership of the person on the podium. And, in equal proportions, the members of that band returned to Mr. Begian their inspired performance. I was that listener, and to this day I know perfectly well that that performance changed my vision and comprehension of what I hoped to attain during my professional career. I shared this personal experience with Dr. Begian on more than one occasion, and like the humble person that he was, he just smiled and said that he was happy to have been part of my early perception of the joy in teaching and the goal of attaining inspired performances.

In a recent GIA publication titled *The Conductor's Legacy*, compiled and edited by Paula Crider, I spoke of starting lessons on trombone because of "the glamour of the glissando," but quickly found out the real expectation was that I had to *practice*. Not wanting to miss out on all the "fun" activities with my friends, I quit (shame on me).

However, the new band director in our school district came to my rescue when I failed to sign up for junior high band. He found our farm (not easy to do), knocked on the door, introduced himself and asked why I had not signed up for band. His name was Don Zimmerman. He was a great teacher, motivated, innovative and most assuredly, *inspiring*. I wanted to please him and work hard for him in a most dedicated manner. His love of music, young people and dedicated vision led me to *know* I wanted to become a re-creation of Mr. Zimmerman.

Between my sophomore and junior year in high school Mr. Zimmerman left to take a new job, and I did not have an opportunity to see him again. In mid-career I tried to locate him to find out about his life—if he was still teaching or retired. I wanted desperately to share with him how much he inspired me in my life and career choice. When I inquired about Don Zimmerman in the town he had moved to, I was told he had been in very poor health and perhaps by this time had passed away. There was great disappointment in knowing I had missed a very important opportunity to share my sincere appreciation with the person who "saved" me into a life of richness, depth and satisfaction.

You are probably shaking your head, thinking I made a terrible mistake for not making contact sooner and giving my sincere thanks to the person who led me to an inspired life in music. End of the story? Not quite! Earlier this spring I received an email from none other than Don Zimmerman. (No, Entourage does not have a connection in heaven.) It seems there were two Don Zimmermans living in the same town, and the information I had received earlier was for the "other" Don Zimmerman, who in fact had passed away.

Well, "my" Don Zimmerman had done some of his own investigating and called the main office in the Jacobs School of Music to obtain my contact information. As protocol dictates, the school would not give him any contact information other than my email address. I received a long email from Mr. Zimmerman to which I quickly responded, and we shared phone conversations soon after.

I came to find out he had a son living in Denver and was coming to visit his son and to attend one of his grandchildren's graduation from high school. Since I and my wife now live in Colorado Springs, we arranged to meet half way in-between for lunch. His energy, his smile, his zest for life and yes, his sense of humor had not changed a bit in the ensuing fifty-four years. I expressed to him how important and inspiring he was in my life and how many times in writing and in clinics I have mentioned his name and the positive influence he had on my life and career. With that same twinkle in his eye and smile he responded, "Gee, Ray, I don't remember receiving the check!"

Thank you again, Don Zimmerman. This illustrates a very important point in all of our lives. Time seems to propel itself even faster as the years drift by. All of us have mentors that have crossed our path or moved in step with us for a period of time in our lives. Do not miss or pass up the opportunity to express your appreciation to those who have inspired you in your professional life.

The Reality of Being Uninspired

Imagine for one moment that you are sitting in a crowded room of fellow educators waiting for the beginning of an in-service seminar on motivation and leadership. You are deeply in need of *inspiration!* The guest speaker ambles to the podium to deliver a Powerpoint presentation, outlining the important topics to be discussed in a flow of uninspired "edu-babble" while you and your colleagues begin to count the number of ceiling tiles. Are you raising your eyebrows right now, shaking your head up and down and muttering to yourself, "been there, done that?" Probably, because at one time or another we have all been there.

When we arrive at a mindset that what is taking place around us does not pertain to us, then we have landed on the first step of becoming uninspired. Being uninspired is a serious problem, and honestly, all of us go through periods of feeling the pinch of working in an uninspired manner. Authors and composers call it writer's block. No matter how much we love the work we do, and I truly believe that music teachers, conductors and composers love their work, our passion for doing our work is much more difficult to perform when we feel uninspired.

The worst possible thing we can do is *nothing!* Producing work or a musical product that is uninspired can lead to feelings of exasperation, to acts of desperation that can lead to professional failure. Unfortunately, in music we are only as good as what people remember about our last performance. Success is not a tradition; we have to earn respect each time out. This is a difficult topic to talk about—or in this case write about. If a Gallop poll were to be taken among active music teachers, asking if they believed inspired teaching was their daily focus, the positive response would be overwhelming. We all want to feel that when we stand in front of students or put pen to manuscript paper the inspiration juices are flowing full tilt.

So what can we do when we feel that we are just going through the motions in our daily routine?

Analyze

Analyze your situation with careful thought. Ask your friends or a respected mentor for advice. (Be willing to take a little sting.)

When you begin to analyze your circumstances, don't do so in your usual surroundings. Get away from your office or even the school building, take a walk, find a very quiet place and listen to the sounds of nature. Then as you begin to think, make sure you have paper and pencil (sorry, perhaps your laptop or iPad) to write down your thoughts. As you write, begin to formulate a plan of action that will lead you back to productive and inspired leadership.

Plan your work and then work the plan! For years I have strongly suggested to students the importance of writing down the advantages and disadvantages of their work as they look at a prospective job. The problems and the solutions usually become more clearly defined.

Do Something Entirely Different

Do something entirely different from your normal routine. In each place my wife and I have lived we made it a point to establish friendships with people outside of the music profession. Obviously, all of us have many friends within the profession, which is natural and important to establish close friendships in our field of choice. However, making friends with people who work and live in different circumstances and surroundings gave us a different perspective on life. That is why we have enjoyed our teaching opportunities in Japan, as not only is that a different situation but a striking culture change as well.

Participating in an area of life outside of our regular occupation reduces stress and gets our minds off ourselves. While that takes place, our subconscious mind is working on the dilemmas we might be facing in our regular work.

It is far too easy to get down on ourselves. Don't pound on yourself over the feeling of being uninspired; we have all felt that way at one time or another. The biggest mistake we can make is to reject the notion that we are uninspired, as that only our motivation and keeps us frozen in place. Our feet feel like they are attached to a ball and chain, rendering our mental mobility to nil.

One of the more challenging aspects of teaching is keeping our students turned on or on task. Working without inspiration for a prolonged time only contributes to stagnation in our program. Forward momentum and vision for our work is lost. The longer we are mired in the mud of uninspired teaching, the more we sow the seeds of insecurity. The anxiety we experience as a result only creates a lack of self-confidence and vulnerability.

Perhaps one of the simplest solutions to being uninspired is to just go back to work. Doing nothing, waiting for the Dove of Inspiration to alight on our shoulder never works. Stop thinking about yourself so much; throw off the shackles of self-doubt and know that your effort and vision will bring inspiration back to your work.

> You are successful the moment you start moving toward a worthwhile goal.
>
> *–Chuck Carlson*

Can we overcome uninspired work? A positive attitude, self-evaluation and logical planning can certainly help, along with the following points.

- Maintain your self-esteem.
- Keep your individuality.
- Work to keep sameness from bogging down your organizational structure.
- Avoid tunnel vision when it comes to procedure. Nothing stays the same. This helps prevent procedural gridlock.
- Let your students help you create the vision for the future, rather than what it has been before.
- Know your place—know peace.

> Motivation is an external, temporary high that pushes you forward. Inspiration is a sustainable internal glow which pulls you forward.
>
> —*Thomas Leonard*

I have always liked this quote; it strengthens and validates what I have always believed, that charisma emanates from the outside while inspiration is born from the heart.

The Reality of Living and Working an Inspired Life

Even the most experienced and successful teachers must continue to inspire and be inspired themselves. Dwight Eisenhower once stated, "Leadership is the art of getting someone else to do something you want done because he wants to do it." A very true statement for sure, but it is difficult to inspire others to accomplish what you haven't been willing to try yourself. In other words, our students will respond in a positive, enthusiastic manner when they see dedication and effort in our own work ethic.

If we are not inspired, then we have nothing to inspire others with. We have to be fueled by inspiration. Inspiration is like dropping a rock in a pond: the circles continually move in ever-widening circles of influence. Additional rocks dropped into the pond represent developed internal leadership and the circles of influence will impact even more of the surface.

Early in this chapter I spoke of the inspiration stemming from the masterworks of Handel and Beethoven. Of course, there are many, many other musical examples born out of true inspiration I could mention, but it would make this chapter far too long.

I also related two personal experiences, one with Harry Begian and the other with my first director and private teacher, Don Zimmerman. There are innumerable other experiences that have touched my heart, inspired me and drove my ambition and vision to new heights. Such experiences do not have to come from the great masterworks or icons in our profession. Inspiration can come from everyday experiences, working and living with people who share pure *joy* in living an inspired life.

I have been tremendously inspired by performances of outstanding elementary bands that displayed great desire and effort in their musical triumphs, and by individual musicians, less gifted than their peers, who work diligently to overcome their deficiencies in order to move to a new plateau in their playing. I am continually inspired by the stories I read or see of young people with disabilities achieving musical satisfaction through their efforts to become a contributing member to the success of their school program.

If you are a parent, or plan to be one someday, it should be your hope and prayer that you will be an inspiration to your children. More often than not, children become inspirations to their parents. Our own children provided great inspiration in our lives. Our son was a fantastic elementary teacher who is now an elementary principal. His work ethic and his ability to forge strong bonds with staff and students is a constant source of inspiration. Our daughter, who suffered from Rheumatoid Arthritis, refused to let that illness stop her from being a wonderful mother of four young children and to be as strong as she could be through regular swimming, biking and weight training in order to be able to compete in Triathlons. In these events (called Triway-Myway), she was allowed to participate in two events twice since she could not run. Her determination and positive attitude were not only a source of pride but inspired us every day in her far-too-short life.

Joy, after all, is a matter of attitude and choice. All of us need to focus on this aspect of our life. Ultimately we have to make the decision to be happy or we become part of the masses that gripe and complain that life did not give them a fair shake. Be a winner, not a whiner. The choices we make about how we choose to live our lives will *make a difference,* not only in our own lives but in the lives of all with whom come in contact. I am reminded of the poem "The Road not Taken" by Robert Frost, and am drawn to the final phrase:

> Two roads diverged in a wood, and I—
> I took the one less traveled by,
> And that has made all the difference.

As musicians actively involved in teaching, conducting, or composing, we share the same goals, the same love for music and the same sense of wanting to achieve special musical remembrances.

Some of our greatest and deepest enjoyment as conductors can come not in performance, but the quiet and intense process of learning during which the simple but profound truths of the score reveal themselves. We must constantly strive to come closer to the simple truths, so that we may stimulate (inspire) our musicians toward such a search of their own.

–Julius Herford

Is that not what we strive to do? It's *all* about the music and the musicians. Great musical moments provide unforgettable experiences providing a never-ending thread of inspiration. Often these special moments can occur during rehearsals. Make sure you take the time, right then, to share with your students how powerful the moment was. Remind them it might not happen that way in the performance, but encourage them to remember the feeling it produced at the time. I can honestly say I have had many of those moments that brought tears to my eyes (no, not because how poorly they played), and as I looked at the faces of the students in the ensemble, I could tell they felt it with the same passion. Your students only get one trip around as a student; make it memorable and they will forever remember your inspired leadership.

What are *your* sources of inspiration? What are the attributes of inspiration? Your list might be much longer than mine, but here are a few thoughts to jumpstart your thinking. Sources of inspiration for me can be found in great music, literature, art, laughter, family, faith and accomplishments achieved by students. Outdoor activities that encompass everything from skiing to mountain climbing bring my focus back to the marvelous creation that is around us. Inspiration is something you give away, it is constantly moving, a moving force that has to be going somewhere or it dies.

The greatest good you can do for another is not just to share your riches, but to reveal to him his own.

–Benjamin Disraeli

If your main inspiration is to make everybody happy, no one will be happy, including you. Be honest with yourself always. Our profession of music education is currently in a highly fragile state. Throughout the United States music programs are being reduced or eliminated at an alarming rate. We all understand the importance and necessity of an active, vital, dynamic music program. The benefits have been outlined in articles, papers and publications around the country.

Michael Martin, a research analyst for the Arizona School Boards Association, delivered a short, powerful message pertaining to the arts. Here are just a few brief excerpts from his presentation.

> Suppose we stopped teaching math and science and schools only taught singing, dancing, painting, photography, acting and music. How impoverished would we be? Many people consider the arts to be an educational frill on the function of schools to provide workers for the information age. But in many respects the arts are the fundamental engineering of the information age. It is simply wrong to think the arts cannot contribute to technological society. Art is about engineering things so that humans feel they are harmonious and elegant in their context. Art is the harmonizing of things and context that creates elegance and beauty. This is not to say that we should have the arts kill off the math and science in the public schools, but we surely should fear that others would have math and science kill off the arts.

It is more urgent than ever that educators at every level teach with creativity, enthusiasm and inspired leadership. We must endeavor to stand strong at every opportunity to create an atmosphere of inspired teaching. Nelson Mandela spoke fervently when he said,

> Education is the most powerful weapon which you can use to change the world.

Edward Hollowell, a noted Harvard educator and psychiatrist stated,

> You can test students all you want; you can work with the curriculum all you want; but it won't make any difference until you have a teacher who can connect with and *inspire* students."

Inspired teachers know the way, go the way and show the way to provide opportunities to direct individual accomplishments towards organizational successes. Create an environment that will motivate and inspire students to attain their highest potential. The mark of a great teacher is seen when students are inspired to perform above what others think their expectation level should be.

Do not go where the path may lead, go instead where there is no path and leave a trail.

—*Ralph Waldo Emerson*

My inspiration for this chapter came from my personal commitment and professional belief that these four iRoad ingredients have dramatically driven my career. And I might add enthusiastically, they still do! My great desire is that you will read, digest and contemplate "The iRoads to Inspired Teaching: Ingenuity, Insight, Integrity and Inspiration.

Is this the end? Never. We must continue forever to inspire with passion, compassion and joy.

CHAPTER 9

Flexibility:
Bending Is Not Breaking

Ray E. Cramer

Blessed are the flexible, for they shall not be bent out of shape.
···Anonymous ···

Introduction

I love this quote because it speaks volumes about our lives and how we need to approach each day regardless of our chosen profession. It just so happens that in our chosen profession, having the ability to exhibit flexibility in day-to-day situations can mean the difference between success and failure, happiness or discontent, a healthy attitude or deep-seated resentment. Daily we are bombarded through every media resource with the many different ways of how being flexible or inflexible can dictate our lives, our school, our community, and our country. As I look back on my early years of teaching, there were numerous occasions when I could have employed a better sense of compromise to achieve positive results for all concerned.

When I was teaching in Iowa at Harlan High School, I had a tremendous respect and admiration for our principal, Merle Deskin. He was an outstanding person and administrator who had the ability to put every aspect of the school's goals in the proper perspective. To stay in contact with him and to let him know about the needs of the band program, I would make it a priority to stop by his office on a regular basis (usually without an appointment) to let him know what we were doing, my latest request for additional money or schedule suggestions, or anything else I thought he might need to know about our growing program and how he could assist. One day I knocked on his door while sticking my head into his office, and when he looked up he said, "Cramer, what is it today?" He did not look pleased to see me on this particular day, as he most assuredly had other agenda items that needed his full attention. So I lightheartedly said, "You know the old saying, the squeaky wheel gets the grease." Mr. Deskin looked up from his work and with a knowing smile said, "Yes, and it is the first one replaced." With that, I bid him a good day and made it a point to show up less often and for serious topics, made appointments that fit into his very busy schedule. Even though that was good-natured banter between us, I learned something very important that day. My work at Harlan High School was not just about me or the band program; it was also necessary for me to understand how the band program fit into the big picture and to make sure I did not become the central feature of the picture. Mr. Deskin was one of our program's biggest supporters. One of his children was in the band program, but Mr. Deskin knew the importance of flexibility and compromise in seeing the entire picture and just not my part. Experience is a tough teacher because the test comes first and the lesson afterwards.

In the next few pages, I will examine various skills in flexibility as they relate to different situations directly impacting our work. This question will be the central focus of the chapter: **How flexible are we?**

It is a proven element that allowing some flexibility in our personal style of dealing with problems is of extreme importance. Do not misunderstand, this does not mean we should abandon the principles that guide our professional and personal standards on which our everyday expectations are founded. Rules and regulations are most necessary in establishing a rewarding teaching atmosphere. Having the ability to identify situations where flexibility will work or not work is the top priority.

Flexibility in Teaching

Teachers spend countless hours in preparation and study to provide positive leadership and experiences for their students. There are times when one questions the amount of effort devoted in preparing for a lesson or rehearsal. Abraham Lincoln once stated, "If I have eight hours to cut down a tree, I will spend six hours sharpening the axe." Isn't it interesting that the more time we devote to organization, planning, and expectation the less need there is for compromise? We are driven and focused in our intent, and the students understand and respect our motives. A regular routine, positively enforced, solidifies our goals and expectations. Theoretically, in most situations this approach will work beautifully. However, we all know that situations arise where there is disagreement between the teacher and student, and sometimes the whole ensemble. Our inclination is to immediately become negative, perhaps angry, and begin to hand out punishment that does not reflect the depth of the deed. Mark Twain once stated, "Anger is an acid that can do more harm to the vessel in which it is stored than to anything on which it is poured." Quick to anger will be destructive to any relationship. The positive relationship you have established over a period of time with your students or the ensemble is in jeopardy of collapse.

Generally, most teachers can foresee these potential conflicts and defuse the potential of it getting out of hand. Even if these situations are few and only occur occasionally, it is paramount that teachers be flexible and willing to make adjustments. It is of exceeding importance that we maintain our self-control, thus earning even greater respect from our students. Teachers, after all, are human, and mistakes will be made even when we try our best not to make errors in judgment or decisions that create stress and tension among our students. Students are very sagacious and will see through any attempt on our part to "lay blame" away from ourselves or to ignore the circumstance hoping the students will soon forget. The fastest track to forgiveness is for the teacher to apologize. This is tough, but necessary, to reinstate a positive relationship between students and teacher and to restore their confidence.

Perhaps you have worked with, under, or have observed people who are totally inflexible, intolerant, and dogmatic, expounding the philosophy of "my way or the highway." I have attended rehearsals where conductors with this philosophy were working. Observing these conductors allowed me to gain valuable knowledge, for they were excellent musicians, well respected in the profession, and successful in their own teaching situations. I began to assimilate some valuable and positive points from these observations. They also led me to understand I needed to be very careful that my words did not hurt and that I did not direct criticism towards individuals or attack musicianship and ability with insensitive remarks. In some situations, this style of teaching/conducting works very well, producing wonderful musical results. On the other side of the coin, however, I have known teachers who lost their jobs because of their inflexibility and their lack of insight to understand situations calling for sound reasoning and compromise.

Understand and comprehend the fact that winning can mean losing. In life, parenting, and teaching, we must choose our battles carefully. Some battles are not worth the sacrifices that come from winning every time. The goal is to win the war even if some insignificant battles are lost along the way. The most vulnerable time for teachers in this regard is perhaps when they have just taken a new position. Our inclination is to want to make changes immediately with little consideration for what had taken place in the past or for long-standing traditions. No matter what had or had not taken place with a previous teacher, some students, parents, and perhaps even administrators felt the former teacher did outstanding work. I used to tell my students at Indiana to remember this whenever they took a new position: "You can't change the course of the Ohio River in one year." It is important to settle in, get a feel for the situation, sense the general attitude about the program, and carefully observe to find out who the perceived student leaders are in the program. Then begin to make careful, calculated steps in the direction you want to go with a deft and gentle touch. I firmly believe everyone wants desperately to succeed. But there are times when we are so focused on our desire to succeed that we overlook the fact that our primary goal is to share our love of music and to be an inspiration to our musicians.

Success, over time, can harbor the feeling you can do and say anything to attain your projected goals. This generally results in an immovable and unyielding stance. As soon as this occurs, a person begins to build an enclosure, resulting in the inability to communicate effectively with anyone outside of that enclosure. The message is, "Look at me, I'm very successful, my track record is impeccable and there is no need for me to consider flexibility in any way." An inflexible attitude or being totally rigid can also be exhibited in such sayings as: "That's just the way it is," or "Those are the rules, ma'am/sir." This is not the kind of attitude we want people to perceive in our work. Approaching difficult situations head-on, fully entrenched in a position of no compromise or flexibility of established rules and regulations, with a "yes or no" attitude, leaves no "wiggle" room for either the student or the teacher. Being the "professional" and "role model" for our students, we must be ready to show some flexibility in our thought process, allowing disagreements to be resolved rather than having a student's self-esteem resemble a balloon being popped with a pin. This is a very difficult skill to attain, but it is a skill that you must have when you are at your wit's end; you must be able to rise above the natural tendency to over-react. We all need to adopt this phrase of Thomas Jefferson: "When you get to the end of your rope, tie a knot in it and HANG ON!"

Are there serious disadvantages of being too flexible? Of course, this is a rhetorical question, as we all know students will take liberties in stressful situations, knowing we will be tolerant as they recall past encounters. As teachers and parents, the natural expectation of a daily routine is for students and children to test the limits of our commitment by "bending" the rules as far as they think we will accept without "breaking," which usually leads to an uncontrolled response. The worst-case scenario is to be perceived as a soft touch. It is an incredibly thin line we must walk to maintain a balance between an uncontrolled reaction or too much flexibility.

Just recently I had a discussion with a high school director who related a recent encounter with the football coach. It seems the director had been given permission and was scheduled to use the larger (full) football field for a specified time to have marching band rehearsal. The football team was also practicing at the same time on another field, which was a bit smaller but certainly adequate. The coach kept letting the team encroach onto the larger field to allow for additional space for specialized drills. The coach approached the band director and said the band needed to move off of the field, as the team needed the full-sized practice area for their practice. Do you see the potential for an uncomfortable "face-off," with each party raising his voice claiming top priority? The band director, a person with many years of an outstanding teaching record and a person of integrity and goodwill, knew exactly how to deal with this situation. He explained in very controlled and well-chosen words that the band had been assigned to that field in the designated time allotment. The band had been given the field for ninety minutes of their rehearsal. The director told the coach that he certainly understood the need for a larger practice space for the team. The director offered the coach a solution to the problem in a clear and concise manner. He told the coach that he could certainly finish what was needed in his rehearsal in the next forty-five minutes, and then the team could utilize the space for the remainder of the time. He continued his conversation with the coach by offering a permanent solution, which caught the coach off guard but gave him renewed interest. The director explained that since his band was much smaller in number, they did not need a full field and suggested that they could switch practice spaces on a regular basis, thus avoiding any further conflict. The coach's anger meter dropped several points; he thought this was a great idea and said they would take care of lining the band field for the rest of the fall.

Sound familiar? For most of us who have taught in high school, similar circumstances most likely surfaced regarding some aspect of "shared" time and space. In two different high schools where I taught, there were several members of my band who also were members of the football program. I knew how much both of these organizations meant to the students. Both of these high schools were not large, and neither band program had an endless supply of musicians, so I had to be very careful not to place the students in a position where they had to make a choice. At both schools, I had become good friends with the football coaches and was a strong supporter of their programs. They, in turn, had a solid respect for the band program. A compromise was determined between the coaches and myself that if the band student was going to dress for a football game, they did not have to participate in the band activities for that week. The students did not have to make a choice, as they felt part of both organizations and served a practical and needed contribution to both groups. This kind of flexibility was natural for me because I was one of those students in high school. From seventh grade through graduation, I had two great loves: band and football. If my band director had put me in a position where I had to choose between the two, he knew full well which direction I would go. My director understood that as soon as football season was over, I would commit totally to music activities and practice diligently to add my musical voice to the band program. During the fall marching band and football season, I would practice with the band at every indoor rehearsal and continue my private lessons and participation in small ensembles. It was a win-win situation for the director, the football coach, and me.

Do these circumstances resemble some of your situations? The scenario we want to avoid in any of these situations is raised voices, faces that become red with anger, and words spoken that can never be recalled. I remember seeing a poster some years ago that reminds me to always be in control; the picture showed two men, face to face, veins sticking out of their necks, faces red with anger, fists clenched, shaking in rage towards each other, eyes bulging out, and obviously vicious words being exchanged. The caption at the bottom of the poster read, "Never argue with a fool, onlookers will not be able to tell the difference."

Suggestions and Questions for Flexibility Control

Analyze the situation very carefully:

- By maintaining a rigid and immovable stance, will that only cause the situation to escalate?
- Will you choose your words carefully? Before saying anything, take a few seconds to formulate in your mind exactly what your first words will be. This allows you the opportunity to not "spout off," leading to a heated debate.
- What are the issues involved? Is the point of friction the real issue or is there a hidden agenda waiting to bubble to the surface?
- Is the timing of the situation creating the tension? Is it the end of the school day following a long difficult week? Are there problems on the home front? Is this the result of a poor rehearsal or test grade? Are you, the teacher, excessively tired and stressed over issues within the school system beyond your control?
- Do you give students breaks in your rehearsal routine, especially during a long marching band rehearsal? During intense, focused rehearsals, they need to have a chance to let off some of their pent-up energy.

Individual confrontation with a student must be carried out one on one, never in front of the student's peers. Sometimes it is better to allow a "cooling off" time with the student, creating a breathing space for you and the student. Focus on praise for outstanding achievement rather than negativity for less-than-stellar work.

Many other questions come to mind, but the bottom line is that we must adjust our thinking according to the current situation. These are not the times for a "zero tolerance" stance, but rather an opportunity to make adjustments and negotiate alternative decisions.

Firmness in support of fundamentals, with flexibility in tactics and methods, is the key to any hope of progress in negotiations.
—Dwight Eisenhower

Flexibility on the Podium

I have often wondered why we spend so much time, energy, emotional drain, and mental fatigue reflecting on what transpired yesterday and stress out about what might take place tomorrow. Please don't misunderstand, we gain great insight by examining the past and confidence in planning for the future. However, does it help to become so driven that we forget to enjoy the present?

My original idea about the title of this chapter was "One Day at a Time." As I began to formulate my thoughts, I realized that being flexible is so much a part of living one day at a time. During my research, I came across this short paragraph, which beautifully provides a window to our lives, our jobs, and the great reward that comes from working with young musicians and living each day as it is given. When I read this brief statement, I knew I had to use it at some point in this chapter. I searched for the author but could only find it listed as "author unknown."

> There are two days in every week about which we should not worry, two days which should be kept free from fear and apprehension. One of these days is Yesterday with all its mistakes and cares, its faults and blunders, its aches and pains. Yesterday has passed forever beyond our control. All the money in the world cannot bring back Yesterday. We cannot undo a single act we performed; we cannot erase a single word we said. Yesterday is gone forever. The other day we should not worry about is Tomorrow with all its possible adversities, its burdens, its large promise, and its poor performance; Tomorrow is also beyond our immediate control. Tomorrow's sun will rise, either in splendor or behind a mask of clouds, but it will rise. Until it does, we have no stake in Tomorrow, for it is yet to be born."

In short, life is fleeting when we try to live in the past, the present, and the future all at the same time. By living one day at a time, we can savor every day. It is a privilege, a gift, to stand on a podium and make music on a regular basis with people who are fully dedicated to the conductor and the music in front of them. As conductors, the responsibility we have is choosing music, bringing the music to life, making musical decisions that effect everyone in the ensemble, inspiring the musicians to perform at their highest level, keeping up with current composers and compositions, continually developing our conducting skill. Honing rehearsal techniques is only part of our professional growth process. Growth is moving forward; no growth is stagnation.

The next part of this chapter will deal specifically with this area of professional growth. When I think about flexibility on the podium and how it relates to the work we do, I can't help but think of another word that immediately comes to mind: *imagination*. We become limited in our vision without inspiration through imagination. Einstein said it best when he stated, "Imagination is more important than knowledge," and then followed that statement with, "Knowledge can get you from A to B; imagination can take you anywhere."

Knowledge is easily obtained in our culture today through the Internet. I readily admit that I am not tech savvy, but I don't believe there is an app for imagination. There is not a year, a month, or a day when we are not required to be creative and flexible, and have a gifted imagination.

It's All About Making Music

Music selection is the motor that drives a program. The decisions directors make concerning literature determines the kind of drive it will be. The *Teaching Music through Performance in Band* series is all about literature. What I would have given for a resource like this when I began my teaching career in 1961. My sources for information included attending concerts by local high school bands and the University of Iowa band performances, attending the Midwest Clinic and state association conventions every year, asking directors for suggestions. Going to Eble Music Company on Saturday mornings, I would paw through the latest band publications that Charlie Eble had accumulated and stacked in the hallway on the second floor of his music store.

My goal has been the same throughout my career, like your goal today—to find the best literature to place in front of my students. With the publication of the *Teaching Music through Performance in Band* series, every director teaching at any level has the opportunity to choose the best literature, with a well-written resource guide and outstanding recordings available for most grade levels with each volume. No other publication can match the breadth and depth of this series when it comes to music selection and the sharing of educational information.

My focus in this section of the chapter is to examine how we go about putting the music together as well as the matter of trust in our musicians as they desire to add their voice to the process.

During the years I was teaching in public school, I felt it was extremely important for each member of the high school band to participate in a small ensemble. Each member was responsible not only for preparing his or her own part, but also sharpening their listening skills and becoming more sensitive to how the individual part fit into the whole. Many musicians feel that performing in small groups is the ultimate experience in demonstrating individual musicianship. To make this work, I had to be very flexible with the time commitment of the students as well as my own schedule. There were times when I would give up full rehearsals and assign ensembles to different practice rooms, and I would rotate from one group to another to monitor their progress. (Also, there were a lot of early morning and after-school sessions.) Individual trust and musicality became a huge part of the learning process. The students always felt a sense of ownership and took pride in their efforts to achieve. I expected each small ensemble to participate in the state solo and ensemble contest. Solo participation was optional for individual students, but small ensemble participation was mandatory. This participation requirement paid huge dividends in the overall performance level of the full band. The confidence level, musical sensitivity, attention to detail, and tonal concepts heightened the expectations for the entire band.

One rather unusual experience regarding small ensemble participation in my high school band occurred when a group of six very close friends came to me and said they wanted to form a small ensemble and participate in contest. Each of them was already playing in other ensembles, but this was something they very much wanted to do together. When I looked at the instrumentation involved (flute, oboe, clarinet, alto saxophone, bassoon, and contrabass clarinet), I explained that I knew of no published piece written for that group of instruments. The students knew I had written arrangements for other groups of instruments, like the brass choir, clarinet choir, and saxophone choir, so with a big smile on their faces they said, "You could write something for us."

Very few people who know me professionally realize that when I entered graduate school at the University of Iowa, I was accepted as a composition major. At the time, I thoroughly enjoyed composing and wanted to pursue this degree in graduate school. My undergraduate band director, Dr. Suycott, was a graduate from the University of Iowa with an earned doctorate in composition who inspired me to enroll in this degree program. As a result, I have always been very interested in writing and supporting new works for band. As I thought about the request from these young students with the strange instrumentation, an idea formed in my mind. Lucas Foss was a contemporary composer who I grew to appreciate and admire during my undergraduate training. One of his early works, called *Time Cycle*, was set to contemporary poems of the day. In between each poem was an interlude where a small group of instrumentalists improvised. I was struck by these interludes as the musicians played off of motives presented by different members of the ensemble. It was the first time I was aware of "classical improvisation." The display of their individual musical voices made a tremendous impression on me. It all made perfect sense to me and did not sound at all disjointed or out of place.

I took my record to school for these six young musicians to hear and talked about the nature of the composition and the "improvisatory" section. All six of the students were members of the jazz band and understood improvisation concepts, but they had never heard anything quite like this recording. They were fascinated and motivated. I agreed to write them a short twelve-tone piece that would include a section of "improvisation" where they could "play off" motives presented by each member of the group. The piece was titled *Dialogue and Discussion*, and as you might expect, the "discussion" part of the piece was the improvised section. They had so much fun with this piece; they diligently worked to make the improvised section coherent and even made the decision on how and who would end that section. I told the students that the adjudicator's reaction to the piece would result in one of two responses, they would either get a "I" or a "V." They assured me the rating did not matter; they were just enjoying the experience and knew it would be an ensemble like no one would hear the whole day. It just so happened the adjudicator was one of the toughest of the day, but he loved their work and the enthusiasm they exhibited during the performance.

The purpose of sharing this story with you is to demonstrate that without some flexibility in thinking and a desire to assist a group of young musicians willing to take a musical risk, a memorable experience would have been missed.

This experience led me to think about commissioning a work for our high school band. The members of this small ensemble became my student leaders in helping to promote the importance and excitement of this commission. It became a fantastic teaching tool and generated unbelievable excitement throughout the community. The composer was asked to write a five- to six-minute composition, but he was having so much fun that he ended up composing a twelve-minute work. He came for a couple of pre-concert rehearsals and discussed with the students the nature of the piece and how the piece was constructed. The Art Department became involved in designing publicity posters to place around the school and community. The local newspaper was kind enough to provide us with a story and advertised the concert. Attendance was quite impressive for a small, rural community, with nearly a thousand people in attendance. I feel this kind of involvement for your band program can still provide tremendous benefits for your students.

Continuing with a few thoughts about large group contest involvement: it was never my practice to work for several months on two or three pieces preparing for large group contest. Too often young musicians get bored and burn out in this method of preparation. I have always felt that if the group is well grounded in the fundamentals of good musicianship, then the music will come together rather quickly. I am aware there is pressure to produce high ratings at contests and festivals, and many directors feel that the only way to achieve these results is to focus on a few selected pieces. Unfortunately, these performances often come across as chasing notes rather than inspired music making. The objective in contest and festival participation needs to focus on making the performance the most musical and exciting as possible for the listeners, which may be other bands, the adjudicators, parents, private teachers, or school officials. But if the music delivers passion and commitment played from the heart, the rating will take care of itself. A musical and stimulating performance of excellent music, motivated by the desire to achieve, far surpasses the desire to just beat others.

I believe it takes courage and confidence in your players and a personal commitment for your program to present a well-balanced selection of top literature for the entire year. Each program from the beginning of the year should have a specific goal on which we will build our next program. How do we build musical flexibility in our players? The answer to this question can take many directions, the first of which requires a little self-examination of our own philosophies.

Perhaps we all need to analyze our teaching/conducting procedures to determine if we are "spoon feeding" (i.e., rote teaching) all musical aspects of the music to our students. Are they waiting for us to tell them how to play the music? Are we providing ways for them to find their own musical voice? These are tough questions and sometimes difficult to implant, especially in a full rehearsal, but here are a few considerations.

When solo passages are present in a work, try not to dictate how you want the soloist to perform that particular passage. It is important that the soloist has a chance to express his or her musical ideas. If later there is a stylistic concern the soloist may not understand, then it would be appropriate to share your thoughts. Try not to over-conduct a solo passage unless it is absolutely necessary for full ensemble success. At times, it is vitally important to let the ensemble play by themselves. Stepping off the podium and having the ensemble play together, breathe together, move together, feeling the steady flow of time, releases, and attacks without our direction, can lead to a tremendous sense of musical confidence. This also serves as a different mode of listening between the players and the director who might be hearing the band for the first time from a totally different perspective. I like to ask the students what they are hearing during rehearsals. That tells me if they are passively or actively listening to what is going on in the music or if they are just warming a chair and moving fingers. If our students are not really engaged through careful listening, then our rehearsal procedure is lacking a very important ingredient. If our students know we are going to ask specific questions about what is taking place in the music, then they will heighten their sensitivity to their musical surroundings very quickly. I am aware of programs where the director meets with the section leaders on a regular basis to discuss specific issues they feel need to be addressed. In some situations, this leads to called sectional rehearsals by the section leader to improve on the weaknesses. Sometimes there are private meetings if the director senses a problem with an individual student who might be hindering effective participation for one reason or another. More often than not, the problem is stemming from a school-related issue or a problem at home.

Being flexible as a teacher/conductor, employing creative means to achieve the best interpretive results, will build a strong bond and trust between the students and the teacher, helping the students to find their own musical voice. In today's society, it is easy for us to follow the adages of "work hard, play hard," "just do it," and the like, but in reality, we need to show flexibility and creativity in laying the foundation of mutual respect and understand the collaboration necessary in making music meaningful to our students. Our ability to be flexible humanizes us as conductors and pulls our students into the intimate circle of music making, which is our ultimate goal.

> People excel and learn, not because they are told to, but because they want to.
> —Peter Senge

We can't assume that our students will just follow us like sheep. Achieving a sense of collaboration with our students demands a clarity of purpose, devotion to an ideal, and the vision to see that our acts of compromise and understanding can result in incredible moments of rewarding, musical satisfaction for our students and ourselves. We must not neglect the inner desire of individual musicians to help their musical voices make a difference.

Flexibility in Professional Growth

It is fascinating to observe teachers at every level and see the growth process critical to professional development. During my first few years of public school teaching, I would make it a point to visit the classrooms of the best teachers in the school regardless of the subject. It was an instructional and motivational use of my time. We can learn so much by witnessing firsthand the manner and methods of outstanding teaching. What we do not want people to say about us is that we have become too "set in our ways." How we grow, think, and work determines how others observe our productivity. For musicians, this carries over into every aspect of our teaching/conducting endeavors.

I know that I do not do some of the great standard repertoire pieces the same today as when I did them for the first time many years ago. My last performance of *Emblems,* for example, is far different than the first time I conducted the work. Several years ago, Frederick Fennell was invited to guest conduct on our campus. One of the compositions he chose to do was on the very first recording he made with the Eastman Wind Ensemble in the early 1950s. He told me he was going to send me his personal score before his arrival so that as I rehearsed the piece, the interpretation would be as his score indicated. As I looked over his notes in the score, I could not help but notice that he had written specific information about how he would do certain passages differently the next time he conducted them. On more careful examination, it became apparent that he had conducted this piece *many* times during the previous forty-plus years and that there was musical growth in interpretation all through those intervening years. No matter how well we think we know a particular work, keep studying, analyzing, and growing with each rehearsal and performance. When Mr. Fennell came to conduct this chosen work, it was magical how he was able to bring musical elements to the fore, making it a very rewarding experience for all concerned.

Growth is the epitome of transforming our ability and openness into flexibility. It is about us and what we do that will make a difference in how we approach the rest of our professional career. Following are a few questions meant to be a self-examination. No pressure...allow a minute to formulate answers in your mind and hopefully it will give you something on which to reflect.

What do you want your legacy to be?

Those of you reading this chapter who are relatively young in the band profession may be thinking, "Are you kidding?" I am just trying to keep my head above water and do all I can to put the best band together with a limited budget and time! That is understandable, but at some point you need to look ahead and determine just what it is you most desire from being in your chosen field. Your legacy doesn't have to include becoming the next director of bands at a major university or president of a national association, but if that is your goal, then give all you have to attain that goal. Perhaps your ambition is to enjoy the middle school program you have built and to have a great impact on many young musicians' lives. The thing to remember is that you will have a legacy, and as you continue to work in the profession, that legacy grows each day.

What values are most important to you?

This question may seem similar to the above, but the intention of this question is to examine your total life—not just your professional life. Everyone at some time during their teaching career has to make choices and establish priorities that become important in life. It may be your profession, but if you are married and have a family, then those priorities have to become more flexible with what is appropriate to the specific needs of your family obligations.

How do your students view you?

This one is a bit scary. You hope their perception of you is one of respect, dedication, caring, motivational, and a person of integrity. In short, we want to be a role model for our students in both our professional and personal lives. With Facebook, Twitter, and other social media, it can be "enlightening" to see what students, alumni, and parents might be saying about you and your work. Be careful here; you might want to decline active engagement in these social networks, even though I know they can provide valuable assistance for quick communication with the members of your program. The main point remains intact: we want to be recognized as a person who has the best interests of our students at heart and who will "go to bat" for them to help the program succeed.

How does the community view you?

When I began my teaching career, the school system required all faculty to live within the boundaries of the school district. They wanted their teachers to become part of community life and to have the people of the community see them out and about apart from their positions within the school system. This may not be part of your school's expectation today, and I know many teachers want to live away from their school to maintain an element of privacy. That being said, it is still important for you to be somewhat visible in the community. Our profession is one of public imagery. People see us and know our work through what our organizations do in view of the community. Therefore, it is important for the community to have a good impression of what we do and also have a sense of the kind of people we are because we have daily contact with the children in the community. My family achieved this aspect of our lives through our church affiliations and by joining other community organizations. We felt it important to establish connections and friendships with people in the community in addition to our professional colleagues. It is these kinds of relationships that can enrich our lives in a very special way.

These questions require thoughtful framing of your answers and should give you encouragement to remain flexible in your approach to each topic.

Flexibility to Attain Greater Excellence

It is inevitable that every person reading this book is dedicated to building a fine band program and has a deep-seated desire to bring excellence to their work and life. Be exceedingly careful not to waste time or opportunities. Life can change so quickly that it is necessary to approach our teaching experience "one day at a time." It is amazing what we can accomplish in a day that contributes generously to our growth. Several factors come to mind that can build the bridge to attaining greater excellence.

Contribute more than is expected.

Certain responsibilities are expected in our jobs. Most are pretty visible to the casual observer, but to achieve an even greater level of excellence, it takes additional behind-the-scene effort that will probably not be recognized. Not many people know that my mentor, Frederick Ebbs, would examine and adjust bass clarinet reeds for his players knowing full well that they would not make the same effort or have the knowledge to ensure better tone quality and intonation. A minor point, you say, but the end result was most noticeable and appreciated by the players. Examine the extra efforts you contribute, and the list will be long and important knowing that, in the end, perhaps only you will notice the difference it will make.

You can never be too passionate about your profession.

When you talk to people about your job, or as your students observe your efforts, do they see in your eyes a sparkle that reflects a genuine excitement for your work? I have never heard of a person losing his or her job because he or she was too passionate. Without enthusiasm, boundless energy and, yes, passion for what we do, the work becomes normal and lackluster, resulting in a bland existence and poor work habits.

Believe that your work is important and that it will make a difference.

I firmly believe that none of us would have become band directors if we had not been inspired by a director in our previous band experiences. Every time I attend a concert or hear a fine recording of an outstanding band or orchestra, I greatly appreciate and respect the efforts of the inspirational teacher of each person involved in that concert or recording who instilled in them the joy of music. We have to grasp and hold tight to this belief that we can make a difference in the life of our students.

Help your students understand that you expect the best from them.

I taught at Indiana University for thirty-six years. During most of those years, the IU basketball coach was Robert M. Knight. There was, and still is, quite a "love/hate" feeling about his coaching style and general personality. Let me just say this: he did not always recruit the "top"-rated players in the country, but from most that he did recruit, he was able to get their absolute best. The result was outstanding success for the IU basketball program. It is not an easy task to extract the best efforts from our students, but the success of our program depends on our ability to do just that. Let each student know he or she is important to the program. We often overlook the necessity of seeing and showing appreciation for each student. Build your program and your expectations one student at a time.

Establish priorities but deal with them one at a time.

The proverbial "to do list" is always present on our desk or desktop. There were days on end where I felt like the list only grew longer instead of being able to "cross off" completed tasks. I even tried at one point having two lists: one labeled "urgent" and one labeled "until you have time." Then I kept losing my lists and couldn't remember what was on the "urgent" list. I so much appreciate my wife Molly for many reasons, but she is definitely a "to do list" person. I learned from her early on in our now forty-nine years of marriage that you can only do effectively one task at a time. There are still moments when I have a hard time prioritizing which is the most important. Incessantly something pops up that appears to be more important, and before you know it, nothing gets accomplished. Today with so much focus on "multitasking" to be effective and to utilize our time to the best advantage, it is still necessary to focus on the completion of one task at a time. Often we begin a task with enthusiasm, and then its importance diminishes and it becomes so much drudgery to continue. Perhaps with a bit more effort, that job could have been completed. The point is to make sure you finish the job. Otherwise, don't begin that particular project until you know you can finish the task successfully. I believe this quote from C. S. Lewis is appropriate, as it alludes to setting priorities:

> Aim at heaven and you will get earth thrown in.
> Aim at earth and you will get neither.

Flexibility Finale

As I draw to a close, a few final thoughts come to mind that hopefully will summarize this chapter and bring this topic to a resounding finale.

Bending is not breaking in anyway. In fact, bending increases flexibility and strength. Bending, in reality, is necessary to ensure that breaking does not occur. This is an unusual example, but since I travel to Tokyo on a regular basis, I have learned a great deal about earthquakes because that country has one of the highest incidents of earthquakes every year. As I look up at some of the very tallest buildings or the newly constructed Sky Tree, which is the highest freestanding communications tower in the world, I can't help but wonder what would happen to those structures during a very severe earthquake of 8.5 or higher with the epicenter in or near Tokyo. I have been assured those buildings and the new Sky Tree tower are designed to bend significantly during such quakes without danger of breaking or collapse. I will let someone else test that fact while standing in the observation area at the top of Sky Tree, which is nearly 2,000 feet in the air. I do, however, plan to visit the observation deck on my next visit…not sure if I can talk Molly into going up with me though.

Don't allow yourself to become inflexible; stay healthy and strong. If you are dealing with an inflexible person, it is very easy to respond in kind. This will only lead to a collapse in compromise, and it won't even have to be an 8.5 intensity. Be above this type of confrontation and your life will be less stressful and your work more enjoyable. One of the ways to avoid such a breakdown in communication is to take the focus away from you. If you want to catch a disagreeable, entrenched person off guard, gently say that you certainly see the person's point. Once the pressure has been relieved, you can then begin discussing the points on which you might agree; there are always some agreeable points. As tempers subside and agitation diminishes, you can then engage in an open discussion of the points creating the contention. Be an active listener, as often the other party feels like we are not paying attention. Listening without interrupting and looking people directly in the eye can de-escalate a stressful situation. Using good old healthy common sense can create a workable atmosphere of collaboration. Knowing how to compromise can strengthen your position and earn desired respect among your colleagues. Human beings are competitive by nature, but we must be careful not to become involved in confrontational circumstances just to prove that we are right! We then become what we don't want to become.

We must believe that our calling is a high calling. We are a sensitive, devoted, empowered vehicle for bringing beauty, culture, and sensitivity to the world. Abraham Booth (1734–1806), an English pastor and author, said, "To constitute a work truly good, it must be done from a right principle, performed by a right rule, and intended for a right end." Our good work is not truly good unless it is motivated by a deep sense of commitment to an ideal and an abiding love for our work. Continue to be *flexible* as you grow, continue to be *amazed* in the joy of sharing music, continue to *trust* your abilities to achieve success, and be *honest* with yourself and others, in your work and your life.

> To love what you do and feel that it matters—
> how could anything be more fun?
> —Katherine Graham

CHAPTER 10

Goals—A Relentless Pursuit Learning to Identify, Attain, and Appreciate Achievement

Ray E. Cramer

"You must be passionate, you must dedicate yourself, and you must be relentless in the pursuit of your goals. If you do, you will be successful."
··· STEVE GARVEY ···

It seems as we travel life's pathway that we are often following footprints of those who have traveled before us. Many of our predecessors have been inspirational, creative, and broad minded, blazing trails of adventure, creativity, and productivity. Sometimes we feel inadequate in our own quest for success or status in our chosen profession. Our vision is often focused on things we can quickly grasp or comprehend in our limited scope of what is immediate. Beware of today's culture of instant gratification stemming from success and accomplishment; how it makes us feel or look can lead to prideful attitudes.

This is the tenth volume of what has turned out to be an amazing series with the aim of assisting teachers in all aspects of their professional career. Little did any of us know when first discussing this project that there would be a second, a fifth, or a tenth volume in the series, or that it would expand to cover so many topics in the music education profession. All of us are delighted that the series is being used in so many music education classrooms across the country and that it is found in many teachers' personal libraries. Of course we are pleased by the positive response from music teachers around the country. Our objective from the beginning has always been to make a difference in teaching experiences.

As people journey through life, they leave footprints wherever they go—footprints of kindness, courage, compassion, humor, inspiration, love, joy, and faith. We leave footprints of knowledge, inspiration, motivation, musicality, and outstanding leadership. Some footprints are bigger than others, but everyone leaves a footprint. Even when they are no longer with us, we can clearly see the trail they left—a trail blazed with a clear imprint of their professional accomplishments that can lead us to a better understanding of what it takes to direct us to a successful teaching career.

It is important that we examine and learn from those who have traveled the educator's road before us. After taking a new job we often hear, "Those shoes will be hard to fill." During our young and inexperienced years, it is not a matter of "filling someone else's shoes," but it is a matter of determining how they were worn and where they walked, and then carefully planning our own steps. Be careful not to throw out the old shoes, for in them you will find a shoe that earned every worn-down heel, broken shoe string, and hole in the sole as they pressed forward in their day-to-day quest for achievement. Throughout our teaching career, we will also leave footprints as music ambassadors that will lead our students to the joy and satisfaction of participating in music.

I am sure that everyone who enters the teaching profession desires to be successful. From the first minute we choose to be an educator, we feel the need to "prove" ourselves to our former teachers, our classmates, and our parents. If we are serious about what we want to make of our career, then certain wheels are set in motion that will hopefully lead us to a successful tenure.

> *"I have found in life that if you want a miracle you first need to do whatever it is you can do—if that's to plant, then plant; if it is to read, then read; if it is to change, then change; if it is to study, then study; if it is to work, then work; whatever you have to do. And then you will be well on your way of doing the labor that works miracles."*
>
> —Jim Rohn

The first obstacle seems to come very quickly as we attempt to determine just what it is we want to accomplish during our "productive" years. Let me clarify that last sentence, as the perception among many people is that as people age, their efficiency, energy, and enthusiasm for what they do tends to fade into the horizon.

> *"Age is an issue of mind over matter. If you don't mind, it doesn't matter."*
>
> —Mark Twain

As a point of reference regarding age and being educators, I have found that many of the most inspiring individuals in our profession have been well into their "senior" years, and they still approach their work with as much energy, enthusiasm, and creativity as the day they entered the profession. It is all about *attitude* and *passion* for what we have chosen to do in our life's work and the goals we set out to accomplish.

Society says that success is the bottom line of everything we do. Really? Does the "end game" bring us happiness, health, wealth, fame, prestige, or security? Maybe in the short term, but perhaps in our quest for acceptance there are other benefits that do not show up on the plaque hanging on the wall, a trophy on the shelf, or thousands of "hits" on YouTube. One of the cultural ills we face is the constant striving for the approval of our peers. Much can be said about our desire to develop musical ensembles, regardless of age, to reach levels of execution that will bring satisfaction and recognition to our programs. This is a worthy goal and one we all pursue with diligence and persistence. But in our quest to attain, we must be careful not to lose sight of those students in our programs who have the desire to excel and enjoy the excitement of participation, but who lack the skills of their peers. There must be a place for those students as well. They may need extra support and guidance, but the opportunity exists for us to open up a pathway to help them appreciate music in their lives.

Directors have a great desire to walk into a new job and try to change things quickly. In our fervor of wanting to have our students progress faster than their fundamental skills can take them, frustration sets in and the early enthusiasm the students felt about the "new" director begins to rapidly decline. Instead, we need to take a look at our expectations and set realistic goals for our particular group of students. When accepting a new or different job, you may find established procedures and traditions that you do not particularly agree with philosophically. The first reaction is to go into these situations without regard to any of the former procedures and make quick changes. While this can be effective in certain situations, it can also create problems in the attitudes of students and parents. It is important to realize that we cannot play the "blame game"—blame the students, blame the parents, blame the administration, blame the facilities, and so on. We accepted the job and recognized potential that has perhaps been untapped. But change will not happen overnight. Progress tends to change less quickly than we desire. Patience must control our perspective and emotions. Learn to appreciate the daily progress of your students and applaud their efforts often. Take care to embrace each day.

I used to tell music education students that you could not change the course of the Ohio River in a day. Take your time, evaluate, plan, and formulate a strategy for the long term. Instead of speeding up, slow down. Re-evaluate and consider all aspects of your particular situation. Accept each new challenge and approach it as if it were a career move. Only then will you achieve the goals you desire. If and when you do choose to leave for another job and you have given totally of yourself in building the program, then you can leave without guilt. You have provided everything that your training, background, and energy could bring to that job.

As music educators, if we focus on what we do not have (e.g., numbers, instrumentation, player quality, budget, administrative cooperation, parental cooperation, etc.), our frustration level is amplified to the point of total discouragement. On the other hand, if we focus on what we do have (e.g., music, students who want to achieve a level of skill, the excitement of attaining a performance goal that pleases everyone concerned, etc.), we feel more satisfied with each new accomplishment. Always remember, the higher the accomplishment (regardless of the age of the ensemble) the greater the satisfaction.

> *"To accomplish great things, we must not only act, but also dream; not only plan, but also believe."*
>
> —Anatole France

So what is it that we pursue relentlessly? There are personal and professional pursuits that impact how we control our day-to-day work ethic. We must focus on prioritizing time commitment that impacts our ability to function with effectiveness at work and at home. Here are a few things to consider as we examine the "layers" of pursuit.

Personal and Professional Pursuits

Attitude

Initially I was going to title this chapter "A Half Century of Teaching and Conducting: Would I Do It Again?" The answer to that question would be a resounding *YES!* I would then follow that remark with a quick thank you and good luck, thus making it the shortest chapter in the history of the *Teaching Music through Performance in Band* series! Since I knew that wouldn't be acceptable, I had to come up with a different subject and provide a few thoughts that hopefully will help us all in our desire to grow personally and professionally.

How we approach life in general is dictated by our attitudes. Those attitudes are demonstrated in everything we do. I think we have to continually ask ourselves the question, "How do we want people, students, parents, and colleagues to see us?" I know we have heard the analogy of seeing the glass half full or half empty. Positive thinking will always elevate our approach to life and work. A person who only sees the negative side of things will only generate thoughts of failure. What we think about is usually what transpires. In our profession, we have to continually identify the difference between minor frustrations and serious problems. There is always a resolution to both with open communication. I believe the answer is in our attitude. No problem is insurmountable if we approach it with creative thinking and a positive attitude.

"If you say you can or you can't, you are right either way."

—Henry Ford

Personality

When I graduated from high school, one of the teachers I highly respected told me that with a friendly smile and a positive attitude, anything you want to accomplish is possible. I have commented in a previous volume on the importance of utilizing personality to our greatest advantage. We can only be ourselves. Our students immediately detect when we try to be someone else or assume a different persona to fit a circumstance; our "phoniness" comes through loud and clear.

There has been a great deal written by our most iconic conductors that the power of one's personality carries music to emotional levels that cannot be attained by others who approach the ensemble and the music without the infusion of their own personality. If you look at videos of conductors like Leonard Bernstein or Frederick Fennell, the power of their personalities is infectious not only to the music and the musicians, but to the audience as well. A strong personality can change the atmosphere of an ensemble from one of dull mediocrity to one with vitality and passion.

Following the passing of our daughter Heather, we received hundreds of messages from people whose lives she had touched. One of the most heartwarming notes said this about her, "When Heather walked into a room, she didn't just light up the room, she lit up the people inside it." That is our job— to instill passion about what we do, why we do it, and how we do it so all students know in their heart that they want to be a part of the action. Here is an excerpt of a letter from a student writing about a former teacher: "You were an excellent role model. You are passionate about what you are doing and you demonstrate this by always being prepared, wasting no time, pushing yourself to grow and improve throughout your career, and giving freely of yourself to your students." I think it is safe to say that the power of that teacher's personality touched the lives of every student in that program.

To this end the greatest asset of a school is the personality of the teacher."

—John Strachan

Expectation

Nothing of worth can be accomplished without expectation. How we communicate our desire to attain visualized goals must match the vision of our students. Helping students to believe they can reach those goals becomes the primary source of realization. Our job as the teacher/leader must somehow infuse the desire to excel in our students. There are many different methods of inspiring students to strive for those goals. Some conductors rely simply on external methods of encouragement, such as the perception of threats, yelling, brow beating, negative challenges, or other destructive means. Each of us can likely recall names and programs that grew and succeeded with this form of external motivation. However, I would guess that students coming from that kind of program failed to gain a real love of music and music making. As conductors, we should strive to instill a love for music in students that inspires them to continue their association in some form with music, either as a teacher, a participant, or a lifelong patron of the arts. I firmly believe that one of our top goals is to bring such a joy in music to our students they will want to make it a lifelong pursuit. In short, we have to be great leaders. Not long ago, I came across this "recipe" for leadership. I think it is worth sharing here.

L	Loyalty
E	Endurance
A	Activism
D	Dependability
E	Enthusiasm
R	Realism
S	Sensitivity
H	Honesty
I	Initiative
P	Persuasiveness

Another goal we must help our students attain is the desire for personal growth. That desire must come from within. Internal motivation can be the most effective means of gaining the greatest work ethic and productivity of our students. Internal motivation cannot be taught; it must come from the director's style of leadership and personality. Our students must see that we have high expectations, not for our own personal satisfaction or notoriety, but for sharing music for the pure and simple pleasure of making it meaningful and emotional. The love of music is what makes us human. Any program without expectations will wander aimlessly.

There is a reason that a target has a bull's-eye. It is the ultimate goal, one that is attainable but often missed because of a lack of focus and improper aim. A target has several outer rings. They represent growth, not failure. If we happen to hit within any of the rings, it means we are on target but still have to improve our aim. To hit the bull's-eye, we have to continue to practice and work hard to achieve the ultimate goal. No performance will be perfect. I have never heard a perfect performance at any level. There is always some minor error, even in professional ensembles. Does that minor error destroy my appreciation of the performance? Not at all, for if the music making is at a high level and the performers are playing with passion and heart, the errors are moments forgotten in the joy of listening to the magic of the music. Here are a couple of brief examples of young musicians who kept their eye on a goal that proved to be an inspiration to many.

> There is a young Japanese girl who was born with only a thumb and little finger on each hand and no feet. She is an accomplished pianist who has captured the enthusiasm, respect, and joy of audiences wherever she performs. She is a picture of determination, relentless pursuit, and perseverance. When she was born, the doctors told her parents they should not take her home because she would not be a long-term survivor. The parents were told they certainly could not care for this severely handicapped young child at home. They took their daughter home anyway. Their own determination, vision, and love proved that all the professional medical advice had no impact on what the human spirit can achieve when the dynamics of love, passion, and devotion take control of goals. She sells out concert halls around the world, as people are truly amazed by her talent, musicality, and pure love for performance despite her tremendous handicap. She plays piano not for self-glory or the accolades of the audience, but for the sheer joy of making music.

> I also want to share a story about a young man in my university marching band many years ago. He was an extremely intelligent, enthusiastic, dedicated, friendly, and polite student anyone would want in his or her program. He was a talented musician but lacked the physical coordination to be in the selected "block" for pre-game shows. On some standing formations, I would provide a spot for him to utilize his playing skills. However, his greatest desire was to become a member of the "block" so he could participate in the quick-tempo pre-game show. Every day during the regular rehearsal, he would work diligently on marching fundamentals to develop his skills. After rehearsal, he would continue to work on his own, but everyone on the staff was willing to help him because his desire to succeed was so sincere. He did eventually make the "block" through sheer determination and personal goal setting. He and his parents felt great satisfaction in this achievement, and he was an inspiration for every member of the band. You would have thought that he had just won a position in a major orchestra. Following graduation, he was offered a very prestigious job, one

that usually went only to people with many years of experience. The company recognized not only his incredible intelligence but also his self-motivating work ethic and goal-oriented focus. They knew these traits would make him a great success. He never missed an Alumni Band outing in the following years.

Another possible title for this chapter was "The Relentless Pursuit of Excellence." This is a phrase that is often heard in our profession. What does this phrase really mean to individual musicians or to bands at every level? Does the word "excellence" mean or imply the same thing to top professional musicians or fine university ensembles as it does to bands with unbalanced instrumentation, players with limited ability, or youth ensembles? Of course we can hear "excellent" performances from any of these groups. Again, it comes down to our level of expectation. For ensembles at any level to attain the kind of performance we envision, we really are striving for the relentless pursuit of *improvement*. To move from the outer rings of the target to the musical bull's-eye takes a clear vision and keen ear for improvement. To foster that steady improvement takes dedication, hard work, inspiration, and high expectations like those of the two people I wrote about.

> *"Whoso could kindle must himself glow."*
>
> —Haim Ginott

Honesty

> *"You cannot build character and courage by taking away people's initiative and independence."*
>
> —Abraham Lincoln

Build for integrity and character, not for fame! Eiji Oue, former conductor of the Minneapolis Orchestra, once stated, "The more acclaimed the performer, the more humble of character." Just waving our hands and arms in thin air cannot exude a masterwork for band. Perhaps you have seen the YouTube video of a young boy standing on a footstool passionately conducting a recording of a Beethoven symphony. It is marvelous, heartwarming, educational, and inspiring just to see the intensity and passion this young boy puts into each phrase, reflecting the rise and fall of the music with determined gestures. Even though he has no musicians sitting before him, he is feeling and expressing every dynamic turn of the music. It is our obligation with musicians in front of us to help them return the passion and expectation we have for the music.

We live in a world that breeds egotism. Our egos can get in the way of being the kind of individual who can remain humble in success and popularity.

Egos are detrimental to our character and how people perceive our intentions. Chuck Swindoll states it better than I can, "Nobody is a whole chain. Each one is a link. But take away one link and the chain is broken. Nobody is a whole team. Each one is a player. But take away one player and the game is forfeited. Nobody is a whole orchestra. Each one is a musician. But take away one musician and the symphony is incomplete."

We need each other. We need the musicians and the musicians need us. Standing on a podium conducting an imaginary ensemble doesn't "cut the mustard." Guiding and leading musicians, and expressing and bringing to life a composer's intent is an awesome responsibility. I have often shared with young teachers how important it is to build a program one student at a time. Every student is important and can contribute to the success of our programs in ways we might not anticipate. Some years ago I came across this quote of Pablo Casals. It is to the point, dramatic, and speaks to the importance of each individual student:

> "Each second we live is a new and unique moment of the universe, a moment that never was before and never will be again. And what do we teach our children in school? We teach them that two and two make four and that Paris is the capital of France. When will we also teach them what they are? We should say to each of them: Do you know what you are? You are a marvel. You are unique. In all of the world there is no other child exactly like you. In the millions of years that have passed, there has never been a child like you. And look at your body—what a wonder it is! You may become a Shakespeare, a Michelangelo, a Beethoven. You have the capacity for anything. Yes, you are a marvel. And when you grow up, can you then harm another who is, like you, a marvel? You must cherish one another. You must work—we must all work—to make this world worthy of its children."
>
> —Pablo Casals

Treating our students with dignity and respect will pay rich dividends both musically and personally. We cannot deceive our students. They have great perception of us and can discern if we are sincere and honest in our approach to them individually and collectively. Be honest, personally and intellectually. Over the fifty plus years I have been involved in music education, I have witnessed that honesty, integrity, and character are the trifecta that produces great success.

Humor

> *"Step lightly; do not jar the inner harmonies."*

—Satchel Paige

An effective use of humor in rehearsal can build a healthy environment. It can be a fantastic stress reliever and carry students past those moments when ridicule and embarrassment seem to be inevitable. However, there are times when we just don't feel like being humorous during rehearsal. The stress level is too high, the next performance is crashing towards us at a mind-boggling speed, and we still can't manipulate the notes let alone the music. Nothing is funny! If that scenario sounds familiar, don't feel bad; we have all been there.

The most humbling, embarrassing, and profoundly disturbing incident I was involved with occurred during an indoor marching band rehearsal. Becoming increasingly upset with the poor intonation one section of the band was producing, I went over to the old upright piano that was near the podium. I struck several keys at the same time trying to emulate what I was hearing to make the point that it was unacceptable. I guess I struck the keys with more force than I realized because two of the black keys broke off and fell to the floor. The pressure of the situation (three straight days of rain with only a five-day preparation for an all-new halftime show) just caught up with me. That moment became the straw that broke not the camel's back, but rather the two black keys. I realized immediately that I had crossed a line, and I felt terrible. The band was shocked knowing full well that I had gone too far; they tuned me out with penetrating stares that gripped my heart. During a very sleepless night, I knew that the following day I needed to apologize for my over-the-top reaction and for causing a great embarrassment to not only the section with poor intonation, but to the whole band as well. I went back to the rehearsal hall that night and glued the keys back on the piano.

The next day, prior to rehearsal, I could hear the students assembling in the rehearsal room as usual, but there were no sounds, no warming up, no talking, just the quiet mummer of sulking students. I guess they were waiting to see if I was going to continue my tirade or sheepishly launch into the rehearsal without regard to the previous day's episode. As the starting time neared, I knew that I needed to do something to "break the ice" before I offered my apology. With absolute silence, and two hundred plus sets of staring eyes following me, I proceeded to the front of the room. Then it hit me. I strode to the podium, stopped and looked at the band, and then continued to the piano, where I made a huge gesture of carefully closing the piano lid and then turned and smiled at the students. Thankfully, they broke into exuberant laughter. It was then that I offered my humble apology to the section and to the whole band for my inappropriate lack of control. What followed was one of the best rehearsals of the entire season. After rehearsal, one of the upperclassmen came up to me and said, "How did it feel to have a band back today, Mr. Cramer?" An honest appraisal of a situation, a sincere apology, and a sense of humor can mend strained relationships very quickly.

On a regular basis since 1990, I have had the pleasure of guest conducting at the Musashino Academy of Music in Tokyo. When you are not conversational in the language and the students speak very little or practically no English, humor in rehearsal becomes tenuous at best. I once told my manager, "The band doesn't seem to get my 'off-the-cuff' humor." A couple of days later the manager asked me, "Professor Cramer, you must explain to me, what is cuff humor?" But according to a note from one of my bassoon players, I have become somewhat better at this "off-the-cuff" humor: "I'm poor at English but your body language is very clear to understand for me. Your musical guidance that has a sense of humor will be a wonderful remembrance of my school days and my life." Yay! Success.

The use of humor does have an important place in the rehearsal. Humor is a tool that can help students focus and learn important details and remain engaged. But humor must be real, not contrived or laced with innuendo or insincerity. Rehearsals are serious business. There is never time to get things right, which can make everyone uncomfortable and stressed. Interjecting humor can help make the rehearsal easier, more efficient, and more enjoyable. Learning is then enhanced with a higher retention than a rehearsal without a touch of humor. The use of humor must be administered very carefully at just the right time, like the use of a fine spice. Sprinkled in a rehearsal, humor will build a wonderful atmosphere and help to establish a great rapport between the director and the students.

Some directors can use sarcasm effectively, but younger students often do not know how to take sarcasm and can quickly become put off. Sarcasm never worked for me; it was not part of my personality and was not effective. Using sarcasm can be dangerous if done on a regular basis. I have witnessed students leave a rehearsal in tears after having sarcasm directed towards them and not knowing how to respond except through the release of tears. A less-than-productive outcome, wouldn't you agree?

Finally, remember that the use of humor can be motivating. Music education students are taught how to teach important music fundamentals to make a band sound great, but they often have to learn as they go how to pace and keep students attentive and attached throughout the rehearsal period. An effective use of humor is the link in the chain that binds us all together.

"The most wasted of all days is one without laughter."

—E. E. Cummings

Outside Assessment of Our Work

Throughout our teaching career our work is being evaluated either formally or informally. Remembering that the focus of this chapter is about the attainment of goals, this is a necessary ingredient of our personal development. All too often when receiving critical assessment, one's normal response is to react very negatively and defensively. Following are a few thoughts to explore these negative reactions, which are only intended to help understand the nature of our response.

Denial

The initial reaction to negative criticism is denial. We don't accept criticism because we think the person offering the assessment doesn't know what they're talking about. We think: They have no understanding of the situations I have to deal with on a daily basis. The results I am achieving with the limited assistance I receive are better than what they deserve!

Sound familiar? We all have experienced this kind of reaction. Talking about that person behind their back, tearing down their credibility and giving credence to our work most often will backfire. We cannot elevate our own status by destroying another person's. Human nature and our society have taught us that we must counterattack when we have been attacked. Our refusal to look inward and accept constructive criticism hinders our growth potential. Through denial, we protect ourselves.

Accepting the views of others about our work takes courage and strength. The solution is to find a trusted mentor who you know will give you a clear, concise, and honest evaluation. Be prepared to take a pinch or a punch every now and then. Sometimes honesty hurts, but it also makes us better.

> *"The greatest barrier to someone achieving their potential is their denial of it."*
>
> —Simon Travaglia

Anger

Everyone gets angry at one time or another, usually over some minor incident that we tend to blow out of proportion. Dealing with criticism directed toward our work can produce degrees of anger that can very often result in an action that takes an unnecessary wrong turn. I have known directors who have resigned their positions because of a moment of serious anger. However, those same directors realized too late that with a "cooling down" period, the reason for their anger would have dissipated revealing a realistic evaluation and solution of the situation. Those moments of lost control can be devastating to our professional life. Rational thinking without elevated emotion needs to be restored before we can continue to pursue our established goals.

Some people's nature is to be just plain angry about almost anything. Those individuals need to take a break and consider managing their anger. I don't expect anyone to throw a chair across the band room like a famous basketball coach once threw a chair across the court during a game. That didn't turn out well for the coach. Uncontrolled anger can take a toll on both our health and our relationships. How do we conquer anger issues? Following are a few helpful suggestions provided by the Mayo Clinic Staff for dealing with anger issues:

- **Think before you speak.** In the heat of the moment, it's easy to say something you'll later regret. Take a few moments to collect your thoughts before saying anything—and allow others involved in the situation to do the same.

- **Once you're calm, express your anger.** As soon as you're thinking clearly, express your frustration in an assertive, but non-confrontational way. State your concerns and needs clearly and directly without hurting others or trying to control them.

- **Get some exercise.** Physical activity can help reduce stress that can cause you to become angry. If you feel your anger escalating, go for a brisk walk or run, or spend some time doing other enjoyable physical activities.

- **Take a timeout.** Timeouts aren't just for kids. Give yourself short breaks during times of the day that tend to be stressful. A few moments of quiet time might help you feel better prepared to handle what's ahead without getting irritated or angry.

- **Identify possible solutions.** Instead of focusing on what made you mad, work on resolving the issue at hand. Remind yourself that anger won't fix anything and might only make it worse.

- **Stick with "I" statements.** To avoid criticizing or placing blame, which might only increase tension, use "I" statements to describe the problem. Be respectful and specific.

- **Don't hold a grudge.** Forgiveness is a powerful tool. If you allow anger and other negative feelings to crowd your positive feelings, you might find yourself swallowed up by your own bitterness or sense of injustice. But if you can forgive someone who angered you, you might both learn from the situation. It's unrealistic to expect everyone to behave exactly as you want at all times.

- **Use humor to release tension,** Lightening up can help diffuse tension. Use humor to help you face what's making you angry and, possibly, any unrealistic expectations you have for how things should go. Avoid sarcasm, though—it can hurt feelings and make things worse.

- **Practice relaxation skills.** When your temper flares, put relaxation skills to work. Practice deep-breathing exercises, imagine a relaxing scene, or repeat a calming word or phrase, such as, "Take it easy." Do whatever it takes to encourage relaxation.

- **Know when to seek help.** Learning to control anger is a challenge for everyone at times. Consider seeking help for anger issues if your anger seems out of control, causes you to do things you regret, or hurts those around you.

—Mayo Clinic Staff

"It is wise to direct your anger towards problems—not people; to focus your energies on answers—not excuses."

—William Arthur Ward

Excuses

The above quote summarizes the previous section on anger and leads beautifully into the next segment in this section—excuses. Excuses are easy to fabricate and conveniently place blame on someone else. Dr. Leon Fosha was a music education professor at Indiana University for many years and a person I highly respected. His philosophies on education and the training of teachers provided a solid foundation for students entering the profession. When students visited his office, they couldn't help but notice a very large poster Dr. Fosha had hung on the wall behind his desk, which read:

RESULTS, NOT EXCUSES!

Humans are really good at making up excuses. Students are exceptional at this, but adults can be even better. We have had more experience and can be more creative in spinning our stories. Excuses can be complex like, "I don't have my horn because my dad went to work with the horn in the trunk of the car," to being much more direct, like when students admit, "I just didn't feel like practicing today." The reason for the excuse is the same, but the latter is more forthright. The crux of the matter is the student didn't want to practice.

When adults are facing a performance review, where their work is being evaluated, a common reaction is to make excuses. Obviously there are many reasons we make excuses, but a few come to mind that might help us understand our rationale.

We do our very best to avoid the truth. We don't enjoy finding out that we have not done something well. It is much easier for us to not admit there is a problem. We often make excuses for ourselves to avoid addressing a particular situation. When I used to think a problem would go away if I ignored it, my dad used to tell me to "take off the blinders."

We sometimes try to turn the attention away from our mistakes by using excuses. We try to cover up our lack of focus. This is when the quest toward our *goals* becomes blurred. Looking in the mirror and seeing ourselves as others see us can be the determining factor in making changes to resolve the problem.

Finally, making excuses reduces the fear factor. It is out of fear that we contrive a myriad of excuses: fear of repercussions, fear of failure, fear of change, or fear of looking bad. Reducing the fear factor takes confidence. Stand tall, be confident, and take ownership. Admitting our mistakes without making excuses can make us larger than life to those who matter. As educators, infusing our students with the expectation of "Results, not excuses" will help our students and ourselves attain projected goals.

> "He that is good for making excuses is seldom good for anything else."
>
> —Benjamin Franklin

Balancing Professional and Personal

> "You cannot be really first rate at your work if your work is all you have."
>
> —Anna Quindlen

The life of a music teacher/conductor is demanding and time consuming. If you are married and have a family, you already know this and understand your obligations as a spouse, parent, and teacher. Each responsibility has specific goals, and the desire to attain satisfaction in them must be a high priority. The same considerations are present if you are single. Setting goals that will allow you to function in a manner conducive to a stable and effective lifestyle at home and at work is possible—not easy, but no worthy goal comes easily. We know how important it is to connect with our students every day, every rehearsal. It is no different where we live. Our spouse, our family, our children need and deserve that same connection from us every day. When we are preparing for an upcoming performance, our role as the conductor is to make musical decisions. Maintaining a healthy and stable home life also requires decision-making to ensure that every relationship has our undivided attention and sensitivity.

As I reflect over my personal life, the choices I made to be involved with my family have provided rich and rewarding memories. There were times when unavoidably the job required my full attention and presence, just as it does in yours, but when I was home, the job with all its pressures and demands stayed at the office. My goal at home was to give my full attention to my family. I wrote in a previous chapter, but it is worth repeating: The *quality* of time spent with your family is more important than the *quantity* of time! Now as a grandfather, I find the same focus is necessary with our grandchildren, except I don't have to put them to bed.

Another important goal in family life is for you and your spouse to present a united front. Only then will the children know that it makes no difference which parent they go to; the decision/position will be the same. When our children were involved in music and sports activities, we were present. I turned down many weekend engagements during their school years just because I wanted to be there for them and just be a nervous dad. After they both graduated from college and were on their own, they individually expressed how much they appreciated that we were both present for their school activities. We would not have wanted to miss any of those experiences.

Molly and I do a clinic together titled, "The Balancing Act: The Realities of a Professional and Personal life." It is a sincere and honest look at our married life and how as a "team" we handled the issues of dealing with this topic. If you are married, perhaps it would be a good idea for your spouse to read the following few paragraphs from my wife's perspective. I believe it will help to solidify our thoughts on this subject.

Molly's Thoughts:

Looking back over our fifty married years (as of this writing), there have been so many blessings, spiritually, personally, and professionally. If we had to think of only one key ingredient in all of them, other than our faith, it would be setting *goals*—his, mine, and ours. There is no one set of priorities that is set in stone and will always stay the same. It takes setting those goals together and then being flexible to make necessary changes when and where needed. Not too long ago I watched a YouTube video of a man using river rocks to build interesting forms and shapes. Obviously they do not balance easily, but with patience and an eye on the goal, the end result was very impressive.

It is the same way with the goals we set as a married team: they aren't all of the same weight and size, but each one has a place in balancing the whole. Often the smallest rocks are the most important: moved slightly out of place or removed altogether, the whole thing collapses.

The goals in our marriage have varied in size and shifted, out of necessity at times. However, the top priority of *us*, not *me*, has always stayed the same. We have always been a partnership, not competitors. We each brought different things to our marriage, things that compliment each other. We have always been proud of and brought out the best in each other, starting with "who you are" rather than "what you do." Just as Ray knows I support him in all he does, I know he supports me in what I do. We have interests in common and interests that are separate, believing that our outside interests are things that keep us interesting to each other.

We had two children. When they were growing up, we loved and maintained our "family together time," doing lots of indoor and outdoor activities. That being said, we also protected our "us" time. Our children were raised understanding that "we were the two of us before we were the four of us and the time will come when we will be the two of us when you are on your own." All too often parents lose sight of each other during the child-raising years. After the children leave home, then all of a sudden the parents realize they have lost their own connection. We never felt guilty when we did things by ourselves to keep us connected so that when we would become "the two of us" again, our bond and life was still balanced.

You get the picture: The goal for the family unit is what you do *with* and *for* each other. We modeled our mutual love, respect, and admiration in front of our children. They never heard a harsh word or raised voices between us, and they knew we were a united "parental unit."

In an article on maintaining balance in your life, Jim Kennedy says, "FIRST, you need to realize you have *unique* contributions to make. Don't try to do yours *and* someone else's, too. NEXT, you need to understand you'll never have time to get everything done. Prioritize and do what's important. And LAST, don't confuse opportunity with responsibility. There will always be more opportunities than you have time to do. You are *not* responsible for doing everything."

Set your goals for a balanced life at home and at work. Thanks for letting me share a few thoughts.

—Molly

Now you know that I made a *great* decision when I married this woman. And that mutual decision was made during our third date! We have had a blessed life and look forward to the next chapter of our lives.

Believe in Your Goals

> *"You are successful the moment you start moving toward a worthwhile goal."*
>
> —Chuck Carlson

> *"Forgetting the things that are behind and reaching out for the things that are ahead, with this goal in mind, I strive toward the prize of the upward call of God in Christ Jesus."*
>
> —Philippians 3:13–14

There are five key words in this scripture that need our focus: 1) *behind*, 2) *ahead*, 3) *goal*, 4) *strive*, and 5) *upward*. The first two words, *behind* and *ahead*, are critical in our thinking. To look ahead, it is important that we look behind to see where we have been. There is a reason that the rearview mirror is small and the front windshield is large; looking back allows us to see where we have been with a much smaller view but still provides us the opportunity to learn and grow from our past experiences. The front windshield gives us a full, clear view of the fantastic goals that lie ahead. No further comment is necessary about the third word, *goal*, since this entire chapter focuses on this topic. The word *strive* implies that we need to be an industrious worker; nothing is achieved without the diligence to succeed. The final word, *upward*, means that we want to elevate ourselves to a higher standard than what we have accomplished previously.

> *"It is fine to look back…just don't stare."*
>
> —Maj. Gen. John Borling

I came across an article written by M. B. Owens titled, "Set Goals to Get Ahead." Here are his opening statements from the article.

> *"Setting up a clear path for your career is something that is important for everyone wanting to get ahead in life. Unfortunately, it is something few of us actually do. The reason for this is few of us actually know what we want in either life or a career. It is important to set goals to help achieve success in both since they are interrelated. Focus on what you want, not what someone else wants for you.*

*Well-meaning friends and family members don't really know what
you are about. However, they can offer some general guidance."*

For as far back in my family history as I can remember, everyone was a
farmer: my father, my grandfather, my great grandfather, my older brother,
and my two sisters both married farmers. I loved growing up on the farm with
all the challenges and freedoms that were part of that lifestyle. I thoroughly
enjoyed all the things that a kid growing up on a farm loved to do. As the
youngest member of the family, I also got my tail worked off by everyone in
my family and the neighbors. As I look back, not stare, I realize that is where
I learned about work ethic and the necessity of getting things done when they
needed to be done. This was a very important life lesson to learn. In the long
tradition of my family's heritage, I always thought I would be a farmer, which
would have been okay with me, but my father, who always struggled financially
to make ends meet, was adamant that I would do something else. Thank you,
Dad. The career and life that I have enjoyed over the past fifty-plus years have
been a great pleasure filled with memorable experiences. Did I have goals
when I began my career? Of course, we all have goals, and the longer we are
in a given profession, goals can and often do change. That is normal, and we
must always remember, only when we look ahead does the front windshield
open up new vistas for us to conjure new goals.

What does it take to reach a goal? Earl Nightingale has put together a list
of the traits generally found in creative, innovative people. Here are just a few
points on his list:

Goals	a sense of direction
Drive	a high degree of motivation
Courage	tenacity and persistence
Knowledge	and a thirst for it
Good health	for an active lifestyle
Honesty	defines our integrity
Enthusiasm	instills excitement and motivation
Dynamism	energy
Outgoingness	friendly
Adaptability	capable of change
Humor	ability to laugh at self and others
Individualism	self-esteem and self-sufficiency
Imagination	seeking new ideas, combinations, relationships
Communication	ability to articulate
Receptive	alert

Is it necessary for all of us to have all of these traits to be successful? Probably not. And this is only a partial list, as there are many other traits that could be added. Don't panic if you read this and realize you don't possess all of these. There are a lot of very successful people in the world who do not find all of these qualities in their arsenal. It is, however, a gauge that allows us to look at ourselves to see if there are areas where we could improve our effectiveness.

The objective of this chapter has been to provide a picture of how important it is to have goals and to consider the various aspects of what it takes to achieve them. For my wife and me, our faith has always been a strong component of how we operate as a family and as educators. We do not flaunt our faith, and I certainly do not use the podium as a pulpit, but it is a driving force in how we strive to live our lives and interact with people.

I recently received an article written by Emily Belz about Manfred Honeck, conductor of the Pittsburgh Symphony Orchestra. The Austrian maestro has been winning the hearts of music critics everywhere the orchestra has performed. Maestro Honeck is a devout Catholic and firmly believes that his faith plays an important part in his music making. In the article he stated,

> *"You can be a good conductor without having faith; if that is the goal, just to be a good conductor, then I would live without faith. But I don't regard leadership and conducting only as a profession where I earn money."*

He continues with his thoughts on music making:

> *"Through music you can touch the soul, and you don't know why. Why is it that people sometimes cry if they hear beautiful music? Why? Even if you hear, 'I love you,' you don't cry necessarily all the time. But if you hear music sometimes, it goes so deep in your heart."*
>
> *"There are humans, humans make music there. You are sharing something which you never can repeat in your life again. A CD, yes, you can. You put the CD in and you have the same mistake or the same wonderful phrase. You can hear it a hundred thousand times. In a concert, no, you hear it in the moment, and if it is good music made on the stage, you hear the music in a way that is only right in this moment. It is compared to architecture and painting— this is forever, it is here. But music, once you have played a tone it is already history. So music lifts from that moment. And I always encourage people to understand there is no way not to come to the concert."*

—Manfred Honeck

"I have come to the conclusion that the most important element in human life is faith."

—Rose Kennedy

Recently, a director shared a story about two members of the marching band whose goals were far different from the normal expectation for a competitive marching band experience. The philosophy of this director is to not exclude any students who have their heart set on being a member of the band program, regardless of personal or musical limitations. There are two students in this year's band with health-related issues that would normally keep them from any kind of band participation.

The first, a young girl, has to deal with seizure disorder, mental cognition issues, hyperopic astigmatism, a history of subarachnoid hemorrhage in her retinas (requiring surgery in both eyes), and social difficulties (has an adult aide much of the time in school). Needless to say, she is in a separate severe special needs class. Talk about working under a handicap! Some directors would simply not allow a person with so many issues to participate. The student went to the director last year and asked if it might be possible to be a part of the band. She had band class in middle school but encountered problems. She loves music and just wanted to be a part of something, but she was scared that she would be overwhelmed and not fit in. After a discussion with the director, it was decided that the best place for her would be in the sideline pit.

Her director shared that she loves learning new things and wanted to learn the pit instruments. In the beginning, she was very nervous but was well supported by her peers. Her student leaders helped get her going and were with her every step of the way. They learned from the director the philosophy that every single person is important. At the end of every rehearsal, the band has a wrap-up session where the students share with each other positive statements from the day. These usually consist of statements like, "Way to go, trombones, your attention positions were awesome today!" or "The flutes had such a great attitude!" The director feels it is really important to recognize the good that happens every day knowing that is when the band truly comes together. This young lady raised her hand and said, "I want to thank you all because for the first time I had people to eat lunch with me." Her goals don't include winning or beating another band; they are about growing as a person with newfound friends and feeling worthwhile.

The second young student suffers from Asperger's Disorder, Type 1 diabetes, and Misophonia, literally a "hatred of sound." It is a neurological disorder in which negative experiences (anger, flight, hatred, disgust) are triggered by specific sounds. His Misophonia is triggered by finger snapping, lip smacking (when speaking), knuckle cracking, and the rubbing together of hands. For him, hearing any of these sounds is like being stabbed with a sharp object or touching fire. His brain is sort of misfiring, which causes his brain think he is in pain. He gets angry about the pain and sometimes reacts by hitting himself in the head and cringing. For people who don't know what's going on, this can be a difficult thing to witness. He is also a percussionist in the pit.

The director shared that the students in the band have worked hard to have a clear understanding of his challenges so they can help him overcome his hardships. This has helped his sense of inclusion in the band immensely. When asked about why he feels comfortable in band, he responded with these thoughts: "I feel good because I know the staff works to make band work. The director is willing to adjust, making everyone a part of something special. It is good to know you have friends who will be there for you during band rather than being alone. If you are alone, it turns music into a chore rather than a passion. The director has a big influence on how students treat each other, so if the director treats everyone like real, quality people, so will the students; when the director is open, trusting, and passionate, something special is created on a different level."

This director has worked diligently to create a trusting environment where every student is able to participate without fear of ridicule or bullying. High school can be a really difficult place. It is hard to feel like you can be yourself. The best music is made when students let go of their armor and just embrace the love of music. The director is convinced the students will play better and be better people knowing they will not be judged for their thoughts and ideas. The overriding culture of the program promotes the belief in pursuing well-rounded goals, rather than a goal of beating others or winning at all costs. Students in the program desire to pull together to have an amazing musical experience, fully understanding that the director's goal is to teach the whole person, not just the musician.

That says something to me about the attitude of the director and the students who make up the membership of that band. The caring and compassionate camaraderie they have extended to these students is making a huge difference in a very special way. The students are learning very important life skills: how to be inclusive of all their fellow members and their musical drive for success. They have already attained a very respected goal in interpersonal relationships. Please do not take this the wrong way: they may not win the state championship, but the important fact is the band will strive for improvement with their eyes fixed on an established goal. The price of leadership, both director and student, is the willingness to see what we can bring to others before self.

"I am only one,
But still I am one.

I cannot do everything,
But still I can do something;
And because I cannot do everything,
I will not refuse to do the
something I can do."

—Edward Everett Hale

I firmly believe that band directors have been well prepared to be *doers*, *problem solvers*, and *catalysts* to "make a difference" in the lives of young musicians. We are who we are today because we had a teacher who cared enough to fully expose themselves and their vulnerabilities to their students' lives. We have all followed in the footprints of our mentors because they represent a trail of success. As we leave our own footprints, our greatest desire is that others will identify those steps as ones setting the right course.

A director shared this note received from a former band student. The student was an enthusiastic, energetic leader in the band program for four years. This student did not go into music as a chosen profession, but the student did become a very fine teacher. What the student learned through band well prepared that student for a very successful teaching career of his own. Here is an excerpt from that letter to his former band director.

> *"Aside from all the tremendous opportunities in band are a number of things you modeled which have served me well as a teacher and a coach. Things like bringing enthusiasm and energy every day... letting people see how much you love what you're doing...the constant quest for perfection...the unmatchable skills you have for knowing people's names...just one more way you let students know how much you cared. Thank you for being an excellent example of a Master Teacher."*

Conclusions

Every time I see the word "conclusion" or hear in a speech, "in conclusion," I think, pay attention, here comes the most powerful part of the writing or the speech. A writer is never sure how material will be received, but my hope is that this chapter has provided some things for you to think about. There may be new thoughts for some, and for others a reminder of things you have discovered on your own or learned through experience. Sharing my thoughts on setting goals, along with guidelines that go into attaining those goals, was my purpose in contributing this chapter. So, in conclusion (sorry), here are a few of my final thoughts.

Attaining a goal is not the end; it is the beginning of a search for a new goal. One of the great challenges of any teacher is to know and understand the unique abilities and goals of our students. If *your goal* is all that matters, you can hinder others from attaining *their goals*. Where is the "I matter most" line crossed? As conductors, our musical goals will not be reached without the musicians in front of us. The musician's desire to play well and be lifted from rote notes to musical satisfaction cannot happen without our leadership. A band or any musical organization is a very complicated assemblage of desires, personalities, ability levels, moods, intellect and, yes, individual goals.

Teaching music is a powerful profession and an even more powerful message in the hands of dedicated, talented, creative teachers who desire to *teach* and *interact* with students in a personal, focused, musical environment. We must always have a goal for almost everything we do in life. Goal setting and achieving *is* a relentless pursuit. But do understand that circumstances over which we may not have any control may force us to change or redirect those goals. Certainly our lives changed dramatically with the loss of our daughter.

The kind of teacher, husband or wife, father or mother you want to be requires that you determine and pursue worthy goals. Let's remember that not only must we set personal goals, but we also must not ignore the goals our students wish to attain. It is perfectly okay, even necessary, to ask them what it is they want to achieve and what their goals are with their participation in band. Setting a goal is easy, but relentlessly pursuing it with the right attitude and purpose is the joy of teaching. Goal seeking is a lifelong pursuit. A music career is the *pursuit of happiness*. Leave your well-defined footprints for those who will follow.

> *"What you get by achieving your goals is not as important as what you become by achieving your goals."*
>
> —Henry David Thoreau

About the Author
Ray E. Cramer

Ray E. Cramer
b. Galesburg, Illinois
June 28, 1940
Emeritus Professor/Director of Bands/Wind Conducting
Indiana University Jacobs School of Music
Emeritus Professor, The Musashino Academy of Music

Ray E. Cramer holds a BA in Education from Western Illinois University, an MFA from the University of Iowa, and Honorary Doctorates from Western Illinois University and Vandercook College of Music. In 2009, he was awarded an Honorary Professorship at the Musashino Academy of Music in Tokyo. Prior to his appointment at Indiana University, Mr. Cramer taught public school in Bardolph, Illinois (1961-62); West Liberty, Iowa (1963-65); Harlan, Iowa (1965-68); and Parma, Ohio (1968-69).

Ray E. Cramer was a member of the Indiana University School of Music faculty from the fall of 1969 through May 2005. In 1982, he was appointed Director of Bands. Under his leadership, the Indiana University Wind Ensemble earned an international reputation for outstanding musical performances, including the 1982 American Bandmasters Association Convention, Indianapolis; the 1984 joint American Bandmasters Association/Japan Bandmasters Association

Convention, Tokyo; the 1988 MENC National Convention, Indianapolis; the 1991 National CBDNA Convention, Kansas City, Missouri; the 1994 National MENC Convention, Cincinnati; the 1995 American Bandmasters Association Convention, Lawrence, Kansas; the 1997 National CBDNA Convention, Athens, Georgia; a 2000 spring tour to Japan performing in six cities and the Japan Band Clinic; the 2003 CBDNA National Convention, Minneapolis; a December 2003 performance at The Midwest Clinic; plus numerous other regional and state conventions.

In addition to his administrative responsibilities as Department of Bands/ Wind Conducting Chair, Mr. Cramer taught graduate courses in wind conducting, history, and literature. He also conducted the University Orchestra during the fall semester for seven years (1994-2001). Mr. Cramer enjoyed a 36-year tenure at Indiana University with the final 24 years as Director of Bands.

Ray E. Cramer is a member of ABA, CBDNA, NBA, WASBE, MENC, CMEA, CBA, CIDA, and is affiliated with Phi Mu Alpha and Phi Beta Mu. Mr. Cramer is a recipient of the Student Alumni Council Senior Faculty Award (1983); the Kappa Kappa Psi Distinguished Service to Music Award (1988); the CIDA Director of the Year Award (1988); the Phi Beta Mu, International Assembly, Outstanding Bandmaster Award (1988); the Kappa Kappa Psi Bohumil Makovsky Memorial Award (1991); the Edwin Franko Goldman Award (2002); the MENC Lowell Mason Fellow Medallion (2003); the Midwest Clinic Medal of Honor (2005); Bands of America Hall of Fame (2006); and Lifetime Achievement Award (2006). He has been awarded Honorary Life Membership of the Colorado Bandmasters Association (2007), Honorary Life Membership Iowa Bandmasters Association (2007), and has received the 17th Japan Academic Society of Winds, Percussion and Band Award (2007). In December 2008, he was named the Academy of Wind and Percussion Arts honoree by the National Band Association. The AWAPA was established by the NBA for the purpose of recognizing those who have made truly significant and outstanding contributions to furthering the excellence of bands and band music. In 2010, he was elected into the NBA Hall of Fame of Distinguished Conductors. He was recently awarded Honorary Membership in the Japan Band Directors Association.

He is a past national president of the College Band Directors National Association, the American Bandmasters Association, and has served as president of the Indiana Bandmasters Association, the North Central Division of CBDNA, and the Big Ten Band Directors Association. He is a past president of The Midwest Clinic, an international band and orchestra convention held in Chicago each December.

Mr. Cramer remains actively involved in clinics and guest conducting engagements nationally and internationally. He serves as a regular guest conductor for the Musashino Academia of Music in Tokyo, Japan, which began in the fall of 1990 and continues to the present. He has conducted the Musashino Wind Ensemble on tours throughout Japan and two performances at The Midwest Clinic in 1995 and 2006.

He and his wife Molly of 53 years reside in Colorado Springs because they love the mountains, and to be closer to family and grandchildren.